Crime Scene Documentation

Crime Scene Documentation

Preserving the Evidence and the Growing Role of 3D Laser Scanning

Robert S. Galvin

CRC Press
Taylor & Francis Group
Boca Raton London New York

CRC Press is an imprint of the
Taylor & Francis Group, an **informa** business

First edition published 2021
by CRC Press
2 Park Square, Milton Park, Abingdon, Oxon, OX14 4RN
and by CRC Press
6000 Broken Sound Parkway NW, Suite 300, Boca Raton, FL 33487-2742

British Library Cataloguing-in-Publication Data
A catalogue record for this book is available from the British Library

Library of Congress Cataloging-in-Publication Data
Names: Galvin, Robert, author.
Title: Crime scene documentation : preserving the evidence and the growing role of 3D laser scanning / Robert S. Galvin.
Description: First edition. | Milton Park, Abingdon, Oxon ; Boca Raton, FL : CRC Press, 2021. | Includes bibliographical references and index. | Summary: "When a criminal act or vehicle crash occurs, most often a local law enforcement agency responds and is responsible for to both investigating the scene and documenting it. It is critical that scene evidence is collected and recorded efficiently, as the scene can quickly change. The sooner evidence can be collected, reviewed, and analyzed, often the better an understanding investigators will have as to how and why the incident occurred. Crime Scene Documentation: Preserving the Evidence and the Growing Role of 3D Laser Scanning demonstrates at length the value of laser scanning through the use of numerous case studies of investigators who have utilized various 3D technologies and laser scanning to document scenes. Thorough and accurate scene documentation is an essential function at a science and proves particularly valuable in courtroom presentations to help jurors understand a crime or accident's likely chain of events. The more advanced a scene documentation method is, the better it can be utilized to capture details that will lead to optimal scene diagramming. Currently, 3D laser scanning is the most advanced method of scene documentation available, capturing detailed and realistic digital scans-and captures scenes in their entirety-yielding a permanent representation of the scene for study and analysis at any time, even years after a crime scene has vanished. The book explains current technology, the latest advances, and how to best utilize the technology. The case examples come from various applications , from tools to programs, can help crash scene investigators understand how scanning can improve scene documentation, provide better and more evidence details, and build more credible diagrams that possibly may be used in court presentations to help support a case. Key features: Describes 3Dscene recording methods in use and how well they work Outlines the variables and inherent challenges associated with documenting crime and crash scenes Illustrates the positive, and dramatic, impact of having a well-documented scene, particularly in the courtroom Explores how 3D laser scanning has vastly changed the way and extent to which crime and crash scenes can be captured accurately and completely, and subsequently analyzed Explains how laser scanning is highly flexible and presents strategies to integrate it into other crime scene incident recording techniques and technologies Crime Scene Documentation details the many benefits of 3D laser scanning technology relative to its reliability and accuracy as well as the multiple case scenarios in which it can be used. The book serves as an invaluable resource to crime scene technicians, investigators, and reconstructionists on the best ways to document a crime or crash scene"-- Provided by publisher.
Identifiers: LCCN 2020038150 (print) | LCCN 2020038151 (ebook) | ISBN 9780367652302 (hardback) | ISBN 9781003128465 (ebook)
Subjects: LCSH: Criminal investigation--Methodology. | Three-dimensional imaging.
Classification: LCC HV8073 .G2922 2021 (print) | LCC HV8073 (ebook) | DDC 363.25/2--dc23
LC record available at https://lccn.loc.gov/2020038150
LC ebook record available at https://lccn.loc.gov/2020038151

ISBN: 978-0-367-65230-2 (hbk)
ISBN: 978-1-003-12846-5 (ebk)

Typeset in Caslon
by Deanta Global Publishing Services, Chennai, India

Contents

PROFESSIONAL BIOGRAPHY

ROBERT S. GALVIN

Robert S. Galvin has been a professional writer for more than 40 years. He has worked as an editor of a community newspaper, and a correspondent for *The Oregonian* newspaper in Portland, Oregon. Galvin also worked as a freelance writer for various Pacific Northwest newspapers and trade publications.

In 1989, Galvin launched his own public relations consultancy, which eventually enabled him to work with clients in the law enforcement and public safety sectors. He authored articles on the benefits of tactical boots and knives, but primarily published articles on various crash and crime scene diagramming software as well as pre-fire planning software. During the last ten-plus years leading up to his retirement, Galvin wrote and published articles that explored the challenges of documenting crime and crash scenes, and how 3D laser scanning, photogrammetry, total stations and other technology tools proved effective at capturing scenes and their evidence.

Specifically, many of Galvin's articles concentrated on how 3D laser scanning, in particular, aided crime and crash scene reconstruction experts in documenting scenes and creating 3D models that could be used effectively in courtroom presentations to help jurors understand the likely events of a crime incident. His articles have been published in the leading law enforcement and forensic trade publications, including *LAW ENFORCEMENT TECHNOLOGY, EVIDENCE TECHNOLOGY MAGAZINE, POLICE MAGAZINE, S.W.A.T. MAGAZINE, POLICE CHIEF MAGAZINE, LAW AND ORDER MAGAZINE, LAW OFFICER MAGAZINE*, and *CAMPUS SAFETY MAGAZINE.*

PART I

INTRODUCTION

The Importance of Crime Scene Documentation and the Drive to 3D Scene Visualization

On February 21, 2014, a student of San Jose State University called the emergency helpline, 911 to report a man with a large knife stabbing the air and acting erratically. Two university police officers confronted the man, who was carrying a footlong, drywall saw and appeared to be mentally unstable or intoxicated. When a Sergeant and Officer arrived at the scene, they ordered the man to drop the saw. When he refused and kept advancing, they used a stun gun to try to subdue him. These actions, however, did not deter the man, and he charged at one of the officers, so the second officer shot him twice in the back, killing him. The officer that the assailant charged at wore a shoulder-mounted body camera that recorded the events from his point of view.

Media coverage of the event focused on how the man with the saw was shot in the back. A civil lawsuit claiming wrongful death ensued, saying the body-camera video clearly showed the man was trying to run away from the officer when he was shot.

A forensic company combined its laser scanner and a drone to thoroughly document the three-block crime scene in a minimum amount of time. The data captured was used to digitally preserve both the smallest details of the scene and a macro, over-head view that included the roofs of vehicles and buildings. This data was used to clarify the body-camera footage that was taken at the scene and determine measurements critical to the case. Ultimately, with the aid of this technology, the shooting was determined to be justifiable[1] (Figures I.1 and I.2).

This case underscores an inarguable point, which is that whenever and wherever a crime occurs, two actions are required without exception: the crime scene must be investigated, and it must also be thoroughly and accurately documented. These essential actions are more technically known as *forensic mapping* because they comprise two separate sciences that go hand-in-hand as crime scenes, and their evidence are probed. More importantly, a forensic investigator has the training and knowledge to understand and identify crime or crash scene evidence, how it can best be documented, and present his or her findings in court.

The scene documentation component of forensic mapping is the emphasis of this book because today's crime scenes are being documented more comprehensively and accurately than ever before, thanks to new, constantly advancing technologies. From the moment

Figure I.1 Shown is body-worn camera footage of an officer chasing a saw-wielding assailant down a street near San Jose State University. When the assailant approaches the officer, the officer shoots him. A forensic scene visualization company reconstructed scene events by using a 3D laser scanner and drone to record a dimensionally accurate, 3D model of the scene to clarify events filmed with the officer's body-worn camera. (Photo courtesy of www.visuallaw.com.)

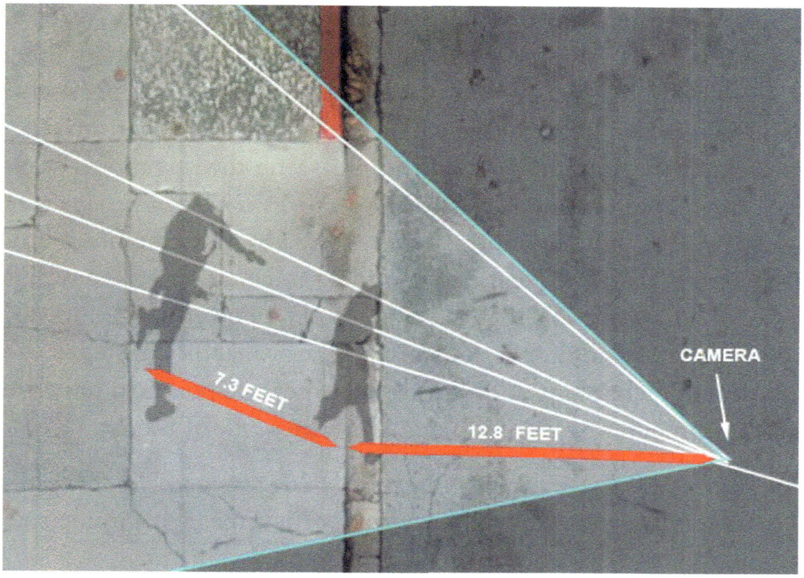

Figure I.2 The scanned data captured from the officer-assailant chase scene was used to create a "virtual camera" that could be matched to the scanned scene's point cloud. Shadows from the virtual camera were accurately placed into the point cloud so distance between the officer and suspect could be measured. (Photo courtesy of www.visuallaw.com.)

a crime occurs, its scene can reveal a treasure trove of information and details as an investigation gets underway. How the scene is documented can be pivotal for a jury to understand the circumstances of a crime.

This book will explore how the latest scene mapping technology supports the investigator or reconstruction technician as he strives to rebuild the scene with the highest of accuracy, but also in a way that jurors can experience actually being taken inside the scene itself via a 3D perspective.

The Drive to 3D Scene Depiction

Crime scene mapping technology progressed slowly at first. For years, tape measures and measuring wheels were the accepted ways to map a scene, and the scenes themselves were portrayed with paper diagrams or sketches. But the diagrams, coupled with scene photographs, had to be explained extensively to juries who may not have fully understood scene events. Eventually, the total station, predominantly used in field surveying, was discovered to have a perfect fit for mapping crash scenes and crime scenes. The total station then secured "king-of-the-hill" status in mapping these types of scenes for decades. It is still widely used today. But when the 3D laser scanner arrived, it represented the tipping point for crime scene investigation because the scanner could map and record the scene in *three-dimension* and in totality, within a fraction of the time required by older methods. From this juncture, there has been, and continues to be, a non-stop prolifera-tion of all kinds of tools that can achieve 3D scene visualization—3D cameras, tablets and drones, for starters. The availability of such a wide spectrum of technology addresses several pressure points in our crime scene documentation environment. Here are a few of them:

- Crime scenes, in many instances, have become larger and more intricate to map and capture, oftentimes with immense amounts of evidence to sift through and document.
- Analysis of evidence, and perspectives of how a crime scene's events may have unfolded, require heightened priority and visualization—especially in 3D—now that juries have become savvier and demanding about how scenes should be depicted in court.
- Vastly improved technology for documenting crime scenes is fueling the need for complete evidence, numerous scene angles and perspectives, and analysis, all of which can be included in and/or supplement software-generated diagrams.
- As crime scenes proliferate, there has been increased pressure within law enforcement to close cases faster, which is prompt-ing the adoption of more efficient technologies that can speed up scene mapping and recording.
- Cost and affordability of crime scene reconstruction technol-ogy continues to be a factor in what technology tool an agency or private reconstruction expert can afford and purchase.

Laser Scanning Becomes a Major Technology, But No Longer Used Exclusively

This book will explore how the various technologies are used today for mapping and documenting crime scenes. It will also explore the relevance, use, and merging of tools in crime and crash scene investigations by investigators and reconstruction experts. There has been a significant shift toward 3D crime scene capture and diagramming, primarily driven by the demand among juries to better understand how events during crash and crime incidents most likely occurred. In the book, as many relevant technologies as possible will be probed and validated by commentary from professional crash and crime scene reconstruction experts who actively use them.

As you read this book, you will see that it emphasizes one crime scene documentation technology in particular: 3D laser scanning. Laser scanning has emerged over the years as a necessary scene recording tool that is used by investigators and reconstruction technicians. However, it is not the only tool in the toolbox for crime and crash investigations. This book will cover a variety of technologies as well as devote the last chapter to how valuable it can be used to combine two or more of these tools to reconstruct a crime or crash scene. Each of these tools—whether it is a tablet, total station, or drone—can play a role in helping to rebuild a scene, while also able to complement laser scanning.

In this book, we will discuss the modern technologies available for crime and crash scene investigations, but by no means does this mean the discussion can be comprehensive with the speed of innovation in our lives. Products are becoming lighter, faster, smaller with each iteration, and mobile phones are mini portable walking computers. New technologies help create new possibilities, but the benefit can only be realized when quality can be guaranteed all-time.

It is only reasonable for forensic science experts to pause in their professional lives to observe just how technology pervades their work and what trends shape how they recreate the crime scenes of today and especially of tomorrow. It seems safe to say that technology is not just here to stay, but that it will continue advancing, helping reconstruction experts uncover how scenes came to be as they strive to solve cases brought before a jury.

Note

1. FARO. "Focus Laser Scanner Used to Clarify Body Camera Film." FARO Technologies, Inc., 2017. https://public-safety.faro.com/assets/CaseStudy_LaserScanner_Visual_Law_PS_AM_EN.pdf.

1

A Brief History of Forensic Science

How Archimedes and Jack the Ripper Shaped Modern Forensics

Archimedes: The First Forensic Scientist

It seems hard to believe, but forensic science has roots reaching all the way back to ancient times, and without even the slightest hint of what we consider the technology innovations of today. But there certainly *was* innovation. One standout example is the period of 287–212 BC, which featured Archimedes of Syracuse, a brilliant Greek mathematician and physicist who had other impressive credentials. History considers Archimedes as the father of forensic science. The most famous example underscoring this accolade points to when Archimedes was asked by then-King Hiero to investigate whether or not his royal crown, commissioned to a local goldsmith, was actually made of pure gold, as the king had mandated.[1] The king was suspicious, which is why he asked Archimedes to, we could say, do a bit of forensic sleuthing. Archimedes figured out that the best solution would be a test of the crown for density and buoyancy, whereby the crown's volume could be determined by the amount of water it displaced. The goldsmith who had created the crown, it turns out, was sneaky, because he only used some of the gold given to him by the king; perhaps he was hoping to save the rest of the gold for his personal use.

The test that Archimedes performed was to calculate the crown's density and, thus, its purity for solid gold. The king's hunch was correct, as the test results showed that only part of his gold given to the goldsmith had been used in making the crown. The experiment marked a true red-letter day for Archimedes, who, thrilled with

Figure 1.1 The tale of Archimedes' "Eureka!" moment is legendary, and one of the first examples of forensic investigation. The famous Greek mathematician/physicist/astronomer was asked by King Hiero of Syracuse to assess the purity of an irregular votive crown he had given to a goldsmith. The king suspected the finished crown was not pure gold and asked Archimedes to test his suspicion. Archimedes did so while taking a bath, discovering that the crown indeed was not pure gold by its density and buoyancy. (Illustration from Wikimedia Commons)

his discovery, ran down the streets of Syracuse shouting, "Eureka," which, in Greek, meant "I found it."[2] Quite the "Eureka" moment! (Figure 1.1).

From this historical period in forensic science's infancy came more innovation, when, in the 700s, the Chinese used fingerprints to establish the identity of documents and clay sculptures. Fast forward to 1248, and in this year a Chinese book was published by Hsi Duan Yu, a noted forensic author, titled *The Washing Away of Wrongs*. It may be the first book published about forensics. The book described how to distinguish drowning from strangulation and offered tips on identifying cases of strangulation and damaged neck cartilage.[3]

Jack the Ripper and Photography as Documentation

It was not until the 1800s that a real breakthrough occurred for being able to actually *document* crime scenes and evidence: the first use of photography for the identification of criminals and documentation of evidence and crime scenes. More exactly, this capability of forensic science was significantly used in 1888, when doctors in London, England, were allowed to examine the victims of the notorious serial killer Jack the Ripper for wound patterns. CSI photography was used at the sites in the impoverished Whitechapel district in the East End of London, where Jack the Ripper committed his grisly murders, between April 1888 and February 13, 1891. Although police accomplished some photography, it was a very new technique and not used to document crime scenes or surroundings as far as we know. In fact, Mary Kelly, the last one of the Ripper's numerous victims, was the only victim actually photographed at the scene of her gruesome murder; the other victims were photographed upon being taken to a mortuary. Incredibly, these photographs were *not taken for investigative purposes* but instead for attempting to identify the victims. Police wanted to use the photos to share with various people in the hope that somebody would be able to identify the victim (Figure 1.2).

Before photography, crime scenes had been sketched or described in written notes. In the 1870s, photography became cutting edge and expanded in its use.

As Forensic Pathologist Dr. Derrick Pounder observes,

> Photography is tremendously useful because, when you look at a crime scene, you're influenced by the emotion of the moment and you're focused on certain elements. But, when you look at a photograph, you remove the emotion, you're looking at it at a distance in time and you can focus on distinct parts of it systematically, and so you see things that you didn't see when you stood in the crime scene.

Mary Kelly's body was photographed as it lay on the bed in her room. These photos were probably some of the earliest murder scene images ever recorded, the website reveals.

Another finding that the Jack the Ripper website offers comes from Professor Robert Flanagan, a toxicologist, who notes that the introduction of photography for documenting a crime scene was revolutionary because no other simple method existed to record the precise position of objects at the scene. Flanagan argues that photography (and video) is the only valid and reliable way to record the exact characteristics of a person.[4]

In summary, photography as a forensic tool used in the late 19th century, and particularly for the murder scenes left behind by Jack the

Figure 1.2 The crime scene of Mary Kelly, the last victim from Jack the Ripper's brutal murders and mutilations of women in the Whitechapel district in London, 1888. Kelly was the only victim actually photographed at the scene of her murder. This is one of the earliest murder scene images recorded, according to www.JackTheRipper.com. (Photo courtesy of Wikimedia Commons)

Ripper, was eventually valued not just for identification of victims, but as a way to record the scene itself and the circumstances of the crime committed. Since then, with advancements and standardization, photography is one of the very first tools that a crime scene investigator or reconstructionist uses to begin documenting evidence at a crime or crash scene. Scene photographs can prove to be critical for identifying evidence that a mapping tool might overlook, and from which measurements can be taken using certain scene mapping technologies.

Newer Methods Reshape Crime Scene Mapping and Documentation

The 20th century ushered in various, new methods for crime scene mapping and documentation. For decades the crime scene specialist used devices like 25-foot steel retractable measuring tapes and

100-foot fiberglass tapes. Next, the 1,000-foot walking wheel (known these days as the measuring wheel) was used. These tools are still used today, but no longer as a primary way to map a scene given the more recent, advanced ways of crime scene measurement.

Eventually, a device called a *theodolite* was perfected from its early origins to become a precision optical instrument for measuring angles between visible and designated points in the horizontal and vertical planes. Theodolite became popular for land surveying but also was used in building and infrastructure construction. It included an infrared electronic distance meter to measure distances from the mounted station to a rod-mounted prism placed over an object. The distances could be measured with high accuracy. Any data from the theodolite is stored electronically later to reconstruct a scene. Even though measurements were still taken one at a time, it offered a higher degree of accuracy from longer ranges compared to a measuring wheel. As a result, the device became a natural tool to use in reconstructing crime scenes and traffic accidents.

The instrument is equipped with an on-board computer that collects data and performs triangulation calculations. The modern theodolite has evolved into what is today known as a total station where angles and distances are measured electronically. The total station began to take hold as a crime and crash scene documentation tool around 2004, and today remains a popular way to map and record such scenes.

Since the adoption of the total station for use in capturing crime and crash scenes, technological leaps have occurred in the 21st century with the introduction of higher efficiency mapping and documentation tools. Rather than capturing one measurement at a time, it is now possible to record large amounts of measurable data points in minutes. Forensic scientists, crime scene investigators, criminalists, and crime scene unit members have turned toward using 3D laser scanners, photogrammetry, 3D cameras, and drones to obtain substantial, three-dimensional point clouds of accidents or crime scenes.

Photogrammetry: A Science with a Long History

Photogrammetry is the science of making measurements from photographs. These measurements are then used to create a map, drawing, or 3D model of an object or a scene.

The science of photogrammetry is hardly new. The principles of this science date back to the late 1400s. And one of photogrammetry's first proponents was Leonardo da Vinci, the same genius who gave the world the Renaissance painting, the *Mona Lisa*. Among da Vinci's incredible range of capabilities were as a scientist, mathematician, and engineer. As a result of his varied skills in these disciplines, da Vinci became a proponent of photogrammetry (he might view this term to be strange and foreign), as he studied how to use projective geometry as a measurement tool.

Projective geometry is a branch of mathematics concerning the relationships between geometric figures and images, or mapping, that result from projecting them onto another surface.[5] Another photogrammetry advocate was Aime Laussedat, who, in the 1800s, pioneered the use of terrestrial photographs for topographic map creation from hot air balloons.

Jumping back into the 21st century, we now apply this science in forensic applications in two major ways: aerial photogrammetry and terrestrial (close-range) photogrammetry. By attaching a camera and specialized software to a drone, multiple overlapping photos of the ground can be taken as the drone flies along a flight path over, most typically, a lengthy crash scene. The imagery can be used to take measurements and build 3D models. As for terrestrial photogrammetry, the specialized digital camera used is located on the ground for capturing forensic and crash scenes. The output is usually drawings, 3D models, measurements, or point clouds.[6]

Photogrammetry can be used in several forensic applications such as:

- Blood patterns
- Skid mark and roadway gouge measurements
- Measuring the height of a suspect in a security surveillance video
- Crush measurements from a vehicle crash (6)

Laser Scanning: A Timely Technology for Crime/Crash Scene Reconstruction

Three-dimensional laser scanning has catapulted to the forefront of the technology wave and has been refined to meet the unique needs of law enforcement and forensic science. It emanated from what is formally known as *LIDAR* (light imaging, detection, and ranging), a surveying method that measures the distance to a target by illuminating the target with laser light and measuring the reflected light with a sensor. Variances in laser return times and wavelengths can then be used to make digital 3D representations of the target. LIDAR was initially considered a portmanteau of *light* and *radar* and is now usually called 3D laser scanning since it is really a combination of 3D scanning and laser scanning.

Laser scanning is not entirely new since it has been around since the 1960s. Yet it didn't break into the engineering field until the late 1990s. Cyra Technologies, founded in 1993, made one of the first scanners to be used by surveyors and engineers. In 2001, Lecia Geosystems, a provider of 3D laser scanning equipment and software, purchased Cyra. Laser scanning was not immediately adopted or affordable. A major hurdle was that it could not advance until bandwidth and hard drive storage improved and became more affordable for those agencies and reconstruction professionals who wanted its cutting-edge capabilities. How to deal with the huge amount of data points that laser scanning produces can still be challenging. Initially, only a few select users saw the benefits of laser scanning, whereas today its usage is widespread across so many industries, especially within public safety, law enforcement, and forensic science.

In 2015, FARO Technologies introduced a small, light, and affordable 3D laser scanner—the FARO Focus. Since then, adoption and usage have become more commonplace across architecture, engineering, construction mining, and more, as well as in public safety, law enforcement, and forensic science. This same trend is true for other leading manufacturers of laser scanning equipment.

The real paydirt of laser scanning, of course, is the output from the workflow aimed at producing a usable 3D model/diagram that, in crime scene investigations, will be admissible in court presentations. The power of scanning lies within the point cloud and the as-built model that is derived from the point cloud, and that you produce with the special software used with laser scanning.[7]

In this chapter, we looked at the early forensic investigation efforts of Archimedes, the use of photography in the Jack the Ripper murders, the utility of photography in crime scene documentation, and the advent and emergence of modern digital imaging solutions. In the next chapter, we look at the challenges of crime scene documentation and the current, reliable, and repeatable methods used based on investigators' skills, training, and experience.

Notes

1. Raut, Santosh. "Development of Forensic Science through Ages." 2008. www.santoshraut.com.
2. "About Eureka." 2011. https://www.bellarmine.edu/learningcommunity/eureka/about.
3. "Forensic Science History. New York State Police." 2008. www.troopers.ny.gov.
4. Jones, Richard. "Jack The Ripper." 1888. www.jack-the-ripper.org.
5. Brunson, Deighton. "Leonardo Da Vinci, Tiny Bubbles, and Photogrammetry?" Brunson—A Blog for Metrology Enthusiasts, 2019. blog.brunson.us.
6. "What is Photogrammetry?" Photogrammetry, 2017. www.photogrammetry.com.
7. "History of Laser Scanning." SurvTech Solutions, 2017. www.floridalaserscanning.com.

2

Crime Scene Documentation has Challenges, But Technology Tools are Meeting Them

Crime, the CSI Effect, and Expectations of Investigators

Regardless of whether crime rises or falls on a national scale—FBI and other statistics indicate that crime rates have decreased in recent years—there will always be ample crime scenes to investigate and record. Naturally, many cases connected to these scenes will head to court, which makes mapping and diagramming the crime scenes carefully so essential to reveal accurate details within their reconstruction. A specific protocol for scene documentation must be followed. Recording crime scenes can be painstaking and require hours. So, it is no wonder that most crime scene investigators and reconstruction experts cringe at television's simplistic portrayal of crime scene investigations, with cases resolved at warp speed, coupled with dazzling 3D techno-wizardry. Some jurors expect seeing the same technology in court as they see on TV. Crime shows fuel their insistence for mesmerizing 3D court presentations regardless of what kind of scene a crime case unveils—broadly known as the "CSI Effect."

Even though the CSI Effect has now become the new reality for court presentations of crime scene reconstructions, there is a silver lining. This technology exists today. With modern technology and its use in forensics, 3D data and crime scene models are courtroom accepted ways and have proven richly rewarding for judges, attorneys, and juries.

The Reality of Crime Scenes

A fresh crime scene to be investigated and captured is challenging right off the bat. It's not orderly or without numerous responders probing as they perform their duties. Crime scene investigators and reconstruction experts must work around first responders to keep the scene as undisturbed as possible while mapping, photographing, videotaping, and/or otherwise recording the entire scene.

Time constraints for scene documentation can be another huge challenge. Vehicle crash scenes are a prime example, where there is typically great urgency to reopen roads or highways. However, measuring any crash scene cannot be rushed, which is why roadways or highways at such scenes are often only partially closed. The longer a road is even partially closed, the higher is the risk of the so-called "secondary" accidents where drivers can become distracted and cause their own accidents.

Whatever the time constraint, the crash scene reconstruction professional must prioritize what evidence to document because once the scene is cleaned up and gone, any crucial, missed evidence vanishes. This approach is especially applicable to large and complicated scenes involving not only vehicles but airplane and train crashes, too, including other events, such as a stadium or building collapse, or a fire. Some crime scenes may extend from within a building or house to a yard, street, or parking lot, or even several blocks from the crime scene. There may be several rooms to investigate and document, and a wide range of evidence, bodies, pools of blood, castoff bloodstain pattern on walls, guns, rifles, knives, keys, bloodstained clothes, and carpeting, among others, that offer clues to what the course of events may have been during a crime.

All of these considerations show why a crime scene investigator must *walk the scene* first and devise a strategy for what parts of it should be the focus of documentation and what evidence captured for further analysis, and how to best diagram it for posterity.

Overlooking key evidence when documenting a scene is yet another aggravating challenge; the case to which the evidence is tied may reopen later for further investigation. There might be pieces of evidence that are requested in a criminal court trial that appear in crime scene photos but are missing from the reconstructed scene presented in court. And, closed crime cases might reopen years later, requiring re-examination of the crime scene and its evidence. Which means a complete reconstruction of the scene, so that additional evidence might be identified.

The actual documenting of a crime scene can be arduous and with not ideal conditions. For example, scenes can have severe weather conditions, making the collection of critical evidence—blood samples, for example—a difficult task. More concerning is that as multiple responders arrive at the scene, the scene and its evidence can quickly be disturbed.

Need for Faster Scene Documentation and 3D Scene Models Has Increased

All of these challenges underscore the need for a reliable method of scene capture and the investigator's competent use of it based upon his skill, training, and experience. Numerous tools to document crime scenes have evolved over prior decades and are still in use today, some emerging just within the past few years. These include tape measures, measuring wheels, total stations (both electronic with prism, and robotic), photogrammetry, 3D imagery systems (i.e., 360° digital cameras), and 3D laser scanning systems. Tape measures and Rolatape wheels probably are fading as ongoing ways to map crime scenes considering their lack of reliable accuracy and the extensive time they require. In the last 15-plus years, crime scene mapping has been accomplished with more advanced, automated tools that yield superior measurement accuracy and richer data with which an investigator or reconstruction expert can then build a meaningful 3D diagram (Figure 2.1).

The Advent of 3D Scanning: Scene Reconstructions More Compelling for Juries

Of the automated solutions, 3D laser scanning has, in recent decades, become the most touted and adopted technology for law enforcement to document crime and accident scenes. It's doubtful that laser scanning will replace most of the other mapping technologies referenced. Even so, it has taken center stage because of its ability to capture a

Figure 2.1 The total station, once reserved for field surveying, has, over many decades, become a trusted tool for mapping and documenting crash and crime scenes. (Photo courtesy of Joe Warren, Traffic Investigator, Chattanooga, Tennessee, Police Department)

scene in its totality, generating millions of data points and within far less time than most other methods. A laser-scanned scene brought into special post-processing software—for building a detailed diagram—yields multiple perspectives and viewing angles and fly-throughs of the scene. Armed with a 3D diagram and these technology advantages, an investigator or reconstruction practitioner can make a highly compelling presentation in court that jurors can more easily understand as opposed to manually produced drawings (Figures 2.2, 2.3, and 2.4).

Older mapping technologies such as photogrammetry and total stations are still in use; they have not only withstood laser scanning's aggressive promotion and growing adoption but are now actually enjoying a resurgence. Decades-old mapping tools are being used as part of an exciting trend: the inclusion of two or three scene documentation tools in combination with laser scanning. And, a welcome newcomer, the UAV (unmanned aerial vehicle), or drone, is actively part of this trend. Not long ago, the drone was a curious hobby object for the general public. Then it suddenly became the new crime and crash scene tech tool on the block. Specifically, the drone has been

Figure 2.2 Environmental durability and range are important considerations when choosing a laser scanner. A professional-grade scanner, such as the Leica ScanStation PS Series, shown here, is designed for maximum performance. (Photo courtesy of Leica Geosystems)

successfully married to photogrammetry and scanning to help record huge crash scenes and selected crime scenes. Drone imaging can also be used to capture heat signatures, and search and rescue efforts and recovery efforts where an individual or remains are being looked for

Figure 2.3 Three-dimensional models like this officer-involved shooting example can make a compelling presentation in court. Jurors will more easily understand a scene like this compared to manually produced drawings. (Image courtesy of Eugene Liscio, founder of ai2-3d, a Canadian firm specializing in 3D forensic measurement, analysis and visualization)

Figure 2.4 The 3D laser scanner is one of the most prevalent tools used by law enforcement agencies and reconstruction experts to document a wide variety of crash and crime scenes. (Photo courtesy of Trimble Forensics)

in a large area. Wide-area scans by drones can be reviewed to look for anomalies or areas that on-the-ground investigators should examine further. Such advances resulting from combining different scene mapping tools add substantially to strengthening crime and crash scene reconstructions (Figure 2.5).

This chapter has presented the reality of crime and crash scenes and how they must be carefully and accurately mapped and recorded since scene reconstructions ultimately may be presented in court.

Figure 2.5 North Carolina State Highway Patrol Trooper Brian Leventhal launches a DJI Phantom 4 Pro drone via the Pix4Dcapture application to capture a scene with photogrammetry. (Photo courtesy of Trooper Brian Leventhal, North Carolina State Highway Patrol)

Advanced, efficient tools are aiding this process, with 3D laser scanning proving to be a leading and widely adopted technology. Drones, as a newer type of technology, are positively impacting crime and crash scene capture and complement other technologies, especially 3D laser scanning.

The next chapter examines the importance of making sure a crime scene is fully secured and protected so that adequate evidence can be collected and the scene itself is not contaminated.

3
Preparing for Crime Scene Documentation

Documenting a crime or crash scene must be done with extreme care. If, as a reconstructionist or crime scene investigator, you are lucky enough to confront a scene that is still fresh and largely undisturbed, documenting the scene thoroughly and accurately should yield ample evidence and details to make the scene diagram effective. Nevertheless, there are still challenges to capturing scene data.

Securing the Scene is the Biggest Test

The size of the area in which a crime unfolds can vary from scene to scene, which is why police must quickly determine the size and boundaries of a crime scene. Securing the crime scene is not easy, as a crime scene might be just a single room or an entire house, everything on a property, or even an entire neighborhood with lots of streets, houses, vegetation, and cars. The biggest challenge is just securing the scene itself. That's the view of Hayden Baldwin, former executive director of the International Crime Scene Investigators Association (ICSIA) who says, "If the scene is not secured, it's more difficult to show where evidence originally was immediately after the incident." An unsecured crime scene can make it difficult, as well, when diagramming a scene and then presenting the diagram in court. "You're telling a story based on facts you can prove," Baldwin said. So, without critical aspects such as being able to show the location of different things—an active shooting scene, for example, where it's important to be able to show where a shooter entered, the scene's dimensions, where he walked to, the final rest locales of bodies, body positions, entry/exit wounds, if any, shell casings, etc.—it will be hard to gain a jury's buy-in (Figure 3.1).

Figure 3.1 A crime scene can have many different types of evidence, so it is important to collect as much evidence as possible while the scene is undisturbed. (Photo courtesy of www.Visionations.com)

Baldwin points out that all crime scenes have a primary and a secondary area. The primary area is the overall scene itself—where a crime actually occurred—whether that's a room in a building or a home, or, say, the total expanse of a collision scene with fatalities. The secondary area is all avenues that lead to the actual scene. It is in some way related to the crime but is not where the actual crime occurred. So, as an example, if a killer commits a murder in someone's home but transports the body somewhere outside the home for disposal, the victim's home is the primary scene; the killer's vehicle and wherever he disposed of the body are secondary scenes.[1]

Prioritizing Evidence Essential

Another big challenge is identifying what evidence is actually part of the crime scene and what is not before mapping of the scene begins. If a scene involves a shooting or an assault, for instance, it may be hard to tell what is fresh evidence and what isn't. Therefore, it's important to consider critical aspects, such as the location and condition of a piece of evidence—is it lying on a floor inside a building, or outside on concrete? Is it clean underneath or dirty? Have weather conditions such as rain, snow, wind, perhaps impacted the evidence?

Regardless of the condition of your scene's evidence, try to ensure it is going to be unchanged or disturbed as little as possible until you can get it photographed, mapped, and documented. Keeping a scene undisturbed can be especially essential if the scene has many different types of evidence. Homicide scenes are a good example, as they often have a variety of evidence, including cartridge cases from shootings, blood spatter, holes in a wall, door, car door, windows, and bodies.[2]

Protecting the crime scene should be the highest priority. This requires not merely securing the scene but also limiting access to only essential personnel and making full, accurate records of all activity at the scene. The first person to visit the scene, whether it is an officer or crime scene investigator, should secure the scene and prevent anyone from entering. If the scene is part of a major crime, the first person responding should help any victims needing medical aid by calling for help. As part of securing the scene, it may be best to obtain a search warrant so that all crime scene officers can investigate the scene and collect evidence. The scene should be enclosed with crime scene barrier tape.

When securing the scene, it's best to tape off a larger area than is needed. There should be officers stationed around the scene's perimeter to stop unauthorized people from entering. Remember, that more people entering and leaving the scene can cause contamination. For complex scenes, such as a murder inside a structure—a house—it may be best to mark off the structure itself in which the actual crime scene is located, then seal off the surrounding property. Two separate logs—one for the main scene and another for the property surrounding the scene—should be kept so that notes can be written about who has entered and what they did. Assuming the logs have been filled with these extensive details, they will become valuable by showing how thoroughly the crime scene was managed during investigation and help deflect any attempts by defense attorneys to question the integrity of scene evidence.

Prevent Scene Contamination

Preventing scene contamination is one of the biggest responsibilities of the crime investigation team. It can be a thorny task. For example, when first responders enter a crime scene to, say, aid an injured victim, they might inadvertently jeopardize the crime scene because they are not concerned about preserving the scene. Consequently, the responders might leave footprints, fingerprints, even DNA evidence, and possibly disturb crucial evidence from how it appears or where it's located—all of which can contaminate the crime scene. Therefore, the lead scene investigator should make sure any responders are interviewed and that their actions are recorded in the logbooks.

Scene contamination definitely was one of many important factors considered as Jeff Gurvis, co-founder of Visionations, a manufacturer of software for managing criminal investigation data, developed and introduced his flagship product, CrimePad. The software enables officers, detectives, CSIs, and supervisors working at crime scenes to log information and photos, generate field reports, and collaborate in real time on all data related within a criminal investigation and a crime scene. With CrimePad, "There's just one step to reducing contamination of the crime scene because you're now eliminating the need for people to go through the scene who don't need to be there," Gurvis said. "Even if they want to know what the scene looks like and to be there, you can still provide them a line of sight through the scene, with this software, without them being at the scene" (Figure 3.2).

Gurvis considers *contamination* to be a very biased word that means a lot of things to a lot of people. But basically, it means preventing any additional and possibly disruptive contribution to the crime scene as much as possible. If a crime scene investigation team is using special software to gather a wide spectrum of crime scene–related information, especially evidence, there is no need for several people to look at the same piece of evidence at the scene. Gurvis argues that the software has already documented the evidence, and in doing so it has reduced the amount of physical presence via personnel needed at a specific location within the crime scene. "And this should reduce the amount of contribution to the scene from other individuals," Gurvis said.

Using CrimePad is a way of bringing the crime lab to the crime scene, the software company founder suggested. The software offers a way to save time because of the sharing of information among investigators, detectives, and crime lab technicians. Previously, expertise that could be applied at a crime scene was limited to just the people who were physically at the scene. Now, by using the revolutionary software the user can invite others to collaborate, communicate, and

Figure 3.2 A tablet designed for documenting a crime scene can be used to log information and photos, generate field reports, and record evidence. It eliminates the need for people to enter the crime scene, people who do not need to be there. (Photo courtesy of www.Visionations.com)

provide expertise without them having to be there. This aids tremendously in controlling potential crime scene contamination, as well. As part of CrimePad's crime scene documentation component, there is an access section which allows the user to document who is coming into the scene and who is going out and where they are going. This information can be notated in a full access log in the software. Also, "We have areas in the software to enter protective equipment that is being worn when you go into the scene," Gurvis said. "So, you can document who is going in and out and when, why they are going into the scene, and what that person is wearing" (Figures 3.3 and 3.4).

Walking the Scene Improves Documentation, Overall Reconstruction

Before you begin to examine a crime scene, gather as much information as possible about it. A slow, methodical approach is best if scene

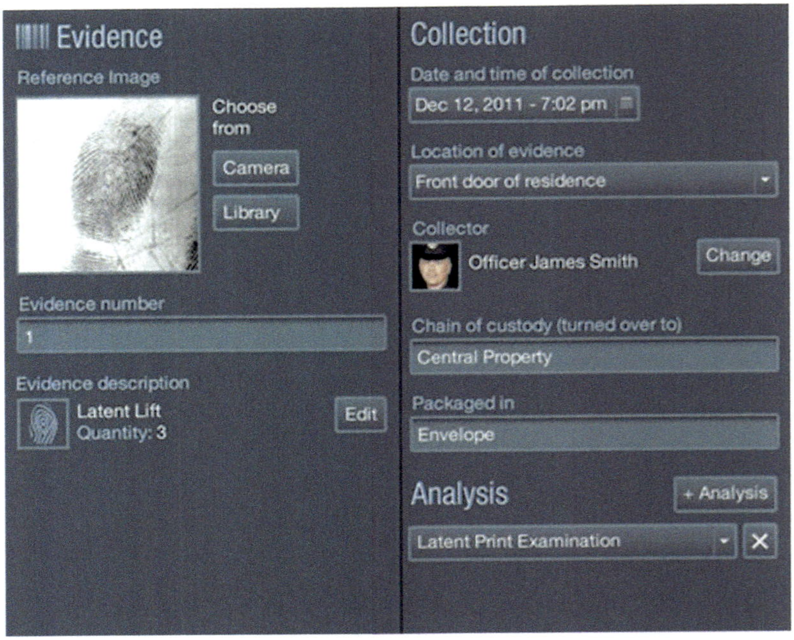

Figure 3.3 CrimePad from Visionations eliminates the need to record data and evidence from a crash or crime scene multiple times, because the investigator only needs to enter any data once. The data is saved on CrimePad and can be shared among various people within law enforcement and forensics departments. A major benefit of a tablet configured for crime and crash scene evidence documentation is that it can help prevent scene contamination. (Photos courtesy of www.Visionations.com)

conditions permit. *Walking the scene is essential* so that you can pinpoint the location of potential evidence and then mentally note how the scene will be examined, mapped, and documented. The walk-through should begin as close to the scene's point of entry as possible. The aim is to gather as much information about the scene as you can so that the crime scene can be appropriately analyzed. The walk-through will prove beneficial in three ways:

- It enables you to set a logical path for identifying and locating potential, crucial evidence that must be documented.
- By documenting evidence in this logical manner, the entire scene can be more effectively reconstructed with whatever technology is used.
- The walk-through allows you to determine what path a crime's execution took and includes all apparent actions associated with the crime.

Figure 3.4 CrimePad from Visionations eliminates the need to record data and evidence from a crash or crime scene multiple times, because the investigator only needs to enter any data once. The data is saved on the CrimePad so that various people within the law enforcement and forensics departments can share it. A major benefit of a tablet configured for crime and crash scene evidence documentation is that it can help prevent scene contamination. (Photos courtesy of www.Visionations.com)

When starting to walk a crime scene, the first place that should be examined is the ground on which you are about to tread. For any evidence spotted, place a marker at the location of this evidence location to warn others walking around the scene to avoid stepping on the evidence. If the crime scene occurred in a house or a room inside a building, the investigator should examine areas overhead, such as ceilings as well as walls. These areas may show additional, valuable evidence (blood spatter, bullet holes). As the walk-through proceeds, the scene should be documented with multiple photographs and videotape, as well as sketches. The more photographs, the better, as they can show how the evidence actually appears and help give context to a scene diagram. Also, the photos prove valuable in case measurements need to be taken from them as part of the documentation being

> used. Of course, capturing the entire scene, preferably with some kind of 3D visualization system, will yield full scene details and preserve the scene for future analysis at any time. Baldwin, the former executive director for the International Crime Scene Investigators Association, agrees and feels that a major change with crime scene evidence preservation is diagramming part of the scene. There is a fine line between the three-dimensional scene capture, which is what 3D lasers and other technologies are doing and being able to animate and walk through the scene in a virtual reality scenario, he affirms. "These are all visual clues to offer a better explanation as to what happened at the scene as opposed to just having a written report," Baldwin said. "A 3D diagram can show perspectives, and distances between objects." And all of these aspects of crime scene investigation underscore the continuous need for scene preservation, as well. With better scene preservation there will be improved documentation of scene evidence and needed details.

The steps discussed in this chapter will help you protect and preserve your crime scene and enable a meaningful documentation of it. And, these protocols will help not only you but another investigator recreate your case years later and help you recall the scene without difficulty and with confidence if the facts of the case must be presented to a jury. Finally, remember, your investigative report and the steps you took to preserve the crime scene can make a difference in the prosecution of a charged offender. You absolutely do not want the report to be the Achilles heel in the investigation and provide an opening for an offender to walk away from his or her crime.

In this chapter, we have examined some of the critical steps needed to preserve a crime scene so that it is not compromised. Chief among these steps is the requirement for ensuring a crime scene is not contaminated as part of the investigation, to prevent scene evidence from being disturbed, damaged, or tainted in any way. This chapter also has unveiled a new technology aimed at helping forensic and law enforcement teams collaborate on capturing scene information without multiple people actually on the crime scene; the result will be more comprehensive, accurate, and compelling presentations of the scene before a jury.

In the next chapter, the emergence of the total station, for decades, a major crash and crime scene reconstruction tool, and its advantages will be explored.

Notes

1. Chase, Jennifer. "9 Key Steps for a Successful Crime Scene Investigation." 2017. www.authorjenniferchase.com.
2. "Crime Scene Documentation." 2016. www.lawofficer.com.

4

The Total Station

Still a Stalwart Documentation Tool

For more than 10 years, Las Vegas, Nevada, has been a hotbed for thousands of vehicle crashes, particularly fatal ones. This translates into a lot of crash scenes to map and document. To assure accurate and efficient scene documentation with so many collisions, it is essential to use the most reliable technology. William Redfairn, former lead detective with the Las Vegas Metro Police Department (LVMPD) Fatal Crash Investigation Detail, knows this need well after mapping hundreds of crash scenes. In 2013, for example, Redfairn and his team used total stations exclusively to investigate and document nearly 300 fatal crashes out of thousands that occurred annually. Today, he is a partner with Dynamic Safety, LLC, a crash investigation and reconstruction consulting firm with offices in Illinois and Las Vegas. Las Vegas remains a focal point for crashes, and Redfairn still uses total stations for documenting crash scenes. He also uses other technologies as they have become available. In many instances, multiple tools are used to map one specific scene.[1]

No matter what a forensic scene reveals , it will be different from any other scene, which means the method of documenting it may differ in almost every instance.

Even though a total station is not the primary crash or crime scene documentation tool used today, it still has a major role in recording essential scene details. Dynamic Safety presently uses Leica reflectorless total stations equipped with data collectors. For selected scenes, just using a total station to document evidence is adequate because a 2D diagram, showing slopes and distances, plus a top-down view, may be all that is required for the final deliverable (Figures 4.1, 4.2, 4.3, and 4.4).

Figure 4.1 Undersheriff Michael Eisenloffel, Nye County, Nevada, Sheriff's Office, lines up his total station to take a measurement.

Total Station, Once a Surveying Tool, Now a Major Solution for Crash Scene Mapping

Total stations, which originally were used for field surveying projects, were starting to be used by reconstructionists roughly 25 years ago to map and document crash scenes. By about 2005, the total station had replaced measuring tapes and wheels because higher and more reliable measurements and accuracy were needed.

Total stations use an infrared wave signal sent from the device to read slopes and measure distances, performing this function one point at a time. They prove very useful for small crime scenes and regular crashes. Among the most favored types of total stations currently used by reconstruction technicians are those offering high-precision,

reflectorless measuring with a narrow-beam visible laser (reflectorless total stations can operate with or without a prism). They can capture distance measurements without needing a prism so long as the objects being measured are within the line of sight.

As a prismless mapping system, the reflectorless total station can measure the distance to certain objects from virtually right up against its scope to several hundred or even several thousand feet away from the reference point location. The total station can be moved easily from one

Figure 4.2 Lt. Eric Murphy, Nye County, Nevada, Sheriff's Office, enters information into the handheld unit of his total station. (Photo courtesy of Nye County, Nevada, Sheriff's Office).

location to another (as in a house, where a crime has occurred in several rooms) by moving to previously established reference points. The device offers increased accuracy of horizontal and vertical angles measured at the scene. Finally, a reflectorless total station can map scenes in 3D after which field measurements/data points are loaded into a computer program designed for reconstructing the scene. This CAD (computer-aided design) program can differentiate among different cars, houses, and evidence, and can also be programmed to move the cars at specific speeds to reconstruct a vehicle accident (Figures 4.5 and 4.6).

Robotic Total Station Needs Just One Operator, and Speeds Up Scene Capture

Using a total station, especially a robotic total station, can be much quicker for collision scene mapping. It reduces the time a highway

Figure 4.3 Reconstruction expert Bobby Jones prepares to map and document a serious crash scene using his total station.

Figure 4.4 Joe Warren, a veteran Chattanooga, Tennessee, crash reconstruction expert, has found that using a total station at major vehicle collision scenes is excellent for documenting skid marks and can generate an after-situation diagram that is almost immediately available for review and study. (Photo courtesy of Joe Warren, traffic investigator, Chattanooga, Tennessee, Police Department).

Figure 4.5 Bobby Jones, a veteran crash reconstructionist, maps and records a crash scene using a Topcon GPT 3002LW total station. (Photos courtesy of Bobby Jones Accident Reconstruction, Knoxville, Tenn.)

Figure 4.6 Bobby Jones, a veteran crash reconstructionist, maps and records a crash scene using a Topcon GPT 3002LW total station. (Photos courtesy of Bobby Jones Accident Reconstruction, Knoxville, Tenn.)

lane must be closed during a traffic accident, which reduces the delay for commuters as well as the potential for additional accidents. And, a total station can cut down time reconstructing a scene with CAD software. Overall benefits include greater accuracy, data accessibility in real time, and faster, more accurate layouts (Figure 4.7).[2]

Redfairn and his fellow reconstructionists in Dynamic Safety's Las Vegas office find total stations still useful in mapping serious injury and fatal crash scenes. They use their three reflectorless total stations with data recorders because 99 percent of Dynamic Safety's work is documenting crash scenes throughout Las Vegas, although murder and assault cases are also handled. Most of the client assignments for crash scene reconstruction come from law firms and insurance companies. According to Redfairn, law enforcement agencies in southern

Figure 4.7 A Sokkia SET550RX Total Station with measuring device. (Photo courtesy of Nye County, Nevada, Sheriff's Office).

Figure 4.8 In Las Vegas, Nevada, where there are thousands of collisions each year, especially fatal ones, the total station is an effective mapping tool, giving reliable accuracy, data accessibility in real time, and fast layouts. In fact, for some crash scenes, a total station can be faster than using a laser scanner, plus there can be time savings back in the office when building the scene diagram to show where the collision measurements had been taken. (Photo courtesy of Bill Redfairn, Dynamic Safety, LLC, Las Vegas, Nevada).

Nevada are investigating and recording nearly 1,500 vehicle collisions a month (Figure 4.8).

Similar to a majority of crime scene reconstruction consulting firms, Dynamic Safety uses nearly every available technology because each crash or crime scene is pretty much one of a kind. One scene may require just one type of reconstruction tool, such as a total station; another more complex scene might call for multiple scene recording tools. The important point here, Redfairn argues, is to mentally put yourself in front of a jury and think about how you must explain a scene to it and show how a crime or crash most likely occurred. It all depends on your end product (the scene 2D/3D model or diagram) and what kinds of questions you will need to answer.

For example, Redfairn recalls a crash incident in which two people in a car had run off the road. There was no roadway evidence, so just the roadway itself and the surrounding area needed to be documented. Only a total station was used because it was faster than using a laser scanner. It saved Redfairn substantial time at the back end as he assembled the scene into a diagram.

Total Station Joined by Other Technologies

As technology evolves, law enforcement agencies and private reconstruction consultants must decide which tools for mapping scenes will best fit their learning abilities, time schedules, and budget. This has become especially clear as laser scanners prove to be a technology that is attractive and more comprehensive for scene documentation. However, scanners require intense training, extensive practice for operating, and can be expensive to acquire. This is the conclusion of Joe Warren, traffic investigator, Chattanooga, Tennessee, Police Department, who, after working for 20 years in his department's traffic division, has straddled the technology spectrum---from using cloth measuring tapes to early versions of photogrammetry, then total stations, laser scanners, and, most recently, drones. It is because he has committed himself to thorough training, especially on laser scanning, that Warren has become a seasoned scene documentation specialist.

As Warren trains agencies throughout Tennessee, he sees a trend that is widespread across the country: law enforcement agencies predominantly use one type of technology because it is what they trained on initially, feel comfortable in using, and are reluctant to learn a newer technology and then have to switch back and forth between two technologies. But relying on one technology for all scene mapping can be risky, as some crucial scene details might be missed. Learning multiple documentation tools is the future direction of crime scene investigation. Also, it is not just the mapping tool that needs mastery, but also the equally critical software that is used for the workflow or post-production part of creating a 3D model.

3D Laser Scanning Making Inroads in Scene Mapping

The technology trend in scene documentation has in the past several years leaned toward laser scanning as almost the de facto tool, even though many more technologies that also yield 3D visualization, such as 3D camera systems, are being unveiled. Even so, the total station has not vanished; it is still frequently tapped to map and record entire scenes or to just provide some quick, supplemental measurements and aid in scene mapping post-production workflow. For instance, Warren works with video evidence as he reconstructs some scenes. Therefore, he may need a few points from a videotaped scene to locate a portion of a diagram of the scene. This may be helpful if scene data may not have been very clearly represented in laser scan data acquired from the same scene, for instance. In a situation like this, Warren will use the total station as a "follow-up" tool to capture these points; obtaining these few points with a total station is far easier than what may be required in office post-production during which he works with massive laser scan data. Getting a few points by using the total station makes it a lot easier for him and others to develop locators for the resulting diagram.

Redfairn of Dynamic Safety, the Las Vegas reconstruction firm, shares Warren's support of the total station's continued strength as a mapping tool. He remembers responding to one of the hundreds of Las Vegas vehicle collisions, this time involving an auto/pedestrian crash on a major thoroughfare not far from the Las Vegas strip and convention center. The roadway was two lanes in each direction, with a center two-way turn lane. The driver of a vehicle struck a pedestrian, killing him. Lighting conditions at the collision scene, Redfairn initially surmised, could have been an issue. The collision scene, pedestrian, and vehicle were laser scanned and the diagram was presented clearly in court without needing to bring jurors to the actual scene. To perform an analysis of street lighting for the collision scene, a total station was used to document the exact locations where measurements of the scene had been taken. Why was the scanner not used in this instance versus the total station? Redfairn noted that by using the total station, it was faster and just as accurate, and time savings was achieved back in the office when building the scene diagram to show where the collision measurements had been taken.

The software used to bring in the laser scan data point cloud was FARO SCENE: the software to pull the total station data and then to process the two combined data sets was FARO Zone. Redfairn also used the Rhinoceros software program which became useful for selecting the desired point cloud data to create the 3D model.

Combining Technologies Helps Grab More Crucial Scene Details

The total station, as it segued into use as a crime reconstruction tool from its earlier field surveying application, has become well tailored for mapping elaborate crash scenes. Warren cites a major crash he and his traffic investigation team recorded that occurred on Interstate 75 in Chattanooga---a scene that stretched roughly the length of two football fields. The driver of a large tractor-trailer truck, who had been driving 36 hours, and who was on meth, and speeding at 82 MPH in a 55 MPH zone, plowed through substantial stopped traffic in a construction zone. The crash involved nine vehicles and led to six fatalities, that included two children, and nine injuries. At this scene, reconstructionists used both a total station and a 3D laser scanner. What Warren noticed with the diagram he was building, based on total station data gathered, was that it represented a dramatic, overall view of the location of vehicles and most of the tire marks left on the interstate highway. With data collected by the laser scanner, *all* of the tire marks were captured. Due to the number of vehicles involved, all of them skidding in different directions, tire marks had overlapped. The scan data picked up all of these crisscrossing marks.

When it came to the post-production process of creating a diagram for this complex scene, Warren found that doing so using total station data was much faster than it would have been using scanning data. The total station was able to generate an after-situation diagram that was almost immediately available for review and study, specifically by the National Transportation Safety Board (NTSB) when their Go-Team arrived the next day. However, the total station did a better job than the current version of the scanner equipment available at that time of documenting the tire marks, as the scan data lacked sufficient resolution at the time of capturing all of the skid marks. At the same time, using both the total station and the scanner allowed a good, clear comparison of point cloud data sets. "The tire marks we measured using the total station were easier to note on the 2D diagram generated," Warren said. "However, because of the number of tire marks at this crash scene, the laser scanner was able to identify more evidence that we didn't focus on trying to capture. While we were able to measure and document final rest positions of all the vehicles involved in this collision, the scan data from the laser scanner picked up the exact crush measurements on scene that we couldn't get with the total station simply because of the sheer number of vehicles involved."

Even though the scanner that Warren was using at that time was inadequate for capturing all of the visible tire marks at the Interstate 75 crash scene, it still was able to record some tire marks that investigators had not identified and whose measurements could be taken with a total station. The total station is entirely dependent on its user to capture whatever evidence is deemed necessary, while, in contrast, the laser scanner is a perfect tool for collecting all evidence that it can see during a scene investigation. "Our newest laser scanner (a Leica ScanStation P40) is much better, with a higher point density capture rate that enables it to see more of the tire marks at a crash scene than we'd be able to see with the naked eye while walking the scene," Warren noted. The Leica ScanStation P40 has a long range (up to 885 feet), speed (nearly 1 million data points per second), and 3D positional accuracy (3mm at 50m; 6mm at 100m).

Be Careful About Replacing Mapping Tools

The total station, although not the predominant documentation tool for crash and crime scenes that it once was, remains valuable as a means now to support newer methods of scene data capture. In some cases, a total station is far easier to use for capture of additional, necessary data to complete scene diagrams during post-production workflows. Unfortunately, many law enforcement agencies and private reconstruction consulting firms have shuttered or sold their total stations in favor of more recent technology tools for mapping crash and crime scenes. Meanwhile, agencies like Dynamic Safety and the Chattanooga Police Department not only still use their total stations with regularity, but have integrated total stations into their technology toolbox. The tendency among many law enforcement agencies and private crime scene documentation firms to buy a new technology and replace other existing tools with it concerns Redfairn. Therefore, he offers a warning: "Reconstructionists need to be careful about adding to or purging their toolbox of certain mapping tools." Ask yourself, says Redfairn, "What am I taking out (of the toolbox, permanently), what am I going to replace it with? And is that new product I'm putting into the toolbox better than what I have now?"

To be sure that adding a new mapping tool, and possibly replacing another tool with it, is the best route, Redfairn suggests that the agency or reconstructionist ask the vendor from whom it may buy a new mapping tool to allow a trial test of the new mapping technology for 15 or 30 days in the environment in which it will be used. This is a great way to learn if the new tool is the right one and will be a good fit, because there probably will be a substantial investment of money required for acquiring the new tool, and, of course, thorough training. Finally, if you, as a private reconstructionist, or your agency buy a new tool and are possibly replacing another tool---like a total station—with it, be sure you actually have enough workload to use the new technology. If you have only a few crime and/or crash scenes to document each year, then the expense of this new solution, and the extensive training and practice needed, may not be worth it.

"Cross-Sensor Validation" a Helpful Strategy for Multiple Mapping Tools

Mike Selves, owner of Collision and Forensic Solutions, Papillion, Nebraska, sees another benefit of retaining a total station—even when another instrument is acquired: "Cross-Sensor Validation." This concept involves validating and integrating forensic mapping outputs from multiple sensors between two different scene mapping technologies, or if more than two mapping tools are being used. Why is this meaningful? Law enforcement and crash reconstruction agencies can always submit sensor outputs from a redundant set of tools (i.e., total station, laser scanner) to courts when the accuracy of a mapping and documentation instrument is questioned. According to Selves, a South Dakota State Highway Patrol Crash Reconstruction expert and forensic mapper/law enforcement instructor for 25 years, the total station is widely viewed as one of the most durable and reliable point-to-point measurement tools available to forensic mappers. Its accuracy can be used as a benchmark to performance-test other measurement devices, such as laser scanners, handheld scanners, and photogrammetry tools, Selves explained. Total stations also are commonly used to calibrate and validate the output from aerial photogrammetry accomplished with UAV drones. A common obstacle for many agencies wishing to buy a laser scanner is the ongoing cost of calibrations. Selves argues that manufacturer-recommended calibrations for laser scanners are usually based on the expectation that users in the surveying and engineering industries deploy their laser scanners continuously. But public safety agencies typically deploy their equipment much less frequently and for shorter durations. "A regular and well-regimented use of 'cross-sensor validation' between a total station and laser scanner can assist agencies in delaying scanner calibrations, saving money," Selves said. "Agencies that use this strategy must ensure that they keep good logs of their regular cross-sensor validations that can be submitted to courts when the accuracy of an instrument is questioned."

Research and Select the Mapping Equipment Carefully; Make Sure It Holds Up in Court

Mike Selves concurs with Redfairn about being careful when selecting mapping equipment for use on crash or crime scenes. He goes a step further, offering this advice: "Make sure you do your due diligence in searching for the right package of equipment that's going to work for your agency, that your trainer is certified, and that you will get 24/7 support." As a seasoned crash reconstruction practitioner, Selves is a strong advocate of the total station because it can validate points within a laser scanner's point cloud of crime or crash scenes. He also uses multiple mapping tools, but only if they can capture data that can be used with a total station. Selves often uses a laser scanner in combination with his total station as well as a drone.

Another important consideration for Selves is the ability of his total station to be verified via a Daubert-Frye hearing in court. Daubert-Frye admissibility hearings refer to a similar set of legal tests used in U.S. Courts to determine the admissibility of scientific evidence (i.e., expert witness testimony and scientific data). A properly deployed total station, Selves asserts, can easily surmount a Daubert hearing as being acceptable for its accuracy. And, again, Selves invokes the concept of cross-sensor validation, saying, "You can validate every measurement made by your scanner or drone with the total station data points."

As always, time saved with capturing crime or crash scene data is always a high priority. And this applies, as well, to workflow. Selves, who has recorded a large number of crash scenes using a total station combined with a drone and/or scanner, has experienced the time savings first hand. "The manpower hours can be reduced significantly, especially if you have a robotic total station instead of a two-man total station," Selves said. "And at certain crash scenes, we don't have to close the roads down anymore because we can scan or drone it. We can get the control points with the total station, then user a laser scanner or drone to get the entire scene very quickly."

Next, everything that is scanned is related back to the control points that were taken with the total station.

Selves prefers extensive effort because he feels it will make his presentation of any scene withstand court scrutiny. The key to combining mapping technologies for scene data capture allows him to explain how he obtained his data. Court presentations can occasionally hit a wall because some scene evidence might not show up. "If you've missed some points, you can still go back to the scene and get more points using your control data set," Selves explained. This also applies to laser scanning of a scene, because the point cloud should allow the reconstructionist to acquire extra points using the control point set.

Throughout this chapter, the transition of the total station's origin as a field surveying instrument to become a major tool used for crash and crime scene mapping has been explored. Although there are newer technologies to capture scene evidence, the total station remains efficiently used, but is also combined with these more recent tools. In Chapter 5, we will look at the advantages that another long-lasting technology, photogrammetry, offers and how it has changed and enhanced crime and crash scene recording.

Notes

1. "Reconstruction Faster, Better." Law Officer.Com, 2016. www.lawofficer.com.
2. "Total Station Technology Helps." Syracuse.Com, April 2012. https://www.syracuse.com/news/2012/04/total station technology helps.html

5

The Value of Photogrammetry Takes on New Importance as Tool for 3D Crime Scene Capture

Photographs are one of the essential deliverables of any crime scene investigation. They capture valuable evidence exactly as it appeared in the scene. However, a photograph takes images from the 3D world and casts them on a flat two-dimensional image plane. Consequently, the depth of whatever object or piece of evidence is shown is lost. Because this information is lost, it is hard to know the full significance of what the photograph is showing. For this reason, photogrammetry, the science of capturing and preserving geometric data from photographs, was created and has become a highly useful tool in crime scene reconstruction (Figure 5.1).

Similar to total stations, photogrammetry has not been exclusively used for crime scene reconstruction in the past several years. Contrasted to its earlier years as a standalone crime and crash scene mapping technology, photogrammetry is now often integrated with other mapping tools, such as 3D laser scanners, and particularly Unmanned Aerial Vehicles (UAV), or drones. The supplemental data captured by these other mapping tools makes photogrammetry a more powerful way to view scenes in 3D detail. Although photogrammetry is a precursor to 3D laser scanning, it tackles many of the same crime scene reconstruction applications that have been credited to scanning, at a fraction of the overall system cost. The drawback, however, is its limited use in particular spaces or at scenes that lack proper lighting, such as night-time crashes.

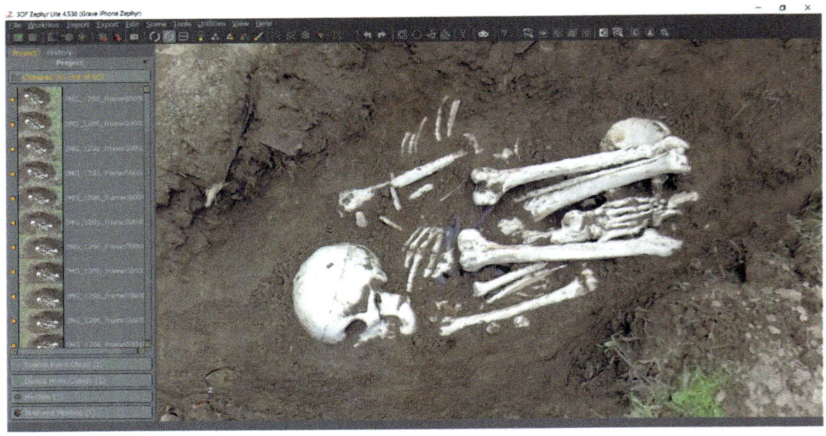

Figure 5.1 Shown is a clandestine grave exercise at the University of Toronto, Mississauga, Ontario, Canada. This model was created using an iPhone with video, and then frames were processed through a photogrammetry program, 3DF Zephyr. (Photo courtesy of Eugene Liscio, Ai2-3D, Toronto, Ontario, Canada)

When a camera is used to capture any part of a crime scene, it can produce views from various positions. The result is several scene perspectives that allow measurements to be represented in numerous 3D formats. Photogrammetry can be useful for crime scene mapping by using multiple photos taken at a crime scene. At the same time, in other instances, all that the reconstruction practitioner will have is a single image from which to extract critical scene data. The single photo can be used for producing important 2D measurement data.[1]

"Retro-Fitting" Scene Reconstruction

Litigation for collisions or crime incidents relies upon whatever scene evidence is available. Several years may have passed for some cases to be litigated, and typically the only evidence that remains is scene photographs taken by crime scene investigators or reconstruction practitioners. In such instances, photogrammetry can be an invaluable documentation tool. Vehicle collisions are a great example of how photogrammetry can be used to determine how severely a car in question was deformed. The aim here is to determine how much energy was required to cause the vehicle's deformation.

Bobby Jones, Bobby Jones Associates Accident Reconstruction, Knoxville, Tennessee, is a veteran crash reconstruction expert who has used photogrammetry for several years. Although Jones has tapped other scene reconstruction technologies in the past few years, he still finds photogrammetry helpful for select crash scenes. Jones is using the PhotoModeler photogrammetry package from PhotoModeler Technologies.

He had used total stations to map scenes prior to acquiring photogrammetry and has always acquired new technologies for scene documentation as they came along. Today, Jones actively uses 3D laser scanning and drones as his latest scene mapping technology acquisitions.

What prompted Jones to adopt photogrammetry when it became available was that it gave what he calls a "retro-fit." For example, Jones explained, "Let's say someone took photos of a crash scene, but they didn't take any measurements. If this person returned to the scene and measured some of the items visible in that scene, such as a utility pole placement or fire hydrant, or any part of the environment that still existed, he could create what we call the control point and match those to the photograph." Jones continued, "The (photogrammetry) software would help us recreate the scene, allowing us to extract measurements, say, from vehicles and maybe the final rest of a body."

Even though Jones primarily documents crash scenes today using 3D laser scanning, he still consistently employs photogrammetry, as well, for smaller projects, and for those cases where photographs are the only evidence available from an older scene. For existing scenes, he likes the fact that he can take 10–12 overlapping photos from various angles, then use the photogrammetry software to create 3D coordinates of feature points of interest, as well as a 3D model that can be used virtually, on a computer screen, and regenerated using a printer.

Many law enforcement agencies have used photogrammetry steadily for more than ten years because their budgets can accommodate the cost. For these agencies, the cost of a laser scanner is simply out of reach, especially when the necessary software, training and equipment calibration are factored into the overall cost. Conversely, those agencies that can afford laser scanning still find that using photogrammetry and total stations help acquire data points that a scanner might miss.

Captures Data that Total Stations and Laser Scanning May Miss

Lee DeChant, owner of Bellevue, Washington-based DeChant Consulting Services, co-developer of the iWitness close-range photogrammetry software system, points out there are pluses and minuses with using photogrammetry. On the plus side is the fact that the images—photographs—create an irrefutable record of where objects in a scene are located. "A lot of times, it's hard to prove that with a laser scanner, total station or other means," DeChant said. "On the minus side of photogrammetry is the fact that it can sometimes take longer to post-process on a personal computer, compared to the near real-time approach of the laser scanner, in order to generate the 3D point cloud data. Countering this PC processing time difference is the relatively faster data acquisition time at the scene for the generation of fully textured, photogrammetrically produced point clouds than from laser scanner data," he added. To summarize, while the generation of a terrestrial laser scanner point cloud is faster than the photogrammetric generation of a fully photo-textured 3D model, the data acquisition time-on-scene for feature point extraction/digitization from the latter is generally much faster than from the former.

In a sense, photogrammetry is kind of a hybrid between a total station and laser scanner, DeChant explained, because DSMs (digital surface models) can be created with it just as effectively as with a scanner. However, it is important to note that photogrammetry must have texture present in the images in order to create the DSM.

In Some Instances, Photogrammetry May Be the Only Solution

Sometimes, getting scene evidence can be difficult, and timing has to be right. For example, Alan Walford, CEO of PhotoModeler Technologies, Vancouver, BC, Canada, offers that there are times when a photograph or video footage *is the evidence.* If you're mapping a scene and have some bystanders taking photos of that scene with their iPhones, a surveillance camera image, or a police cruiser with a dashcam or a body-worn video camera has captured the scene, this may be the only record of evidence before the scene was possibly disturbed and you, as reconstructionist, have arrived. These recordings of the evidence are essential because the evidence might have been moved or the scene disturbed by the time you have arrived and started mapping the scene. Consequently, "You have to reconstruct some very critical data at the scene and all you have are images from any one or all of these sources," Walford said. "Therefore, photogrammetry is your only solution."

To illustrate this point, Walford recalls a domestic abuse case in which an officer responding to the incident scene was wearing a body cam. As he climbed the stairs to the living unit there was a pistol lying on the front steps, but which he did not notice. The officer entered the unit to find the occupants. Next, as emergency teams arrived at the unit and immediately went up the stairs, one of the team's members accidentally kicked the gun off the stairs. It turns out, Walford explains, that as part of the investigation of this case it was important to find out where the gun was located relative to the living unit. The only piece of evidence was the body cam footage of that gun as it originally sat on the front steps to the unit (Figures 5.2 and 5.3).

Photogrammetry has always had an important role in crime scene documentation, even though it has had to compete with other technologies as they emerged and were adopted. In the early stages of scene documentation technology, there were total stations and photogrammetry. Small scenes typically were mapped with photogrammetry and longer scenes were mapped by combining photogrammetry and total stations. As the 3D laser scanner emerged and was adopted by reconstructionists, photogrammetry's use waned slightly, except in cases where it was the only technology available to use because there was nothing more than photography or video footage for evidence. Then, when drones were accepted and authorized for commercial use by the FAA, as a way to help map scenes, photogrammetry became

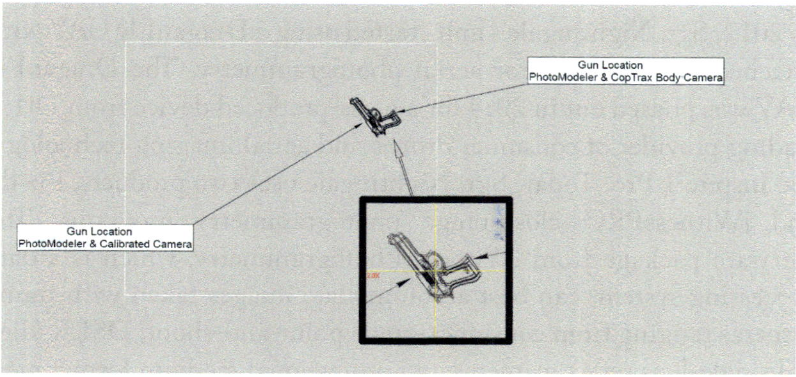

Figure 5.2 Example of photogrammetric measurement of firearm location at a crime scene for law enforcement body-worn camera. (Photos courtesy of Photomodeler Technologies)

Figure 5.3 Example of photogrammetric measurement of firearm location at a crime scene for law enforcement body-worn camera. (Photos courtesy of Photomodeler Technologies)

an important companion mapping tool because of the ability to merge its terrestrial data with the aerial mapping data of drones (Figure 5.4).

Merging Terrestrial with Aerial Scene Data

The trend of merging terrestrial and aerial data has become particularly advantageous for lengthy, complex collision scenes where there is an extensive debris field, and possibly fatalities. Sgt. Brian Nightingale, Level 5 reconstructionist and unit commander in charge of Vancouver Island, BC, Canada, Royal Canadian Mounted Police, has used photogrammetry for the bulk of his crash and crime scenes since 2009. In 2012, Sgt. Nightingale's unit started using a DraganFly UAV with attached Sony camera for aerial photogrammetry. The DraganFly UAV was phased out in 2014 for a mass-produced device from DJI, a leading provider of consumer drones and aerial imaging technology, the Inspire 1 Pro. Today, Sgt. Nightingale uses two products, Pix4D and iWitnessPRO close-range photogrammetry programs. The software package from iWitness Photogrammetry, which is a data processing system, can best accommodate images taken with frame cameras ranging from consumer-grade point-and-shoot, DSLR (digital single-lens reflex) cameras and professional medium format metric cameras. Pix4D works best with cameras that utilize a "rolling shutter" configuration like the X5 proprietary mounted camera used

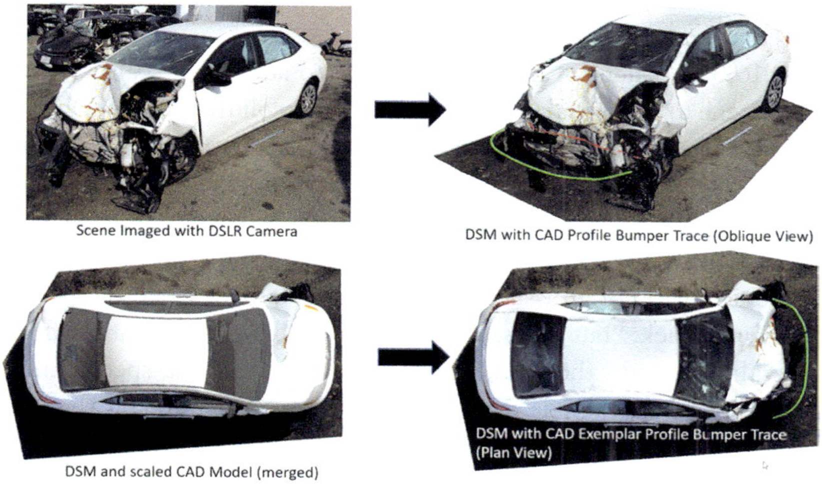

Figure 5.4 Shown is an example of a digital image of a collision vehicle (top left) photographed with a DSLR camera, to a photogrammetric digital surface model (created with iWitnessPRO photogrammetry software—top right). At bottom are drone views of the image of a CAD exemplar model of this same vehicle (left) and DSM (Digital Surface Model) "merged together" (right). (Photos courtesy of www.photometrix.com)

on the DJI Inspire Pro UAV, Sgt. Nightingale explained. As with PhotoModeler's photogrammetry offerings, iWitnessPRO can also process full-motion video, and images recorded from both terrestrial and aerial camera platforms can be accommodated, as well. The iWitnessPRO product has been optimized to automatically generate digital surface models, ortho-imagery, and 3D reality meshes from UAV/drone photography. The inclusion of Pix4D photogrammetry has further streamlined the processing of Nadar images (Felix Nadar was a 19th-Century French photographer famous for the portraits of his great contemporaries, and whose name became a brand) in the office with additional enhancements such as Google Tiles and quality densification point clouds, all from a single photogrammetry project.

For Sgt. Nightingale, the ability to combine terrestrial and aerial photogrammetry was a significant turning point for his crash scene mapping cases. He said it now takes only 10 mins for one aerial flight over an average scene. As a result, "We're surveying the whole scene (on the ground and in the air) plus getting all the photographs we need for a crash scene in about 30 minutes," Sgt. Nightingale said.

Aids in Corroborating Court Testimony

In 2016, the benefit of having the ability to add aerial scanning of a crash scene to terrestrial photogrammetry was solidly confirmed by the sergeant after a driver struck a pedestrian on a sidewalk in a Vancouver Island community, BC, Canada, then drove further down the road. The accident involved an impaired female driver who, after striking the pedestrian, struck five vehicles as she continued driving. "Speed of the vehicle was not an issue," Sgt. Nightingale said, when the pedestrian was struck, "but the issue was when the driver accelerated off the sidewalk and onto the road, traveling slightly over the speed limit." Even though the female driver claimed in a court hearing that she blacked out due, in part, to a preexisting medical condition, the investigation revealed that she had a blood alcohol level that exceeded the legal limit, he further added. The driver ultimately was found guilty. Aerial surveying was a major part of the expert evidence presented and allowed the court to fully understand the dynamics of the incident.

Sgt. Nightingale used photogrammetry to map the collision scene, but in using a drone to also map scene details he had to fly it approximately 115 ft above, which is higher than many other crash scenes would require. Although it might seem that laser scanning this scene might have been a logical option, the sergeant would disagree. "We had a lot of small pieces of physical evidence all the way down the road—the pedestrian's shoes, items he was carrying in his hand.. So, there is all of this detail you can include in a diagram that gets more difficult to locate in a scanner's data set, because the point cloud produces so many points," Sgt. Nightingale continued. Also, scanning such a vast scene would have taken significant time, he added.

By merging data points on the road of this accident scene (50+ physical evidence items called exhibits), using Pix4D, with data captured by a set of NADAR images by the Inspire 1 Pro drone, Sgt. Nightingale was able to produce a 3D diagram showing the path of the vehicles and the dispersal of debris along the roadway.

Drone Images Used to Solve Photogrammetry Measurements

Drones generally work hand-in-hand with photogrammetry, affirms Dan Mills of DCM Technical Services in Toronto, Canada, a user of the PhotoModeler photogrammetry program. "A lot of times," he said, "the reconstructionist can take images produced by a drone to aid in solving measurements taken with photogrammetry." The advantage of doing so is that you're not needing to stand out where the measurement point is being taken. "You can take photographs and do a lot of the processing offsite," Mills said, "which can be helpful depending whether or not you're at a hazardous site and want to minimize the amount of time you're spending there." Mills does not personally use drones for his clients, but often will analyze drone footage provided to him. Mills considers photogrammetry to be highly advantageous if a reconstructionist is trying to perform some inverse measurements from a set of photographs, or when a case's direction changes. Older cases can evolve a bit; a new party might get involved with an old case later on via a lawsuit. Some new details might arise in the case that could be of interest and bring new perspectives.

If you have a large number of photographs that were taken by an officer or investigator at the scene, this will be helpful because even if a measurement for an area of interest in a photograph was not initially taken, "It's still possible to get this measurement off of the photo," Mills said. He added, "From an evidentiary standpoint, the ability of photogrammetry to offer measurements off of photographs that have evidence present is a strong advantage for this technology tool."

Most collision and crime scenes occur during daylight. But nighttime scenes can occur anytime just as easily. Sgt. Nightingale, the RCMP unit commander, recalls one crash scene he was required to map at night. He mapped the scene using both photographs and a 3D laser scanner. However, because of the immense data set produced by scanning, the scene needed to be marked with exhibits; the sergeant routinely marks physical evidence so that the markers can be more easily identified at a later time.

The nighttime crash obscured tire marks that definitely had been left on the road. At the first light of day, Sgt. Nightingale was able to see tire marks and placed identification markers on them. Next, he took photographs of the tire marks and then laser scanned them as well. Although the tire marks were hard to discern, they were still visible in daylight, and the sergeant even noticed that the tire marks extended further back on the road than the location of the identification markers. "Because I had photographs and common points on the ground, I was able to identify the location of this area (the tire marks) in my scan to see if I could extend the skid marks," Sgt. Nightingale said. Skid marks show up as a different color tone in 3D scans. By referencing the skid marks in his scan of the crash scene, Sgt. Nightingale could easily identify where the skid mark had ended.

If street lights are on the road where a crash occurred, a drone can capture the key measurement points. The drone data would be valuable for photogrammetry because it would show the precise locations of the markers from which measurements could be taken.

Photogrammetry an Aid for Scenes Difficult to Map

Another benefit of the aerial survey data created by photogrammetry is that, for a crash scene like the nighttime scene just described, the user could create a broken line for the road precisely the way it is depicted in the images—as the actual broken line on the road separating the two lanes. This capability prevents trying to use a CAD program that is merely estimating the broken line. "So, if you're going into court and you're showing a piece of evidence by a line on the roadway, the line is actually there when using the photogrammetry program and merging it with drone data because it's drawn in automatically," Sgt. Nightingale said.

Mills, of DCM Technical Services, Toronto, Canada, agrees that merging drone data with that of terrestrial photogrammetry has enabled difficult crash scenes to become easier to map. Long, narrow, two-lane roads have been particularly hard to map if a reconstructionist was using, say, just a total station. Working with photogrammetry can be challenging, as well, because it will require taking a lot of photos and getting the needed ground measurements. But when drone surveying is brought in, it is possible to find a vantage point above the road to get measurements as opposed to having to look down the length of the road.

Photogrammetry More Relevant When Used with Other Technology

Angad Singh, Technical Sales Manager for Pix4D, a photogrammetry system provider, believes that drones have given photogrammetry increased importance because of the richness of scene data captured coupled with much faster crash or crime scene documentation. Pix4D

Mapper is an image processing software that is based on automatically finding thousands of common points between images.

As with the other commercial photogrammetry programs, Pix4D can process images taken from any camera and can use perspective lens or fisheye. Singh said that a new app for Pix4D, offered in 2019, allows rapid capture of extensive scene data over a three- or four-acre area. "With the software, you can create a map from the software's photogrammetry imagery in about a minute on a regular computer that's not very powerful," he said.

Roadway and highway safety for collision reconstruction experts or traffic officers is an ongoing concern due to heavy moving traffic and the potential threat of secondary accidents. Therefore, a drone used with photogrammetry can dramatically reduce the time spent on a busy roadway compared to using a laser scanner to map a collision scene.

The merging of photogrammetry programs with drones yields substantial, valuable point cloud data that allow a more detailed scene diagram to be created. The pairing of these technologies has made photogrammetry itself a more important and relevant mapping tool. "The ability to use a drone to get the imagery you need, when you need it—because of the drone's logistical simplicity—has triggered a resurgence in photogrammetry in recent years," Singh added, because the two tools are a natural match (Figure 5.5).

Figure 5.5 Police drone survey, acquiring digital images converted into a DSM (Digital Surface Model) and Orthomosaic using iWitness PRO photogrammetry software, mapping a serious crash scene incident. (Photo courtesy of www.photometrix.com)

Photogrammetry/Drone System Produced Irrefutable Evidence in Collision Case

By having different top-down as well as close-up side views from a drone's flight over a collision scene, a more compelling and clear scene representation can be created. Singh recalls one dramatic crash scene in the Midwest, in which the driver of a car with a passenger was traveling at a very high speed on a roadway to elude police; the driver already had been pulled over by police the same day. The car's high speed caused the driver to lose control as he was exiting onto a ramp off the roadway. As the driver raced onto the ramp and suddenly turned left to a frontage road of an interstate highway, he lost control. The car then hit a metal barrier, which caused the barrier to slice off the top of the vehicle and, in the process, decapitate the driver's companion in the passenger seat.

Singh noted that skid marks from the crash were highly visible and easy to measure. "This allowed us to determine the exact rate of speed at which the driver took his turn," Singh explained. "You can also see, based on knowledge of how the barrier was constructed, how much the car mangled the road's shoulder due to the car's high speed, the slope of the road, and how far and fast the decapitated head flew."

The car's driver survived the crash, and the case did not go to court because the data captured with a Pix4D photogrammetry/drone system showed exactly what happened and that the evidence against the driver was irrefutable. The drone was used for making a double-grid mission (two passes) over the crash scene. Next, the drone was lowered so that the damaged car would be scanned to capture more definition of the damage that could be built into the 3D model. It was critical to focus on one measurement point on the ground, take as many photos as possible from varying angles, and then triangulate where that point existed. Once the point cloud from the scanned scene was processed, an enlarged map of the data set captured by the drone and photogrammetry system was created showing all evidence plus skid marks and gouges. A 3D fly-through video was created, as well.

Photogrammetry, a tested and reliable technology for crime scene documentation, has experienced a resurgence in recent years. While valuable on its own as a scene mapping tool, photogrammetry, when married via software to drones for aerial mapping, is now even more a compelling technology. It has been a significant technology in both accident and crime reconstructions. No wonder. Using a camera from various angles is the quickest way to document a scene, and by using photogrammetry software, the accident scene, for example, can be recreated from the photos and evidence markers collected by the police responding to the accident. The photos not only can depict the damage to vehicles but can also depict tire marks on the road, as well as environmental conditions at the time of a vehicle accident. In a similar fashion, photos taken at a crime scene showing rooms in a structure of a murder scene, weapons, damage to an area, or injuries to a victim can allow detectives and forensic experts to revisit the scene and try to ascertain the likely events. And even an autopsy can reveal evidence that was not obvious during the initial scene investigation, but which later contributes context to the photos. Photogrammetry can produce measurements for a realistic reconstruction to help determine bullet trajectories or blood pattern analysis, as well. When a photograph or an image is your only evidence—such as taken by a bystander, a body-worn camera, a dashcam, or a surveillance camera, then photogrammetry is the only viable solution to extracting key forensic data.

The usefulness of photogrammetry as a crime/crash mapping and recording tool, coupled with its ability to partner with drones to collect more comprehensive data, has been the focus of this chapter. Photogrammetry can capture data that laser scanning might miss, and at times may be the only technology able to map certain scenes.

In Chapter 6, the way in which 3D laser scanning has transformed crime scene documentation will be examined.

Note

1. “Photogrammetry in Forensics Introduction-5220.” 2008. www.hgexperts.com.

PART II

Getting the Most Out of 3D Laser Scanning

A Look at Some Unique Applications

The remainder of this book's content will now examine the basics of 3D laser scanning—how it works, how to work with point clouds and 3D modeling/diagramming, introducing scanned scenes into court—then some applications for laser scanning that forensic and crime scene reconstruction experts have accomplished with solid success. These applications include:

- Active shooter scenes
- Risk assessment and emergency planning for schools and various public buildings and venues
- Officer-involved shooting scenes
- Bloodstain patterns and analysis
- Crash vehicle damage analysis
- Suspect height approximation
- Combining technologies to solve crime/crash scene reconstruction challenges

Once again, it is key to remember that acquiring proper, professional training on a laser scanner is paramount. Not only is this basic scanner training necessary, but so is added training to become competent at using a laser scanner for the above applications. Some scanner manufacturers offer software packages specifically tailored for many of these applications, and they are well worth the added financial outlay.

Finally, the applications for laser scanning described in the following chapters require not only extra training, but increased practice with a 3D laser scanner due to their specific and exacting requirements. The frequency of these applications for which laser scanning can prove invaluable will differ in each reconstruction expert's work environment. But the best way to be ready for any of them is to practice using your scanner as much as possible. Because the results of your work on cases involving any of these scanning applications—the scene reconstructions created from them—may one day come before a jury.

6
How 3D Laser Scanning Systems are Changing Crime Scene Documentation

When it comes to recording a crime scene, most reconstruction experts would agree that it just takes a significant amount of time. Which is a primary reason why so many law enforcement agencies and private reconstruction firms have turned within the past several years to using 3D scene capture technologies. The predominant and highly popular solution is the LIDAR (Light Detection and Ranging), which is also commonly referred to as a 3D laser scanner or terrestrial scanner.

While this 3D scanning technology has been around for several decades and has widespread acceptance across many industries, it has been viewed as the next generation of crime and crash scene reconstruction technology among a majority of crime scene investigators and reconstruction experts. The 3D laser scanner is an effective and efficient way to capture most crimes scenes. Usually, when arriving at a crime scene, reconstruction practitioners must decide which parts of the scene are relevant to their case. They need to quickly determine what evidence to photograph as well as measure and collect. Prior to scanning, this process was accomplished using traditional mapping methods such as tape measures, measuring wheels, 35mm cameras, video cameras, and total stations to capture physical evidence indoors and outdoors. However, these mapping methods could take hours or even days to capture relevant parts of a scene, which also means certain key scene details might be missed (Figure 6.1).[1]

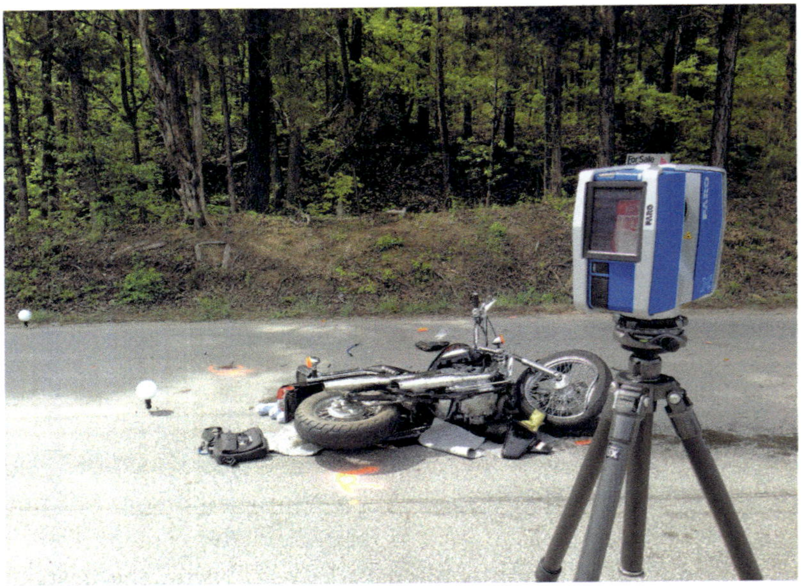

Figure 6.1 The 3D laser scanner is well suited for mapping and documenting crime and crash scenes. (Photo courtesy of Bobby Jones Accident Reconstruction, Knoxville, Tenn.)

Millions of Data Points Are Transformed Into a 3D Point Cloud

A laser scanner can digitally capture the surrounding environment as well as the shape of physical objects using a line of laser light. It is a way to capture the environment, frozen at a moment in time, to include the conditions of the scene and the exact size and shape of items within. The result is a complete digital three-dimensional representation. The laser scanner produces a line of laser light which sweeps across the screen while sensors continuously record the changing distance and intensity of the returning wavelength shape of the laser line in three dimensions (X, Y, and Z) as it strikes the object. As the laser scanner sweeps across a scene and performs a 360-degree scan, it creates an accurate, spatially correct 3D model comprising millions of points called a "point cloud." The point cloud can be easily navigated using a standard desktop or laptop computer as a dense representation of the scene is displayed (Figure 6.2).

This whole scanning process is very fast, capturing upwards of 750,000 points per second, with scene details down to the millimeter. This data set is what is referred to as a point cloud. The point cloud may contain as many as 10 million points after a scan of about 5 mins,

Figure 6.2 As the laser scanner sweeps across a scene and performs a 360-degree scan, it creates an accurate, spatially correct 3D model comprising millions of points called a "point cloud." (Photo courtesy of Eugene Liscio, ai2-3d, Ontario, Canada)

defined in terms of the X, Y, and Z coordinates. The typical file formats of point clouds are ASCII types like XYZ and OBJ, as well as E57, LAS, IGS, and other proprietary file formats.[2]

Typically, an operator usually will set up the laser scanner at a scene and move the device several times to accomplish different scans from many angles. Once the point cloud files are created, they are merged into one big three-dimensional representation of the object and then post-processed with various software packages, each designed for a specific application. The end result is the creation of point cloud data that is a precise reproduction of the scanned scene.[3]

Different Ways to Use 3D Laser Scanners

Terrestrial Scanner

Most common of the various scanners is the terrestrial laser scanner, which is typically mounted on a tripod or, in some cases, can be placed on any flat surface. Terrestrial Laser Scanners have a wide range of applications and can capture dense point clouds with millimeter accuracy. The goal of a terrestrial scanner is to collect data on an environment or an object's shape and perhaps its appearance. The 3D scanner's aim is to create a point cloud of data reflected back from the surface of the object. The resulting data set then can be used to build a 3D model or animation. The 3D laser is well suited for mapping and documenting crime and crash scenes, but also building interiors and exteriors as part of pre-planning efforts.

Airborne (UAVs) LIDAR Scanning

Airborne LIDAR can capture data on Earth surface. The UAV (unmanned aerial vehicle), or drone, is equipped with a 3D laser scanning technology. Airborne scanning can quickly gather large area data for outdoor crime and crash scenes. These do differ from drones equipped with digital cameras for aerial photos which in some cases can also produce 3D data through another technology called "photogrammetry" (the science of making measurements from photographs).[4]

Handheld Scanners

The handheld laser scanner is not prevalent within the forensic sector—so far—but they can provide value to investigators with particular, challenging crime scene aspects such as bodies, small spaces, behind or under furniture or vehicle interiors.

Mobile Scanning

Unlike Terrestrial Scanning, which is performed from a static position, Mobile Scanning collects geospatial data from a vehicle or person outfitted with LiDAR, cameras, and other remote sensors. Mobile scanning is designed for rapid exterior mapping to collect geospatial data quickly and accurately. It is ideal for asset management, planning, and disaster/major incident management.

Reduced Time at Scenes

Because the laser scanner is so fast at recording a scene, it helps reduce the amount of time for investigators to completely clear a scene while grabbing a huge amount of scene data. The scanner does this far more precisely compared to a measuring tape or a total station. After all, if the measuring tape, for example, isn't straight, or the total station is not level, this can greatly affect the accuracy of the collected data. Software for creating a diagram of the scanned scene provides a view of the entire scene that can be studied from any viewpoint (Figure 6.3).

The reduced time spent recording a scene with laser scanning means it is possible to process more crime scenes, and with fewer people. This results in more efficiency with crime scene processing department-wide along with helping agencies to keep on budget. Another benefit with laser scanning is that it captures and preserves the crime or crash scene as it is. In a crime scene, viewing and analyzing data can allow investigators to revisit the scene virtually anytime, which is extremely beneficial as they uncover new information that emerges in the case. And, it is easy to share the scene with others who may have not been

Figure 6.3 With laser scanning technology, public safety officials, like investigator Weston Hadley, of the Santa Ana, California, Police Department's Collision Investigations Unit, can capture an entire scene—billions of highly accurate data points—in less time than with other technology tools. For crash scenes in particular, laser scanning significantly increases efficiency, saves time, and prevents major shutdowns of intersections and highways for collision investigation. (Photo courtesy of Leica Geosystems)

at the crime scene when it was processed. When scanners are used at crash scenes, they yield safety for the reconstruction expert because collisions can be cleared more quickly due to the short amount of time needed to scan a scene. Traffic, congestion, and particularly the chance for secondary crashes is greatly reduced.

Laser Scanning Gives You Tools You May Not Have

The use of 3D laser scanning to map and document crime and crash scenes offers a wide range of benefits to those discussed above, but also some tools you may not have. First, let's review the key benefits that 3D laser scanning offers:

- Acquisition of large data sets – Eliminating the need for revisiting the scene
- Faster, more accurate data acquisition
- Compressed field-to-office timeline
- Selected feature extraction and manipulation
- Security planning analysis
- Creation of Building Information Models (BIM)
- Geographic Information Systems (GIS) interaction
- Data can be viewed, navigated, and analyzed similar to a 3D model in traditional CAD systems.[5]

Second, consider these tools that you get with laser scanning:

- Take 360-degree photographs of the scene
- Overlay scan data over photos and make precise measurements between any two points in real time—even while testifying
- Place a virtual camera at any location in the 3D scan data and view the scene from various points
- Create a fly-through video to take a jury into a crime scene as an effective way to show different perspectives of a scene and its evidence. The video can also be effective for crash scenes by showing the scene in slow motion, then speeding up the video camera to show the actual speed of a vehicle. This can help demonstrate what the driver saw. And, the video can show the scene in slow motion to allow a jury to study details.

- All of this information can be used to recreate a crash or crime scene to convey the investigator's hypothesis as to how the event most likely unfolded.

A significant advantage with scanning is that the photography and scanned data points, registered together, become a compelling communication tool for use with juries. Law enforcement agencies nationwide are using scanning to document crime scenes, show line of sight details, and what scene aspects perpetrators and victims could see from different vantage points (Figure 6.4).[6]

Choosing a Laser Scanner Model

As this technology becomes more widely recognized and used for investigators, reputable organizations like the Forensic Technology Center of Excellence and the National Institute of Justice help provide unbiased information and studies. There are excellent studies to help introduce readers with a basic understanding of 3D laser scanners. The report "A LANDSCAPE STUDY OF 3D CRIME SCENE SCANNING DEVICES" offers a view of what 3D terrestrial laser scanning technology was offered at the time, as well as factors impacting the implementation and use of this technology.

Figure 6.4 A 3D laser scanner, widely used by law enforcement agencies and reconstruction experts, can capture a scene to include the conditions of the scene and the exact size and shape of items within. (Photo courtesy of Trimble.com)

One of the report's key components is comparisons of the capabilities of commercially available 3D laser scanning instruments, their use, benefits, and limitations. It also provides considerations that will affect an agency's or reconstruction expert's purchase, training, and use of a laser scanner.[7]

Preserved Laser-Scanned Scenes are Highly Impactful in Court

The laser scanner is particularly valued for its ability to digitally preserve the stored crime scene point cloud once the scene has been scanned. This enables investigators and anyone else to re-examine the scene and to get additional measurements they may need.

Additionally, a laser scanner lends great objectivity to scene documentation because of its speed and compact nature, meaning that everything in the scene can be documented in its original position. The permanent record provided through scanning allows for detailed crime scene analysis long after the scene itself is gone.

Another tremendous advantage to using 3D laser scanning is the point cloud data it provides. The ability of a forensic team or reconstruction expert to use the laser scanner's point cloud data in their workflow cannot be overemphasized. By bringing scan data into a software program to register the data points, a photorealistic 3D model can be created that proves invaluable in a courtroom presentation to not just show the jury the crime scene, but to actually *bring them to it.* A full-color walk-through is possible, allowing attorneys to *drop the jury right into the scene* so it can see the movements of people and activities as they most likely unfolded. When a case goes to trial, it can be months or years after the crime was committed. Luckily, the 3D model of the original scene remains intact and can be re-examined at any time to see additional information or evidence. The laser scanner is able to document indoor and outdoor scenes in high resolution and with ample measurements of rooms and environments. This powerful capability yields a more efficient workflow in a short timeframe (Figure 6.5).[8]

Utilizing 3D Data in Court

As with any evidence or documentation from a scene, there is a possibility for it to be presented in court. Fortunately, 3D laser scanning

Figure 6.5 Once a crime scene has been scanned, the point cloud can be imported into CAD software to create a detailed 3D model, such as this scene of a homicide victim in an office. (Photo courtesy of FARO Technologies, Inc.)

technology has been around for several decades and laser scan data have been accepted in court. There are also many peer-reviewed reports available about the technology as well as published known error rates on these devices. Contacting the laser manufacturers can help provide this information. In preparing to testify, it is good practice to prepare for questions not only about the technology but also if the scanner was in working condition and if the operator handled the equipment properly. These can be answered clearly with ensuring the device is calibrated per the recommendation of the manufacturer as well as operators completing training to be certified in laser scanning.[9]

Setting Control Points for Any Scene Urged When Using Laser Scanner

A laser scanner is like a total station that functions extremely fast. It can measure distance, direction, and deflection to place a point in space. It does this between 500,000 and 1.5 million times per second, and the scanner establishes all of the point positions from an arbitrary origin, which is why all of the data points taken from a scan will be accurate relative to the scanner's original position. However, according to Senior Trooper William Bush, an Oregon State Police District Lead Reconstruction expert, "Where we start having issues is when you start moving the laser scanner. And we *always* move it."

Bush is a fervent advocate of establishing control points for any scene he will map and document because, he argues, this is how accuracy of the data collected can be assured. Too many laser scanning practitioners count on their post-processing software to calculate a best-fit model to combine multiple scans, Bush said. Therefore, instead of reconciling multiple scans back to a set of shared, fixed knowns, these scanner users try to reconcile datasets by letting the software determine how the arbitrary clouds fit. This is a risky move, cautioned Bush. "The problem is that the user may not know how well, or if, the software is giving him the degree of uncertainty about each individual scan's *fit* as the scanner is repositioned while mapping a scene," he added. In such an instance, it doesn't matter what reconstruction tool is being used because it is still essential to have the same, absolute fixed control positions that are shared among different pieces of technology. And, Bush further adds, it is never a good idea to trust too deeply in any one laser manufacturer. "This (laser scanning) is surveying technology being applied to forensics," he said. "So, we need to apply survey level control to what we are mapping and documenting at a scene." After all, Bush continued, "There is never an instance where a surveyor would *not* control his work."

Spheres are a way of setting known control points that the post-processing software would recognize, and this is how it is possible to reconcile multiple scans. Scanning projects that use spheres can be more easily solved because the spheres can be used to align the scan data with the photographs that are taken during scanning. Spheres are an effective scanning target. They are hollow, typically made of plastic with a distinctive surface comprised of wear-resistant paint that provides excellent reflection.[10]

The further away from the origin that a laser scanner is scanning, the more space is being missed, said Bush. Granted, establishing control points takes time, but, "as long as the controls are there, captured, it's just as good to assign them in post-processing than it would be to execute a resection into those controls prior to scanning," Bush added. The main point here is that the control points still are needed. "We are applying survey industry best practices to the laser scanning of crash and crime scenes and we are asserting that whatever we scan is an accurate representation of the scene," Bush said. "We are forensic surveyors."

This chapter's discussion explained how laser scanning creates a "point cloud" comprising millions of three-dimensional data points of a scanned scene, which can be converted to a 3D model to be used as an effective communications tool for juries. Also discussed was using this data in court.

The next chapter looks at steps for setting up a scanner at a crime or crash scene and then scanning the scene, as well as the post-processing procedures for creating a 3D model of the scanned scene's point cloud.

Notes

1. "Laser Scanning for Forensic Investigations." FARO Technologies UK, 2011. www.faro.com.
2. "Quality Basics – How Does 3D Laser Scanning Work." 2016. www.engineering.com.
3. "What is 3d Scanning." www.laserdesign.com.
4. "Drone-photogrammetry-us-lidar." 2019, October 18. www.wingtra.com.
5. "About 3d Laser Scanning." www.smartgeometrics.com.
6. Jones, T. "Scanning for Forensic Presentations." 2011, February 2. www.landairsurveying.com.
7. "3d Crime Scene Scanning Devices." 2018, August. www.forensiccoe.org.
8. "Laser Scanning for Forensic Investigations." FARO Technologies UK, 2020. www.faro.com.
9. "Hardware 3D Scanners." www.faro.com.
10. "Basic Reference Sphere Set." Laser Scanning America, 2020. www.laserscanning-america.com.

7

Setting Up The Scanner, Working With Point Clouds, and Building 2D/3D Models

Capturing a crime or crash scene with a 3D laser scanner is not just a matter of setting up the device at the scene and pressing a button to activate scanning. Assuming you have received professional training on how to use the scanner, it then will be essential to accomplish some valuable preliminary steps for getting the best possible scans of the scene.

Mark the Scene to be Scanned

The first step is to correctly mark the scene that is about to be scanned. Evidence markings will make it easier to catalog evidence, define its location within the scene to later analyze, and improve the view of evidence items in photographs. Evidence marking before a scan occurs also will make identifying the evidence easier within the point cloud data that the laser scanner captures. Numerous ways of marking the scene can be used, including chalk, reflective chalk, spray chalk, paint stick, or marking paint. Various surfaces work differently with different methods of marking. For instance, spray paint often does not show up on dirt, grass or barkdust in grayscale. It is important to experiment with your laser scanner to see what marking method works best on different surfaces and how the scanner sees it. These can be effective whether working with a grayscale-scanned scene or colorized scan image. Dynamic Safety L.L.C., a Lake Zurich, IL-based consulting firm specializing primarily in vehicle crash reconstruction, experimented with these methods and made some interesting discoveries.

It found that reflective chalk works best when captured in a grayscale point cloud—marks were easy to identify at 60 ft away from the laser scanner, and were even still visible at a distance of 80 ft. What's more, reflective chalk proved to be an excellent marking tool when a scene was scanned in wet conditions. Spray chalk was not reflective, but showed up more successfully with colorized point clouds.

Dynamic Safety's report on the effectiveness of these scanner scene marking tools provided one caveat: the distance where the marks were well-defined and visible varied based on lighting, road conditions, and moisture, among other factors.[1]

Scanner Placement, Height will Affect Scene Capture

Where to place a 3D laser scanner is perhaps the most critical element to successfully capture a scene and must absolutely be accomplished before scanning begins. Scanner placement will determine, in part, how effective the scene will be recorded. So, be sure to understand where the best place is to place the scanner and how far to move it to the next position. Each scan taken of a scene requires some time; you want to take as few scans as possible, yet make sure the scene is captured in totality. Create a diagram or sketch of your scene before you begin scanning and update it as you proceed. This will help ensure adequate scanning coverage and provide a roadmap to assist with registering the scans together (Figure 7.1).

Dynamic Safety LLC recommends staggering the laser scanner placement from one side to another, keeping a 70-foot radius between scanner placements. If the scanner's placement is too distant from other placement locations at the scene, or bigger than the recommended 70-foot radius, essential evidence might be missed. This is totally dependent on scanner settings. For a common outdoor resolution, 70–90 ft works fine, but this can vary based on how a person sets up his scanner and what the individual specifications of a scanner are.

Another helpful step is to make sure that the scanner is set at the proper height. Remember, the scanner can only capture what it sees as it makes a 360° sweep once it is activated. Positioning the height of the scanner is crucial. For example, elevating the scanner's tripod allows for a higher range of points to be scanned on the ground. This is because the scanner's signal angle relative to the ground is

Figure 7.1 Placement of a laser scanner for a crash or crime scene is critical in determining how effective the scene will be recorded. (Photo courtesy of Leica Geosystems)

increased, meaning that the return signal once scanning begins will be stronger upon its return to the scanner. Thus, the higher scanner position on the tripod assures that the scanner can record points at longer distances than if the scanner is closer to ground level. Scanning from a higher altitude also becomes important if you want to capture features like the roof of a car in a crash scene. Likewise, sometimes it is necessary to adjust the tripod downward to bring the scanner to almost floor level so that evidence that might otherwise be concealed—such as a bullet casing behind a chair or couch, or off to the side of a street—can be recorded by the laser scanner.[2]

Determine Resolution Values

A paramount step for making quality scans is what is called *resolution*. Resolution is a setting on the laser scanner that determines the density of the scan points collected. By choosing a small value for resolution, the scanner operator will have a larger distance between points to be scanned in his scene and a lower density of points in the completed point cloud. Selecting a larger value for resolution will translate to a smaller distance between scanned points and, thus, more densely captured points in the point cloud. When scanning a scene, achieving a dense point cloud should be top priority because it yields a more realistic depiction of the scene. There is a tradeoff, however, because the higher the resolution, the longer the scans will take. Therefore, scan at the highest resolution possible within the time allotted. Since the point coverage is a function of point distance you can set a lower resolution but place your scan locations closer together to achieve the same coverage at a higher resolution, but save time. If, for example, the scanner's highest resolution requires a 2-hour scan, you can get the same coverage by dropping the resolution to a lower level. You just need to move the scanner a shorter distance, completing 3–4 scans in 30 minutes and getting the same coverage as achievable with the high resolution scan.

According to Laserscaning Europe, a laser scanner sales and training company, a simple rule for scanning resolution should be followed: don't operate a scanner at its highest resolution, but only with as much resolution as needed. Scanner resolution relies on the scanned object, requirements of accuracy and time available for laser scanning, and the distance between the laser scanner and its object. To find the correct resolution for a laser scanner, it's key to understand the requirements of the scan results. Choosing the proper resolution relies on whether the scene to be scanned is interior or exterior, the distance between the scanner, and the object (the room or area of the scene), and the number of scans to avoid shadowing effects.[3]

Registration: The Key to Tying Scans Together

The goal with 3D laser scanning is to be able to build a three-dimensional reconstruction of a crime scene tied to a case. However, no laser scanner will create a 3D CAD model. What the scanner actually does create is a point cloud using the raw data points captured and that can be used to create a 3D model. And this process is not lickety-split. Through post-processing, the raw scan data points can be connected into accurate 2D or 3D drawings with diagramming software. The drawing software is well designed to enable the user to create 3D visual walk-throughs and 2D or 3D overall design of a crime scene.[4] Armed with the point cloud produced by the scanner, a crime scene investigator or reconstruction expert can find revealing, critical clues to a crime or collision. These clues will be visible when the investigator performs *registration*, a process of "stitching" scans together that is typically part of any post-processing software. In most cases, the registration process is simply a matter of launching the software, importing scan data files from the scanner, and registering them. The size of each scan and how powerful the user's computer is will determine how long registration takes, but it is usually a few minutes for each scan. There are numerous software programs that can model the point cloud. FARO Zone 3D, for instance, can bring the point cloud in after registration, and allows for diagramming and animations, and even Virtual Reality interaction with the point cloud (Figure 7.2).

Point Cloud Segmenting Helps Import Data into Modeling Software

By segmenting the point cloud, it is possible to import the data segments into the 3D modeling software and start modeling key identifiers

Figure 7.2 How much captured scan data is enough for a scene depiction? The key is to show the scene as clearly and powerfully as possible with the information available, so that a photorealistic representation is the result. Shown here is a point cloud of a shooting scene outside of an apartment, showing bullet trajectory. (Photo courtesy of Bryon O'Neil, Criminalist, Clackamas County, Oregon, Sheriff's Office)

such as walls, doors, windows, hallways, and other structural features. The segmentation process makes it helpful to study crime scenes that involve structures, such as a house or public building (i.e., a school) where a shooting may have occurred. Modeling time required will vary greatly depending upon how much or how little detail the user is trying to extract from the scan or scans. The big benefit of having these point cloud segments is that they provide a template to use: for example, walls, floor, and ceiling. Then the user can start working with the actual structure. What's really nice about this whole process is that the laser scanner has captured the entire scene, and so the investigator should have all the information he needs from just that one scanning session. Crime scene point clouds usually are not as big as for a construction project, so it may not be necessary to segment them.[5]

Clean-Up Scan Data, Build Orthoimage

Before starting to work with the CAD software, it's best to clean-up the scan data to remove unwanted items such as reflections. This will help immensely with being able to export the scanned scene into your CAD program and to begin plotting data points. The processed point cloud can be exported in various formats including 3PF, ASCII, Autodesk DXF, VTK, and WRI as reduced data sets for processing in programs like AutoCAD or point cloud processing software offered by 3D laser scanner manufacturers.

When the point cloud is brought into your processing software, it might not carry the image data—the edges and texture—when it appears in the software. If this is the case, an orthoimage, which is a photographic map, must be created. This requires processing the point cloud through several stages—triangulation, meshing, and texturing—with the corresponding position image data and combining the color-textured scan with the corresponding geometric plane of the scanned image. Triangulated data enhance the definition of the scanned objects. In addition, triangulated data can be textured with high resolution images taken by the scanner's digital camera. This is what helps produce a photorealistic 3D model. Texturing means taking every triangle and finding an optimal image to texture it.

Creating the orthoimage or ortho photo relies on the geometry information (the scan data) and image data. Images must be rectified during the scan data processing stage. The orthoimage represents the data for a particular plan on the x-, y-, and z-axis, and can constitute elevation, plane, or section of an object.[6]

Overlapping Scans

Successful scan data processing will depend on having sufficient overlap of scans made at the scene, according to Joel Salinas, a retired police lieutenant and private crime and crash reconstructionist. For example, Salinas explained, if you are scanning a crash scene and the orientation of the scene is linear down the road—for a crash scene—and the scanning does not have sufficient overlap, "You won't know this until you actually see it and start to post-process the point cloud and stitch the scans together. If there's not enough overlap, your scans are not going to come together properly." Therefore, registration of the scanning data depends on how good a job the reconstructionist has done with scanning his scene. Again, using the example of a crash on a roadway—not one on an interstate where there may not be a lot of vertical objects—the scene will need to be scanned differently than if it was, say, a downtown intersection area with a lot of buildings. "You need to understand how to use the targets for the scene to aid in registration," Salinas said. "If you're doing a scene in a downtown area where you have a lot of vertical surfaces, you can use features of the building and the environment itself, and common points, to stitch the scans together," Salinas continued. And, he emphasized, "it's important to take several scans of a scene. If there's a four-way intersection, for example, then each corner must be scanned. For best registration, a 40 percent overlap from scan to scan is recommended."

Hide Unwanted Data/Objects

A most helpful technique often used with post-processing software is to hide unwanted data points/objects in a scene by using the software's clipping box. The clipping box helps users streamline point cloud data analysis by keeping only the parts of scans that are relevant to the captured scene. With this tool, scan data are presented in either point cloud or realistic photo view. The clipping box enables the user to choose those portions of the scan he/she needs and then the remaining parts of the scan are automatically and seamlessly hidden. The points still exist, but the software just doesn't show them; the clipping box in the software hides these points and it can be turned on and off. This capability gives the user the data he/she wants without all other extraneous data that can make analysis stretch way out. Another advantage with the clipping box is that the reduced data point file size simplifies and speeds up export to the user's CAD program.

Bryon O'Neil, criminalist and forensic reconstruction expert with Clackamas County, Oregon, Sheriff's Office, uses the clipping box in his FARO SCENE scan data processing software routinely and finds it to be efficient and time-saving for his post-processing of scanned scenes. When he uses this feature, he does not delete any of the point cloud's data points because they are all part of a forensic scene. He places the clipping box over the points he does not want to see and they are instantly hidden from view within the scanned scene. "You can turn the clipping boxes on and off," O'Neil said. "It doesn't delete the points, but just hides them." However, O'Neil gives a warning to anyone using clipping boxes. "You have to be careful not to hide key evidence," he said.

So often with 3D laser scanning a familiar question comes up: How much scan data captured is enough? The answer probably varies depending on any one user's scanning preferences. O'Neil simply hides all the big items in his finished scans that he doesn't need in his final diagrammed scene. He flies through the scene back and forth once or twice, and if he doesn't see anything that he thinks should be removed, it does not bother him. The scene, O'Neil said, does not have to be perfect or completely clean; it just has to be good enough to show the scene as it was with the right evidence. The key is to show the scene as clearly and powerfully as possible with the information available to show exactly how it appeared when the crime occurred.

Color vs. Grayscale-Scanned Scenes

Similar to determining what data and unwanted objects to hide is the decision of when to use color for a scan and when grayscale will be adequate. Color panoramic images are a great way to put yourself into a scene, as if you are in place of the scanner, and looking around inside it. Color is essential for presentations of a reconstructed scene. Other advantages are that color makes point cloud processing tools such as registration and 3D modeling much easier to use. Finally, color 3D point clouds can capture enough scene data to create an immersive 3D virtual reality experience.[7]

O'Neil, the Oregon forensic reconstruction expert, confesses he favors grayscale, but noted that colored scans have a definite, immediate impact; juries crave colored crash and crime scenes. You can let the type of scene you have dictate whether to use color or grayscale. O'Neil uses color for scans taken in daytime, and grayscale for nighttime scenes. When he scans houses that are part of a crime scene, O'Neil scans in color those areas where specific, important actions happened, and black and white for those portions of a scene with no relevant activity. However, "We still scan the entire house," O'Neil said. "When we're doing a fly-through in a scene, people's attention is drawn to the colored portions," he continued. "It's a subtle way to draw someone's attention to what's important in the scene." The added benefit to scanning in grayscale is time-savings. It takes time to take photographs, so by not capturing color considerable time on the scene can be saved. By the same token, the presentation of a colored 3D scene in court can be considered guesswork about what is going to keep the jury engaged in listening to what you want them to hear. This is why, for instance, O'Neil prefers not to use sphere targets for his scanned scenes because they can be distracting for the jury and steer it away from listening to the presentation.

Should the CAD Model Be 2D or 3D?

For most crime scenes, creating a 2D view in a diagram is adequate. Although it is a bird's-eye, top-down view, it helps the person looking at it, especially a juror, understand the positioning of objects relative to that bird's-eye view. That's the opinion of Bobby Jones, reconstruction expert at Knox County Sheriff's Office in Knoxville, Tennessee, and of Knoxville-based Bobby Jones Reconstruction, who contends that the 2D view is *always* needed; Jones himself routinely starts his scene diagramming with a 2D perspective. "The 2D view factors into building a diagram for almost every crime scene,"

Jones explained. "I need the layout of a building, the way a suspect entered or exited, the layout of a room or hallway, outside the building where there was a body or other evidence related to a crime. I need to show anybody looking at that three-dimensional diagram the two-dimensional illustrations of where all these scene details are in relation to, say, a roadway intersection or something else that they can grasp and understand," Jones continued. And, he added, a key advantage of laser scanning is being able to extract measurements because these will be useful for a 2D diagram and for some type of calculation and analysis. The 3D is more of a visual aid than it is an analysis tool, Jones said.

Building a 3D Model Is the Goal

The 3D Model is ultimately what the investigator wants to have once the point cloud is produced by the scanner because it is the reconstruction of the actual scene, and could be taken to court if the case associated with the crime scene goes to trial. The modeling software gives the ability to look at a scene from different perspectives. It's important to use a drawing program that allows a top-down look, from a 2D perspective, as well as a 3D view. Advanced CAD software makes it possible to rotate an environment—the actual scene—and see it from any perspective while the user is completing the model of a homicide scene in a building or the position of a vehicle at a crash scene. The software has symbols to choose from so that a specific car or streetlight, as examples, can be represented as they actually appeared in the scene. This capability makes the 3D model more realistic and accurate compared to using only representative symbols. The real benefit of the software is that the 3D representation it yields can be used to extract the right information needed to perform the analysis that will help the user and a jury better understand what occurred at the crime scene. But the completed diagram or 3D model can also show spatial relationships between evidence items. To see and understand these spatial relationships, another extremely valuable feature of the drawing program is its ability to enable the investigator and a jury to take a virtual walk-through of the scene. This is an aspect of the CAD software that has become especially well received in the courtroom (Figure 7.3).

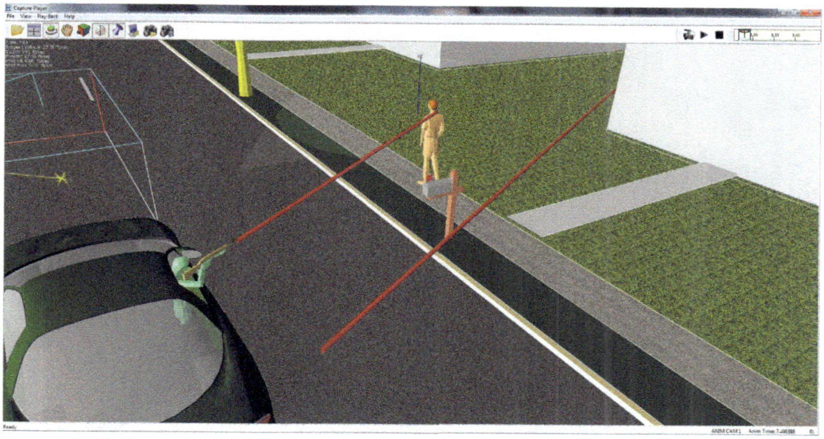

Figure 7.3 An example of a 3D model showing a drive-by shooting scene. CAD software is effective for showing 3D models of crime scenes that may be presented in court trials. (Photo courtesy of Det. Matt Archuleta, Arvada, CO, Police Department)

Today's laser scanner manufacturers offer a wide range of highly specialized software to accomplish this post-processing step of handling the scan data collected by a scanner. The raw scanner data, or 3D point cloud, can be used with software to view, pan, zoom, rotate in 3D; point-to-point measurements can be extracted from this point cloud, as well.

Scenes Are Preserved for Later Analysis Anytime

The point cloud, once captured, and the 3D reconstruction of the scene from the point cloud data is helpful in another respect because it offers a valuable function: to store millions of data points that represent a complete crime scene, frozen in time and as it actually looked, so that the scene can be *analyzed at any time*. And, *this analysis can be accomplished while the investigator is no longer at the scene*. Furthermore, details of this scene can be shared with other investigators and especially jurors. Although the "CSI effect" (exaggerated portrayal of crime solving and forensic science on crime tv shows that influences public perception) has raised jurors' expectations for how forensic evidence is presented, 3D crime scenes nevertheless are gripping and compelling. Jurors become more engaged in crime cases when these 3D depictions are presented in court; they can better understand

Figure 7.4 Crime scene reconstructions like this one are highly effective for showing juries how a crime incident may have occurred. The ability to bring the jury into the crime scene gives it a better understanding of scene events, scene perspectives, and positions of people. (Photo courtesy of FARO Technologies, Inc.)

details when a 3D model shows a crime scene from any angle or a fly-through video takes the them directly in and through the entire scene (Figure 7.4).[8]

There is a wide range of applications for laser scanning. This explains why scanner manufacturers offer software focused on creating deeply targeted scene facets that may help tremendously in solving cases. Chief among these facets include identifying bullet trajectory data points from a shooting recreation to calculate a likely point of origin; suspect height analysis using video surveillance; blood pattern analysis; and vehicle collision damage analysis.

This chapter has focused on steps for properly marking a crime or crash scene to be laser scanned, scanner placement and height adjustment, and the crucial post-processing and 3D modeling stages.

Chapter 8 will look at the key principles of receiving comprehensive training on 3D laser scanning plus post-processing and scene diagramming software, and the necessity for continuous scanning practice to ensure skills always stay sharp.

Notes

1. "White Paper/Laser Scanner Basics for Public Safety Scene." 2017. www.insightsfaro.com.
2. "3d Laser Scanners Forensic Reconstructions." www.ee.co.za.
3. "Correct-Resolution-Laser-Scanning." www.laserscanning-europe.com.
4. "Hd-3d-Laser-Scanning." www.rgasurveying.com.
5. "Construction-Industry." www.constructible.trimble.com.
6. Uploads.tx psprieg/downloads/shortpaper 1044 060 922.pdf. www.riegl.com.
7. "Color-Point-Clouds." www.arrival3d.com.
8. "How You Can Accurately Recreate Crime Scenes with the Focus3d-X-330." www.policeone.com/ police-products/crime-scene-investigation/articles.

8

The Essentials of Getting Trained on the Use of a Laser Scanner

Getting trained on how to use a 3D laser scanner cannot be stressed strongly enough. It also cannot be avoided, as with any equipment used for investigations. The user of a laser scanner must rely on his training on how to operate a scanner so that he's in top form to map and record a major crime or crash scene at any moment. Between crime or collision scene callouts, a laser scanner's operator must practice using his scanner routinely and consistently. This is the only way he will master laser scanning to ensure that a scene is thoroughly and accurately captured. While pursuing scanner training would seem obvious, many think because laser scanners are tools, it is "precious," so they are inclined to put it away until a "big scene" comes. However, the opposite is recommended. Regular practice of scanning, exporting the data, and creating a video or simple animation or reconstruction, even if it is at the office, helps set the agency for success when that "big scene" comes and all eyes are watching (Figure 8.1).

Find Training Tailored to Your Specific Needs

Agencies with lack of training or regular practice with laser scanners is something veteran crash reconstruction technician and laser scanner trainer Joel Salinas is all too familiar with. Salinas has trained reconstruction experts, investigators, criminalists, and crime scene unit members all over the country on the many aspects of laser scanning a crime scene. Before his students plunge into laser scanning training, Salinas prefers to tailor his classes to the needs of each agency. He communicates with an agency's training coordinator to ascertain what specific kind of training the agency wishes to have. If, for example, the agency wants laser scanning training for crash scenes, then Salinas

Figure 8.1 It is essential to get trained on how to operate a laser scanner. This will ensure the operator that is in top form to effectively map a major crime or crash scene at any moment. (Photo courtesy of Trimble.com)

will gear the class to crash reconstruction training only. Some agencies want training for both crash and crime scenes. "We interview the students, find out what they want to use the equipment for and tailor the training course to that," said Salinas. Scanning crash and crime scenes are very different from each other. At an indoor crime scene, for instance, if you are scanning in, say, a house from room to room, you must have enough overlap in scans to tie these scans together, Salinas explained. You must not jump from a hallway to a living room while scanning without taking into account if there enough common points between these scans to see where you are going and where you have been so that you can register these scans together.

One aspect of training that can be particularly challenging for Salinas is that students come to his classes with so many different levels of experience. He vividly recalls one class in which no student had any experience with identifying evidence beyond basic academy training. For example, one class of students could not identify skid marks. When he learned this reality, Salinas took the students to a documented crash scene to show them what to look for regarding not just skid marks but other types of roadway evidence to identify.

Scanner Operation, Post-Processing Techniques Taught

Most manufacturers of laser scanners offer both basic and intermediate training classes for new users prior to carrying out any scanning work. Most users tend to need and want the intermediate training because it provides much more in-depth coverage of the scanner and post-processing software. Topics typically include:

- Basic steps of laser scanner operation
- General scanning techniques—hardware programming and setup
- Scene sketches
- Target placement
- Evaluation of a scene by walking it, estimating the number of scans needed, and determining what evidence is crucial to capture
- Scanning at different resolutions and how this will affect your overall collected scan data
- Organizing and processing scan data
- Registering scan data
- Interior vs. Exterior Scanning
- Data colorization
- Working with data imported from other data capture technology (Figure 8.2)

Training classes are designed to make sure each student demonstrates proficiency with a laser scanner before he can be certified. Salinas requires his students to be able to competently operate the scanner and to work with registration software and CAD software. "Students must show me how to set up the scanner, how to recover from any mishaps in the field, such as the scanner quits working for some reason," Salinas said.

Follow Scanner Maker's Recommended Training; Get Certified

To be truly successful and proficient at scanning, the operator must master the operation of a laser scanner, then be able to effectively work with the point cloud that scanning produces and build a meaningful 3D model. "Scanning and post-processing is an art form," asserts Bryon O'Neil, a crash reconstructionist with Clackamas County,

Figure 8.2 Basic steps of laser operation are part of a thorough, professional training program. Other key components are: scanner setup and hardware programming, scanning techniques, registering scan data, organizing and processing scan data, and more. (Photo courtesy of Trimble.com)

Oregon, Sheriff's Office. O'Neil should know, as he scans no less than 30 crash and crime scenes a year and builds 3D and 2D models with his scan data. O'Neil also has trained many agencies on how to scan scenes and prepare for court presentations.

The most important aspect of scanner training is to follow your scanner manufacturer's recommended training which oftentimes includes certification. This becomes particularly important if you must present a documented crime or crash scene in court and are asked by a defense attorney what training was given on the scanner. It speaks to the Daubert standard, a rule of evidence regarding the admissibility of expert witness testimony, and can only help an investigator who must testify in court about a scene he has scanned that is tied to a case. More specifically, a Daubert Hearing is an evaluation by a trial judge on the admissibility of defined "expert," or scientific and technical, testimony and evidence.[1]

In addition to laser manufacturer certification, the International Association of Forensic and Security Metrology (IAFSM) also offers certification for basic laser scanning. This non-manufacturer-specific training goes deeper into the science of laser scanning to ensure that users truly know and understand how to operate their equipment. Certification definitely helps to add credibility to a scanner operator and is critical for withstanding a Daubert challenge. Furthermore, O'Neil argues, it is not enough to train on a particular manufacturer's scanner just once. The user must keep current with changes made to the scanner. Otherwise, certification is meaningless. "Learn what is different about your scanner and apply this to your scanning," O'Neil said.

Keep Current with Training and Practice, Practice, Practice!!!

O'Neil is adamant that ongoing training should be in place once agencies complete a laser scanning course. In fact, he considers *any* scene that an agency or reconstructionist scans as part of *recurring training*. "Every scene you scan should be considered as training," O'Neil said. "You're learning something in that scanning process, and *that's training*. This is something you can present in court with authority," O'Neil added (Figure 8.3).

During 2018 and 2019, O'Neil and his reconstruction team executed 56 callouts in 52 weeks. "That's 56 scenes that we scanned," O'Neil said. Every one of O'Neil's operators have had two or three scenes that they have personally laser scanned throughout a year. "That's a lot of training right there," O'Neil said. No scene is too small or trivial for scanning. In fact, O'Neil stresses that anyone using a laser scanner should treat every scene as though it's the "big scene." By following this practice, he admits that operators who regularly scan in the field will make mistakes. But by working out these mistakes when scanning scenes that don't mean much (not criminal), this will prepare the user to be more successful on bigger, more critical crime scenes.

The goal for anyone who takes laser scanning seriously and who keeps current with training is to *envision what the 3D model through post-processing will look like*. To achieve this goal, O'Neil considers scanning resolution to be at the core of building an accurate, compelling point cloud for a crime scene. Specifically, it is important to understand what resolution actually does. Scanning at different resolutions enables the user to see what he will get. This, said O'Neil, helps to build a mental picture of what the scene should look like.

Figure 8.3 The only way to become proficient with 3D laser scanning is to practice often and consistently. Every scene scanned can be considered as training in itself, said Bryon O'Neil (shown here), a deputy and reconstruction expert with the Clackamas County, Oregon, Sheriff's Office. The goal for anyone who keeps current with training and is serious about laser scanning practice is to envision what the 3D model of a scene through post-processing will look like. (Photo courtesy of Bob Galvin, RS Galvin & Assoc./Writing Services, Lebanon, OR)

Every Scene Is an Opportunity for Scanning Practice

Once students have successfully completed a training class, the real work begins: using the scanner regularly so that the skills learned on how to use it never get rusty. Most trainers will advise practicing with a scanner on any scene no matter how seemingly unimportant. For example, offers Bobby Jones, accident reconstruction expert with the Knox County Sheriff's Office, Knoxville, Tennessee, "Maybe an officer or investigator should get the scanner out and use it on a simple crash where there's maybe minor or moderate injuries," Jones offered. The veteran crime scene reconstructionist considers learning and practicing with a laser scanner a "perishable skill set." It is not just a physical skill set, but a mental, practical, and technical skill set all rolled into one. "You have to carry this over from the field to the computer where you have to have mastered the post-processing software to be able to exercise the scanner's full potential," Jones said. Without the commitment to laser scanning practice, a user's skill in operating the scanner will be lost and he won't be able to build a reconstruction of his scene to preserve it. This issue tends to plague smaller agencies, because larger agencies usually have specialized crash and crime reconstruction teams and are using their scanners often on multiple scenes each year. "They (larger agencies) just get the scanner and use it," Jones continued. "They already have a plan in their mind of how they will map and document a scene. That speaks to practice, but it's also *experience* and practice."

Develop a Scanning Plan, Have an Idea for End Result Product from the Start

Jones hits on a very important point here—having a plan as to how a scene will be scanned. Remember, the final deliverable from the scanning and post-processing must typically be a 3D model that will hold up in court while keeping jurors engaged in how a scene is being presented and discussed. So, for instance, this might be a fly-through of the crime scene to show viewers how the whole scene came together from a bird's-eye view. It takes them down to the actual scene, walking them around to show critical evidence. With this approach, Jones said, "I'm thinking about the end result *in the beginning*. This is where agencies who don't practice and really use the scanner make big mistakes in not understanding what they can do with this tool. And that sets up a barrier for them to set up correctly or scan in wide positions."

Practice also applies to the post-processing stage. If you're using a scanning manufacturer's 2D diagramming software to create a top-down, bird's-eye view of a scene, for instance, it's necessary to understand how to run the software so you can understand what needs to be scanned at the scene. This helps you know what to scan so you can capture the right data to put into the drawing software. It is a backward and forward learning process—learning how to create the end result product, which means understanding the post-processing software. "You must be proficient with it," Jones said, "and that means you must know how to operate the laser scanner" (Figure 8.4).

Part of getting agencies to practice with scanning falls on supervisors. These people must work with officers to make sure they are practicing with the scanner. Even just letting officers take a scanner home

Figure 8.4 Training on the operation of a laser scanner is a crucial component of getting the best use out of your laser scanning hardware and software. Shown here are professional reconstruction experts being trained at Leica Geosystems' high definition scanning (HDS), University in Norcross, GA. (Photo courtesy of Leica Geosystems)

and practice scanning their property is helpful. "Give them a reason to practice and they start doing it," affirms Jones.

Another idea is for agencies to designate a "training day" once a month for their officers who have been trained on a laser scanner. "We recommend that people schedule training each month, or that someone host a regional seminar for a one- or two-day scanning operation refresher," Jones said. "It's a great way to generate questions and sort through problems. It's like a little rodeo for current users."

Scanner manufacturers should all require recertification on their equipment. It should occur at least once a year or every other year to revisit some of the basic steps of laser scanning that users may have forgotten.

In this chapter's discussion, the central requirements for getting trained on laser scanner operation and scene post-processing software have been laid out. Also emphasized has been the need for training certification, in case a scanned scene is presented in court and must meet the Daubert standard, and why regular, dedicated scanning practice will ensure success with documenting collision and crime scenes.

The following chapter explores the process of presenting a scanned scene in court, along with the role of introducing video evidence, and how critical it is to meet the Daubert standard.

Note

1. "Legal/Daubert." www.omsj.org.

9
Bringing Crime Scene Reconstructions into Court

The advent of 3D Laser Scanning as a means to capture and show crime scene details has become so compelling that it is now welcome in nearly any courtroom. The technology enables either a prosecution or defense team to bring a scene into the courtroom so that everyone can view it at the same time. A forensic expert (choosing to remain unidentified) once said, "To my knowledge no laser scanner data properly presented has ever been ruled inadmissible in any court in the United States. In fact, many police departments and federal agencies use scanners to collect evidence for all types of criminal and civil investigations. It is the best way available to collect data. The data is so graphic and intuitive that it is very easy to see the results and make logical judgments and precise measurements."[1]

The beauty of 3D laser scanning is that it is accomplished with photography and scanned points that are registered together and are calibrated, precise, and accurate. It is the reason so many reconstructionists and police departments now use this method to document their crime scenes and present their evidence of a crime in court. This is why it is so important for serious laser scanner users to take the resulting point cloud data into their workflow, the essential post-processing phase of crime scene reconstruction. When laser scan data have been captured, in the form of a point cloud, it then can be brought into specialized processing software to register data points. Registration is the process of aligning laser scans into one, common coordinate system. From here, additional diagramming software allows for a photorealistic 3D model to be created. This model is used in courtroom presentations to interactively and accurately bring a jury

Figure 9.1 The ability to show a scene in 3D offers perspectives for juries that might otherwise be hard to understand. By showing such a 3D model, it is easier to depict scene perspectives and positions of people during an incident. (Photo courtesy of FARO Technologies)

directly into the crime scene. Once in the scene, jurors can be walked through it, in full color, and be shown the paths, movements of people involved in the crime. This provides a far more convincing argument compared to using just crime scene photographs. Additionally, once a case is brought to trial, it can be months, even years after the crime was committed. Although the crime scene is gone forever, the 3D models of the scene filled with scan data can be revisited and reexamined to extract additional information (Figure 9.1).[2]

Scanner Must Assist "Trier of Fact" in Court

Eugene Liscio, 3D Forensic Analyst with ai2-3D Forensics, Toronto, Ontario, Canada, has testified numerous times as a forensic expert witness in courtrooms, and has valuable insights into the use of 3D laser-scanned models with judges and jurors. A crime scene introduced in court can be one from indoors, outdoors, a shooting from a car, or even a piece of evidence like a shoe or gun. "One of the issues a judge will consider regarding whether or not to allow a scanned scene into court is it has to assist the 'trier of fact' (a judge or a jury)," Liscio explains. This means that the judge will ask how the laser scanner data is actually going to help in the case. "You can't just show a scan for the sake of showing a scan," Liscio said. "There has to be a reason, something useful and not just for effect." Another consideration that Liscio raises is if the scanner has been used in other cases, if it has been studied, and if there are published papers on the scanner's accuracy. Has it been used for different applications? Basically, has the scanner generally been accepted? This kind of information—the results of reports on scanning accuracy—could be shared with jurors to help give them a better sense of the crime scene. Laser scanners have been used for years and are widely accepted. Laser scanning has been sanctioned by the International Association of Forensic and Security Metrology (IAFSM), which promotes the development and use of precision measurement systems, techniques and software to generate 2D or 3D coordinate spatial data. These data are used in documentation, planning, analysis, and presentations. The IAFSM offers a Basic Laser Scanner Certification Course and certifies operators globally.

Juries Connect with 3D Crime Scenes from Laser Scanning

There can be some apprehension among attorneys about questioning the validity of 3D laser scanning in court as many of them do not know how to react to it or know how a scanner works. Reconstruction experts and CSIs frequently confront this situation and will often demonstrate a laser scanner's operation right in the courtroom. Some will do this by scanning the entire courtroom, showing the judge and jury how the scanner captures data and what the point cloud data looks like. Liscio, who has put on this kind of demonstration himself in courtrooms, points out that it's easy to lose a jury quickly when making a presentation of a crime scene reconstruction. So it is important to give jurors a good education on what is happening in the crime scene being presented and in a captivating way that will hold their attention (Figures 9.2 and 9.3).

Once the laser scanner user captures a point cloud from his scanned scene, he can use it with various software to reconstruct the scene, but also to combine it with other media such as total station data points, video footage, and photographs. The benefit from the very start is that a laser scanner captures 3D data, and by its very nature 3D data is visual, making it ideal for presentation before a jury. People like

Figure 9.2 Law enforcement agencies utilize 3D laser scanning technology to capture a complete view of a scene in a very short period of time. Scene details in 3D are valuable for a jury's understanding of events. (Photos courtesy of Clackamas County, Oregon, Sheriff's Office)

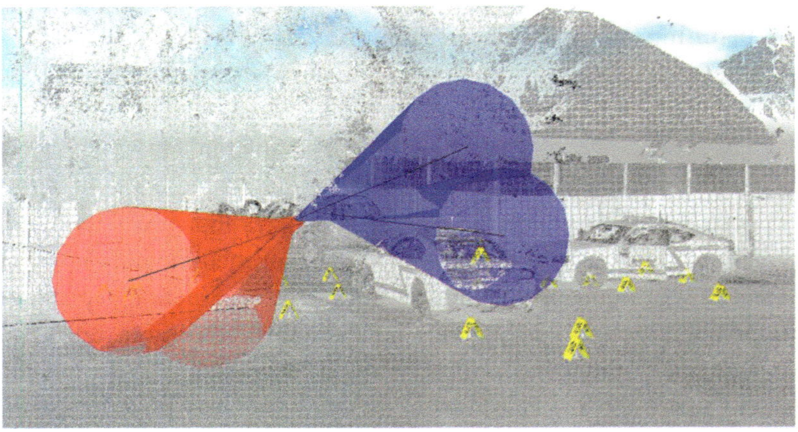

Figure 9.3 Law enforcement agencies utilize 3D laser scanning technology to capture a complete view of a scene in a very short period of time. Scene details in 3D are valuable for a jury's understanding of events. (Photos courtesy of Clackamas County, Oregon, Sheriff's Office)

learning from things that are visual, Liscio said. "It's not abstract. You can see a roadway, skid marks, or bullet trajectories," he said. And if the scanner user does an analysis in 3D, the results are in 3D. Because all of this is very visual, it becomes extremely powerful.

Juries Brought Directly Into a Scene

Remember, during the entire time a reconstructed crime scene is being presented in court the chief aim is to build credibility for how that scene was to build credibility for the scene's creation, its details, and the analysis connected with it. Showing bullet trajectories as part of a crime scene is a good example. Liscio has done so many times in courtrooms. He can show trajectories in 3D and all of their angles in his court presentations. Liscio also is able to bring juries into the 3D models of his reconstructed crime scenes, which gives a clearer perspective of crime scene events. "I need to show the jurors where they sit in the greater environment of the scene, and when I do, that is powerful," Liscio said, "because they can see the bullet trajectory angles and what they mean." Without being enveloped in the crime scene in this way, it is hard to know what exactly these angles would mean, Liscio added. "By bringing a juror into the scene, he can see that, for example, 'Oh, the bullet was going this way, it hit the guy there, and there was a wall behind it,'" he continued. A scene with this kind of visual detail, and the juror's involvement in it, gives the context that jurors need for the entire scene.

Although 3D laser scanning has garnered a lot of attention within law enforcement and is often hailed as the go-to technology for documenting crime scenes, just how should juries treat 3D models of crime scenes generated by laser scanners and then introduced in court? Liscio says: "The visual nature of 3D is what is important because it helps you understand the spatial difference between things, and the context." Liscio shows his full reconstruction of a crime scene while speaking to a jury. In the 3D model he displays, "I can move around. It's very fluid, very dynamic, which means somebody can stop you and ask a question or ask you to move to a different location in the scene."

Liscio uses FARO SCENE 2go, a secure, non-internet-based project sharing solution for SCENE software users (Version 7.1 or later). SCENE 2go makes easy to share, read-only scan projects ideal for courtroom presentations. The user simply saves his scan project(s) on a USB drive or any other external storage medium and can view them on a Windows® or macOS® computer without needing an internet connection.[3]

Liscio considers this software a highly effective way to present scan data. The user can take snapshots, offer a video flythrough of a scene, as examples. SCENE 2go is like a Google Streets for crime scenes, he said. In addition to being able to look around a scene, photographs, lab reports, and videos also can be integrated into the scene. Liscio views the software as a tool that shows the user how to build a comprehensive crime scene documentation package that can be used in a court presentation. And a 3D print can be made from the scanned scene, as well. Three-dimensional printing can be used to help law enforcement agencies recreate detailed models of crime scenes, vehicle crashes, footprints, and fingerprints, as well as for making architectural models of human bones and skulls. The use of 3D printing of a model of a crime victim's skull, in particular, can lead to that victim being positively identified. Laser scans of a victim's bones or skull can be printed in 3D for courtroom presentations.[4] Printing evidence or objects from the scene can ultimately help jurors understand more of the technical details. A study published in the *International Journal of Legal Medicine* found that 94% of jurors understood the technical language of an expert when presented with a 3D-printed model of skull trauma.

Surveillance Video brought into Scanned Scenes

Another major piece of evidentiary support material for crime scene presentations that is now routinely brought into courtrooms is surveillance video. It can be incorporated into a presentation of a laser-scanned, reconstructed crime scene. According to the website Security Bros – Surveillance and Security Product Reviews, digital video surveillance evidence has become an integral part of the majority of investigations and court proceedings. "It is the shock witness, the icing on the cake, and many times the breakthrough in a stagnant court case," the website says. When juries are presented with surveillance footage, the suspect is more likely to receive a conviction than if no video surveillance was used at all, the website continues. However, there is a caveat to using this type of evidence in court. Video surveillance evidence must be clarified by one or several qualified professional witnesses. And it is essential for both plaintiffs and defendants to understand the constraints of using this kind of evidence and not to misinterpret it for the jury. Meanwhile, what a jury believes in a court case offering video surveillance may ultimately hinge on the video footage that is shown in court.[5]

Enhanced Video Yields Added Perspectives

The National Center for Audio and Video Forensics (NCAVF), based in Los Angeles, California, is called upon often to study, enhance, and present surveillance video footage in court cases. It copies original video evidence to its computer servers, then converts the original video into a format ready for analysis and enhancement. This crucial step protects the original video evidence while allowing a new version to be added to special software for clarification and analysis. Clarifying a video or audio properly—using the right tools and techniques—can uncover important case details and make the difference between a guilty or non-guilty verdict.

Among a few of the techniques applied to video enhancement are:

- Enlarging or zooming in on certain parts of a video.
- Studying shadows or reflections to help focus on movement.
- Slowing down or speeding up the video.
- Measuring heights and speed of objects and movements of people in the video footage.
- Editing multiple camera angles to show a plausible timeline of events.
- Adding to time counter to identify individual frames.
- Tracking people, cars, or items over time through several surveillance cameras and systems.
- Showing time elapsed between specific events unfolding in a video.
- Identifying use of firearms, weapons, or other threatening actions from individuals shown in the video through the expertise of NCAVF's gun expert.

Each video that the NCAVF is asked, by a client, to analyze and enhance for use in court requires a unique response and strategy, according to founder David Notowitz. "We enjoy thinking outside the box," Notowitz said. "There is metadata to analyze and compare, and often multiple video and audio sources can be filtered, stabilized, and synchronized. Sometimes, we put circles around certain evidence in the video or add arrows to identify different people within an incident," Notowitz continued. "And we add legends so you can cross-reference what arrows represent what people or items in the surveillance video scene." Examples can be a turn signal, or a stoplight that is green, red, or yellow. Other times, the focus is on tracking people and associating them with their names. Shadows are important to track, as well. "We may circle a knife, or even the shadow of a knife," Notowitz said. "In fact, the shadow (of the knife) can give away that it's a knife better than the actual weapon that you may see in the hand of the suspect in the video, because the shadow is more detailed and clear."

Original Video and Its Enhanced Version Shown Together

In addition to showing a close-up or enhanced view, NCAVF also embeds the untouched, original video into the enhanced video version for court. Doing so helps a viewer reference the original surveillance side by side with the enhancement, allowing easy comparison and better context. This technique allows anyone to go back to the original video while looking at the zoomed-in, enhanced version. "It's important to keep the jury informed of what's happening in the video," Notowitz said. "This gives context."

NCAVF uses a counter in its video surveillance enhancements that measures 1/100th of a second. This enables attorneys and other parties to point out individual frames in the video footage. These frames can be individually referenced by witnesses, jury, and judge, and by the opposing attorneys. Notowitz said most original surveillance videos only show a second counter, but that inside each second there are multiple frames occurring. The counter his firm has built can stop a video and identify each frame so it can be specifically addressed by the court.

When video surveillance footage is brought into court it may be shared with other experts, such as a body mechanics expert, gun expert, or blood spatter expert. A judge often walls off each expert into what he or she is going to discuss relative to the video footage. This helps prevent excessive overlapping in what each expert will testify about, Notowitz said. As an example, "There might be a video of a drowning," Notowitz explained, "and an expert testifying on drownings may look at our video to determine where the drowning occurred, how the person fell into the area of water, and how long the person was underwater based on the enhancement to the video we've done."

Enhanced video surveillance footage will sometimes be introduced and discussed as part of a 3D model of a crime scene. In such instances, a defense attorney will call on Notowitz first to present his video evidence, as this can be the basis for the entire trial. "They will want to know where the video footage came from, how we exported it, how we gathered it." Notowitz, who presents all video surveillance footage for his clients, may not be the one who takes the jury through the video. Often, it is better to have a witness do this, or another expert witness, he added.

Surveillance video enhancement is the only part of introducing this type of evidence in court. Often NCAVF writes a report detailing analysis of the work done and what the video shows, as well as frame rate, resolution, and a description of what may not be shown on the video—missing evidence, items, people, movements due to poor video quality. "All of these things come together to help the case," Notowitz said.

Getting Technology Admitted in Court Critical

When an expert forensic witness, crime/crash reconstructionist, or crime scene investigator goes to court with a reconstruction of a crime scene that he intends to present, he usually must undergo formal court scrutiny of his methodology for the reconstruction. Thus, the so-called *Daubert standard* is applied whereby a set of criteria is used to determine the admissibility of scientific and technical testimony and evidence (Figure 9.4).

The Daubert Hearing is conducted through what is known in legalese as a motion in limine—a motion, discussed outside a jury's presence, requesting that certain testimony be excluded. With a Daubert Hearing, the judge becomes a gatekeeper who determines whether or not an expert's advice is considered reputable and relevant.[6] As gatekeeper, the trial judge employs a Daubert test to ascertain whether or not an expert witness's testimony is: 1) based on scientifically valid reasoning, and 2) whether it has been properly applied to the facts at issue. If the expert witness does not meet the Daubert Standard, his testimony can be excluded. The standard is based on five factors of consideration:

1. Whether the theory or technique proposed can be and has been tested
2. Whether the technique has undergone peer review and publication

Figure 9.4 Point clouds like this shooting scene outside an apartment are comprised of millions of data points once the environment has been laser scanned. To manage these points in post-processing and create a photorealistic representation, CAD software is used to literally connect the dots so that a 3D model can be built. When presented in court, the 3D model immediately connects with juries. (Photo courtesy of Clackamas County, Oregon, Sheriff's Office)

3. The technique's known or potential error rate
4. Existence and maintenance of standards controlling the technique's or equipment's operation
5. Whether the technique has gained widespread acceptance with a relevant scientific community.[7]

How did the Daubert standard come about? It stems from a 1993 U.S. Supreme Court case known as *Daubert v. Merrell Dow Pharmaceuticals*, in which petitioners argued serious birth defects were the result of the prenatal use of Bendectin by the mother. The petitioners testified that the drug caused birth defects based on chemical structure analyses, animal studies, and the reanalysis of previously published studies. But the lower court dismissed the case on summary judgment, stating that the petitioners failed to establish the premise that Bendectin caused birth defects in humans met the "general acceptance in the scientific community" standard.

Up until this case, there was another famous case from 1923 known as *Frye v. United States*, in which the defendant was charged with second-degree murder and who sought to introduce testimony from a scientist who conducted a lie detector test showing he was telling the truth. With this case, the legal system tried to develop coherent tests for the admissibility of scientific evidence. In Frye, the D.C. Court of Appeals weighed expert testimony for the reliability of lie detector test results. But the court stipulated that any deductions for this kind of test had to be generally accepted in the field in which it belongs. Consequently, the court found that the lie detector test "had not gained such standing and scientific recognition among physiological and psychological authorities." Frye imposed a special burden: that a particular technique must be "generally" accepted by the relevant scientific community.[8]

The Daubert ruling of 1993 superseded the Frye standard in federal court and in some state courts. It is still used in those courts today, according to the Legal Information Institute. The Daubert standard improves upon the Frye standard because it reduces "general acceptance" to "acceptance within a relevant community." And, the Daubert standard provides for other, specific scientific factors, among which one of the most important is *error rate.*

Clearly, the ability to present crime/crash scene reconstructions in court and whose methodology meets the Daubert standard is powerful; it can help determine the verdict of a case. In particular, 3D laser scanning, as a scene reconstruction technology, can provide details about a scene and its evidence that otherwise might be overlooked and that you might not have known to look for originally. So, if a scanner was used at a crime scene and crucial detail was captured and it can be viewed in court via a 3D model, after passing a Daubert test, this can be especially useful for jurors (Figures 9.5, 9.6, and 9.7).

Verifiable accuracy of a widely used instrument such as a 3D laser scanner will ensure that the scan data evidence will withstand court scrutiny against the Daubert standard. In 2013, a U.S. federal court issued a ruling affirming the scientific validity of laser scan data. In that case, a Leica ScanStation was questioned, and the judge stated that data from the scanner is admissible as scientific evidence. This ruling paved the way for the acceptance of other laser scanners' data.

Scanner Proves Compelling in Court Case

As this chapter has emphasized all along, there is a special power in walking a jury through a crime scene versus presenting them with still photos and 2D diagrams. Joe Lefevre, Department Chair at the

Figure 9.5 Photo and point cloud of an officer-involved shooting scene that shows the power of bullet trajectory presentation, which is a valuable tool that is offered with most laser scanning post-processing software packages. (Photos courtesy of Det. Matt Archuleta, Crime Scene Investigation Unit, Arvada, Colorado, Police Department)

Figure 9.6 Photo and point cloud of an officer-involved shooting scene that shows the power of bullet trajectory presentation, which is a valuable tool that is offered with most laser scanning post-processing software packages. (Photos courtesy of Det. Matt Archuleta, Crime Scene Investigation Unit, Arvada, Colorado, Police Department)

Public Safety Training Center at Fox Valley Technical College, knows this firsthand. Lefevre assisted on a case while he was a Platteville, Wisconsin, police officer that was the first time a 3D laser scanner crime scene model display was used in a Wisconsin court. The case pertained to a woman found dead in her bed from a gunshot wound

Figure 9.7 Photo and point cloud of an officer-involved shooting scene that shows the power of bullet trajectory presentation, which is a valuable tool that is offered with most laser scanning post-processing software packages. (Photos courtesy of Det. Matt Archuleta, Crime Scene Investigation Unit, Arvada, Colorado, Police Department)

to her temple. A second bullet hole had entered the wall just to the left of the woman's body.

"It took less than 30 minutes to scan the room. Four scans of the room were made with the laser scanner, with each scan taking six minutes, and less than a minute to move the scanner from one location in the room to another," Lefevre said. Although additional work was required at the scene after laser scanning was accomplished, the scanner and operator had left the crime scene quickly after the room had been scanned.

The dead woman's husband proved to be the suspect, and after searching a day to locate him, he was finally found at an out-of-state address. When the husband was questioned, his answers varied but they focused on a malfunction with his firearm, which led to an unintended firing of the gun. According to Lefevre, the possible trajectories for the two rounds fired did not line up. Some lateral movement of the bullets had occurred. Jurors were shown a 2D overhead sketch of the scene, but this did not present the scene as accurately as the 3D model. "As I testified, the jury did not look confused (viewing the 3D model)," Lefevre said. "Moving about the virtual scene illustrating details, I could see comprehension in their facial expressions."

Even today, it is still unknown why the victim's husband fired the two shots with his gun. The strongest theory is that the first shot missed, prompting the husband to fire the second shot. Apparently the jury agreed, and found the husband guilty of first-degree intentional homicide after just two hours of deliberation.

The defense used a strategy of attempting to confuse the jury, Lefevre explained. "They put multiple experts on the stand to talk about firearm malfunctions and ballistics," Lefevre said. "These technical confusion tactics did nothing to undermine the virtual environment we created."[9]

Introducing laser-scanned crime scene reconstructions in court to aid juries has been the focus of this chapter. Surveillance video is an additional, crucial evidentiary tool that can be combined with laser-scanned scenes that are part of a courtroom presentation. Finally, it is essential for 3D technology that is used in a court trial to meet the Daubert standard to ensure accuracy and credibility, such as with laser scanning.

The next chapter will look into how 3D panoramic cameras are a more recent technology whose ability to create comprehensive digital layouts of buildings for increased security has been seen as compelling.

Notes

1. Jones, T. "Scanning for Forensic Presentations." 2011, February .3 www.landairsurveying.com.
2. "Laser Scanning for Forensic Investigations." FARO Technologies UK. www.faro.com.
3. "Scene2go Mobile and Secure Project Sharing." www.faro.com/resource.
4. Honick, J. "How Police Departments Are Using 3d Printing to Solve Crime." 2017, September 13. www.police.one.com/ police-products /3d-laser-scanners/articles.
5. Chris. "Using Video Surveillance as Evidence in Court." 2017, October 16. www.securitybros.com.
6. Lindgren, W.H. "What is a Daubert Hearing?" 2010, April 17. www.omsj.org /legal/daubert.
7. Expert, E., Institute. "The Daubert Standard – A Guide to Motions, Hearings and Rulings." 2020, March 10. www.expertinstitute.com / resources/insights.
8. "The Frye Standard and Rule 702 of the Federal Rules of Evidence." www.forensiclaw.uslegal.com /litigation-history-of-forensic-evidence.
9. LeFevre, J. "Why Police Should Use Crime Scene Mapping Technology." 2017, February 14. www.policeone.com.

10

360° Imaging Systems as a Way to Document Crime Scenes

The appeal of being able to build a detailed, photorealistic 3D model of a crime or crash scene has only strengthened in recent years as newer technologies, offering different, compelling solutions, have been introduced. Specifically, the emergence of 360° imaging solutions represents some of the latest, attractive alternatives to, say, 3D laser scanning because of their tremendous ease of use, quick operation, and substantially lower pricing. This is in no way to downplay the importance of laser scanners as they are still in high demand, have proven to be dramatically effective for scene documentation, and produce point clouds that, with specialized processing and diagramming software, can be converted to 3D models that have proven effective in court. Meanwhile, 360° imaging systems are helping to round out the options available to law enforcement agencies, crime scene investigators, and reconstructionists looking for different ways to map and document crime scenes with the highest efficiency possible.

360° Panoramic Cameras Record Crime Scenes, but also Building Floorplans

One of these imaging solutions involves the use of special cameras that produce panoramic 360° documentation of crime scenes. Just a few years ago, before consumer-grade, low-cost spherical panoramic sensors were available, panoramic photography and 3D modeling involved stitching shots from various viewpoints into one single frame, or the use of an expensive rotating linear array camera. This approach proved time-consuming and did not always guarantee optimal quality of photogrammetric restitution due to various deficiencies with the whole process.[1] Today, a wide selection of 360° cameras are available to create panoramic images or videos in real time, without the need for stitching or additional processing, and which provide high-quality results. These compact cameras also are more affordable. As a result, the 360° cameras are ideal for documenting not only crime and crash scenes, but especially buildings and major venues where security is paramount.

Victor, New York–based L-Tron Corporation offers a special 360° camera for capturing indoor and outdoor crime scenes by shooting a series of photos of any scene with a panoramic range. The solution, called OSCR360, captures scenes and their chain of events in 360 degrees. The OSCR360 creates a virtual tour of ancillary evidence with a photographic timeline.

The OSCR360 consists of a 360° camera, a tripod for camera mounting, and a tablet that connects to the special camera so that photos taken can be viewed in real time. When the 360° camera is activated for scene documentation, photos taken are actually JPEG files that are automatically stitched together. After a scene has been documented with OSCR360, it can be downloaded using the software that is sold with the camera.

As with laser-scanned crime and crash scenes, any kind of additional evidence files can be attached to a scene that is photographed with OSCR360. These include video files (body-worn video or cell phone video), photographs, recorded sound, and close-up views of evidence (i.e., guns, knives, and bullet casings). Such multimedia files provide a precise depiction of a crime scene in its entirety and aid in courtroom presentations because by having a more complete crime scene to present, in a panoramic view, a jury can understand a scene and its events. Also, the fact that a jury can be walked through a virtual tour of the scene is so much more helpful than verbally describing it. The camera captures associated metadata, such as compass direction and GPS location. The result is that a jury can better understand where events at the scene were transpiring, and witnesses can more accurately explain where they were when certain things happened.

L-Tron claims that the OSCR360 is so easy to set up and use, no training is required, and that the panoramic camera's fast set up and operation also help prevent scene contamination.(1)

Canada-based Crime Sciences, Inc., offers the LizardQ (LIZQ) Spherical Imaging System for 3D capture and virtual scene documentation. The LIZQ is a camera system for quickly and automatically creating panoramic or full spherical (360°x180°) images with high resolution and high dynamic range. It delivers full spherical images at 100–500 megapixel resolution. Multiple full frame images are captured and merged into the final spherical image automatically. The LIZQ uses the new Canon EOS 5Ds 50megapixel camera, with which the user can create 500 megapixel spherical images. When the LIZQ is deployed, it can capture scenes in virtually all lighting conditions, or in a completely darkened room.

LIZQ Captures Images from Various Positions; No Disruption with Stitching

The LIZQ camera system also can be inverted to capture images from various positions. There is extensive overlapping between image captures, which means there is no disruption in the stitching process. LIZQ creates JPEG tone–mapped images from every capture position, and so these can be used in the company's photogrammetry software to create a dense point cloud for 3D modeling and for providing measurement accuracies of 2 mm or less. And, images can be enhanced by merging drone images or still crime scene photos in the same project.

Another noteworthy entry for 360 cameras is the Ricoh THETA V360 4K Spherical VR camera. In 2017, a model in this series was used for a test crime scene in a house at the Staffordshire University in the UK. The camera was used for 3D documentation and rapid identification of possible crime scene contamination. A crime scene house, containing seven rooms and intended to simulate investigations in a realistic setting, had some permanent exhibits of crime scene investigation, including examples of various types of bloodstain patterns.

Cameras Useful for Detecting Crime Scene Contamination

Researchers set out with two objectives: 1) To evaluate the performances of a low-cost imaging sensor—the Ricoh Theta spherical camera—for a quick 3D reconstruction of a forensic scenario; and 2)

To propose a methodology for the rapid recording of possible contamination which could have changed the original appearance of the crime scene. The Ricoh camera was combined with algorithms for image pre-processing, photogrammetric 3D reconstruction, data registration, and analysis. The experiment involved qualitative analysis, such as visual inspection of reconstructed objects and quantitative test evaluation (i.e., best-fitting plane analysis on various surfaces). These analyses indicated a strong potential outcome for use of the Ricoh spherical camera's 3D documentation on the crime scene. The documentation produced a dense 3D point cloud (mean spatial resolution in the range of 1–5 mm). In addition, the study's conclusion said, small objects, such as a gun, bottle, can, vase, or pills container could be reconstructed and, therefore, potentially documented as investigation evidence. However, the process failed when higher detail and accuracy were needed for modeling smaller objects, such as a pack of cigarettes, lighter, bullet, or knife.

The other portion of the experiment proposed a method to quickly record possible contamination that could have changed the scene as it originally appeared. The method was based on automatic 3D featured–based point cloud registration and cloud-to-cloud distance calculation. As a result, this process showed successful identification of the largest objects in the crime scene among those objects that were purposely removed. The method also proved how the camera's documentation was applicable to other different types of contaminations (i.e., displacement of objects from the original position within the crime scene). The study cited two limitations with using the Ricoh camera: 1) The approach is not completely automatic, and that manual segmentation of the point cloud is required for the distance calculation to be performed; and 2) Noise of the collected data can negatively impact the analysis, which can result in detection of false evidence. The study's findings conclude that this approach will be improved "by supporting the analysis of the reconstructed 3D geometry with RBG (color model) information available on the original panoramas."[2]

While 360° panoramic cameras have demonstrated effectiveness for documenting crime scenes and creating powerful 3D models, they play an even larger role in the forensic arena: security as a means to better understand how a major facility (school, public building, entertainment and sports venues, etc.) can be protected if a major incident occurs.

A key provider of this technology is Visual Plan, a Seattle, Washington-based company that enables clients to build a custom security plan for their facility using advanced 360° mapping software in a virtual and interactive fashion.

3D Tours of Digital Floor Plans

The Visual Plan software can capture 50,000 sq. ft of a building's floor plan in less than three hours, creating an as-built, measurable 3D photographic record otherwise known as a "digital twin." The software also generates an automated 3D tour of digital floor plans and the ability to create 2D and 3D floor plans. Data capture accuracy is 1 percent dimensional error, or lower, for every 65 ft, according to the company's website, but adding constraints can dramatically increase accuracy. Visual Plan works well for both indoor and outdoor scenes. The software package uses off-the-shelf 360° camera hardware which range in cost from $200 to $1,000. Because technology with these cameras is changing so rapidly, the company can easily upgrade its cameras as its technology changes (Figure 10.1).

Another camera that Visual Plan uses is the Ricoh Theta Z1, which is effective for documenting low-light areas which are often found at crime scenes. In addition, the company uses handheld LED, ruggedized lights that are 30-watts and have 1,500 lumen. In completely dark scenes like a fire reconstruction, a mix of six to eight of these lights is used to illuminate the scene effectively. One of Visual Plan's customers, Mohawk College in Hamilton, Ontario, Canada, uses this method, but also has attached strips of LED lights to safety vests worn by the person capturing the imagery to effectively light any area as photos are taken without the need to stage any scene lighting.

"Digital Twin" Data Sets Helpful for Comparisons

An important part of Visual Plan's work for clients involves comparisons of data for their buildings. Therefore, "We can compare side-by-side, in-sync up to four different data captures of the exact same area taken at different points in time," explained Kelly Watt, Visual Plan's

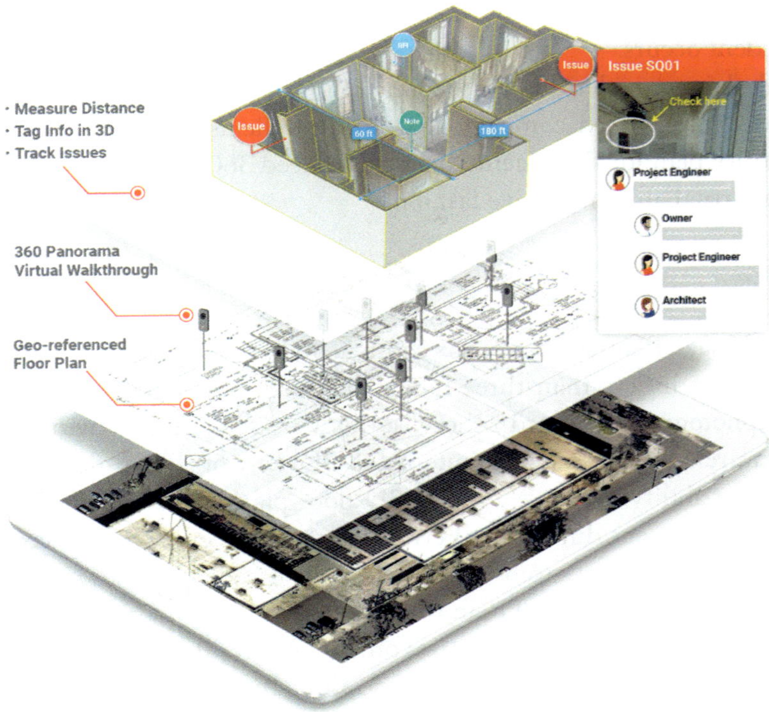

Figure 10.1 This CAD diagram shows the various interior features of an office building scanned with Visual Plan 360°mapping software. The building is a 2D overlay with 3D BIM (Building Information Model) and shows measurements and annotations that are helpful for risk assessment associated with potential active incidents. The 2D overlay and 3D BIM can be shared with various stakeholders such as law enforcement and public safety personnel. (Photo courtesy of www.visualplan.net)

founder. "These data captures are called a 'digital twin' and are meant to preserve a digital carbon copy of the information. Whether it's an image or 3D CAD BIM (Building Information Modeling), we can compare this data side by side," Watt said. Substantial information can be captured at walking speed without tripods using HD Video or stop-and-go image capture. Image capture can be taken inside or outside a building by spacing capture of images between 3 ft and 20 ft apart depending on the environment. You must have images spaced at the minimum distance of the xyz measure of space. For example, a user would use a distance of 3 ft as the maximum spacing of a hallway that measures 3' x 8' x 20' because 3' is the smallest distance of the xyz. A warehouse measuring 20' x 40' x 120' could see an image spacing of <=20' apart to maintain measurability. "You don't need to take a lot of photos if you're just wanting visual information," Watt said. "You can take a single image and walk 100' for the next image. But to create a photogrammetric mesh where you can measure from, you need to photograph enough images to use for measurable data," Watt added.

Panoramic Photorealistic System Useful for Major Venues, Mounting on Vehicles

When considering how nearly all large buildings or clusters of buildings—shopping malls, self-standing retail/grocery superstores, office parks, university campuses, hotels, just to name a few—today are easy, vulnerable targets for major incidents, Visual Plan's spherical environment capture software is timely. The software is equally effective for major venues such as stadiums or large areas used for festivals and special events. According to Watt, Visual Plan is a scene documentation tool designed to help people increase and maintain security. "We're aiming to achieve 360-degree situational awareness that happens with a fast data capture process," Watt explained of his software's purpose. "This allows various stakeholders to remotely identify, discuss, and design countermeasures to vulnerabilities found in the visual model." Stakeholders are able to efficiently address risk without having to be onsite.

In addition to Visual Plan's ability to map and document information via walking in and out of various facilities, the company also can use the software using vehicles whereby a 360 camera is mounted. The software's vehicle mapping solution captures images while driving at speeds up to 25mph. This solution is helpful for very large scenes that involve event planning or a large university campus. "We're looking for vulnerabilities, vehicle choke points, shooter locations, and covered areas where someone could hide and who could be a threat," Watt said. The vehicle mapping solution is also helpful for planning escape and evacuation routes at large event venues and for organizing where law enforcement officers could be placed so that they can direct people in case of an incident. Likewise, if there is something like an explosion and people are running in a certain direction, but you have an evacuation route that first responders are using to move in, this presents a problem, Watt said. "So, you've got to have a route where people can go out and one where people like first responders can come in."

Data captured for a project using Visual Plan is hosted on Amazon Government Secure Servers. Most federal government agencies use cloud-based platforms as their primary method for hosting data. The actual projects that Visual Plan has completed are hosted on its own website.

The Gaylord Palms Resort & Convention Center, in Kissimmee, Florida, is a good example of a potential soft target for a major incident—one that warrants a solution offering thorough risk assessment and a plan for strong security. Visual Plan was able to provide just that solution with its software. It's easy to understand why Gaylord Palms was such a natural candidate for higher security throughout its environment. The multi-building hotel and convention center, which opened in 2002, boasts more than 2 million sq. ft spread across a 65-acre property.

360 Situational Awareness for Hotels

For the Gaylord Palms project, Visual Plan mapped and documented the hotel's entire indoor floor plan as well as the exterior grounds and rooftop access areas. The goal was to create a security plan using a virtual, interactive model. This entire process took four days to capture with a team of five from Visual Plan. To accomplish the project, a MADV 360° camera affixed to a construction hat or on an extended pole was used to capture the hotel's entire floorplan, after which it was uploaded and processed in the Visual Plan software. In the software, captured images were accurately leveled, stitched, and meshed automatically, then arranged to create a complete and accurate model. With this model, symbols, images, training videos, links, and notes could be added to make comprehensive security plans available to view. Equipped with this interactive security plan, Gaylord Palms can develop scenarios, make inspections, review lockdown and evacuation plans, and share all of these components with its key shareholders as well as with first responders (Figures 10.2 and 10.3).

For the Gaylord Palms project, Visual Plan's Kelly Watt said his company imported existing 2D diagrams of the floor plans for the

Figure 10.2 The Gaylord Palms Resort & Convention Center, Kissimmee, Florida, is a potential soft target for major, active incidents. The resort's indoor floor plan, exterior grounds and rooftop access areas were mapped with the Visual Plan 3D software for risk assessment. The resulting 3D model represents an interactive security plan for creating incident scenarios. (Photos courtesy of www.visualplan.net)

resort's buildings where the 360° imagery was laid overtop. "This allows you to navigate through the 2D diagrams to find out where you are in the sprawling hotel complex and to do the same using the 360° imagery," Watt said. "I can take measurements directly on the map or 3D measurements from the imagery in the software's 3D viewer. I just pick any point where I want to measure from. I can also do so using a tablet and a stylus."

Figure 10.3 The Gaylord Palms Resort & Convention Center, Kissimmee, Florida, is a potential soft target for major, active incidents. The resort's indoor floor plan, exterior grounds and rooftop access areas were mapped with the Visual Plan 3D software for risk assessment. The resulting 3D model represents an interactive security plan for creating incident scenarios. (Photos courtesy of www.visualplan.net)

Merging 3D Imaging Results with Laser Scanning

Although laser scanning is also able to make digital floor plans of buildings, 360 panoramic cameras, among other 3D imaging solutions, now compete with laser scanning, yet yield higher efficiency, according to Watt. Yet there is a tremendous benefit to combining critical measurement data from laser scanner data with scene data from 360° image software like Visual Plan. There is also impressive time savings. For example, it would easily require hours more time to scan the Gaylord Palms Resort & Convention Center, using a 3D laser scanner compared to Visual Plan. The scan data are rich, plentiful, and meaningful. However, when combining the scanner with the Visual Plan, a better and quicker result can be achieved so that there is even more robust data to handle. Watt poses the challenge of mapping and documenting a four-story apartment building where a crime scene that started outside suddenly splinters off and travels inside the building, up the stairs and into one room and then another. "If I'm laser scanning this entire scene, I'm going to be there for two days or more," Watt argued. "If I'm using Visual Plan to scan the entire environment, then I can use 3D laser scanning to capture critical evidence (i.e., bullet casings, blood on walls), and merge this scan data with the Visual Plan date, which means these two tools working together will foster a more effective workflow."

Watt describes his software as reality capture or visualization, whereas laser scanning offers more accurate point clouds. Laser scanning is lidar-based and Visual Plan is photogrammetry-based. What crime scene investigators, reconstruction experts, and stakeholders for major facilities and venues need today is visualization and critical measurements, Watt said. By combining laser scanning with software like Visual Plan, critical evidence can be taken from the laser scanner while large environments can be captured quickly with the 360 software. Producing the results faster means investigators can use the data as part of their ongoing investigation, rather than simply as a court exhibit.

The capability of building a 3D model from imagery that is initially captured with a $300 camera (and later processed with specialized software) is a phenomenal accomplishment. "We get next-day results from this technology," Watt said, which is not always the case with laser scanning, especially with large scenes. Merging 3D scanning and 360 image capture workflows is an effective and efficient process for

Figure 10.4 This library at Carleton University in Ottawa, Canada, has been mapped in 3D as part of the school's plan to build emergency management plans for the campus. Carleton considers the Visual Plan mapping solution critical for its goal of a ready and effective response to possible active incidents. (Photo courtesy of www.visualplan.net)

crime scene reconstruction and for security planning. What's more, this trend underscores how today's technology tools for documenting crime and crash scenes and to address risk assessment in large public buildings and various venues are increasingly being combined to solve complex scene documentation problems—a topic that will be addressed towards the end of this book (Figure 10.4).

The introduction of 3D panoramic cameras and new cloud processing software as a different way to map crime scenes but also floor plans of buildings—for increased security—has been surveyed in this chapter. A 3D camera's ability to comprehensively document interiors/exteriors of buildings and numerous venues, and merge with critical measurements from laser scanning data are key advantages.

Tablets, the subject of the next chapter, are another form of 3D imaging that have become popular within law enforcement as another easy way to document crime and crash scenes, with scene details that rival and even expand the capabilities of 3D laser scanners.

Notes

1. Galvin, R. "Crime Scene Documentation for Law Enforcement." 2017, July 19. www.officer.com/ investigations/articles.
2. Abate, D., et al. "A Low-Cost Panoramic Camera for the 3D Documentation of Contaminated Crime Scene." 2017. www.researchgate.net.

11

Rugged Tablets

A Newer Way to Capture Scenes; An Alternative to 3D Laser Scanning

Using a tablet for crime or crash/collision scene documentation means investigators can reduce the number of people who must enter the scene to record it. And that's a huge benefit because by keeping multiple people from entering and probing a scene, there is reduced scene and evidence disturbance, lower chance of scene contamination, plus the time needed to document the scene itself is drastically cut. One person using a tablet can usually document a scene in full, with highly accurate measurements and a high level of photorealistic detail. Tablets are not a new technology, of course, since they have been used on the consumer side at least as far back as 2010. Today, with many improvements, the tablet's versatile utility makes it a perfect tool for use in the forensic field. And the fact that it's a handheld device makes its usage even more convenient and effective. Capabilities, in addition to capturing crime or vehicle crash or collision data, include word processing, digital camera, video recorder, and multiple software apps that can be run on this device.

Built to Meet Needs of Law Enforcement

A tablet configured for forensic use means that it can not only document a crime scene but also map it, and it can be used to make notes about the scene, its characteristics, and each evidence item collected. Software that can work with the tablet to process scene data is essential to making the tablet a tool worth using. The tablet has become a primary tool for crime and crash scene recording, which means, it must handle many other tasks. As a result, tablet manufacturers have found that there ultimately must be a partnership between themselves and law enforcement to build hardware capable of meeting the current software needs for crime scene mapping, documentation, processing, and diagramming. Another issue is that because of the specifically tailored apps needed for the tablet, the device requires a large amount of memory, often well beyond what originally was 1 GB of RAM. Top-of-the-line offerings can deliver up to 32 GB of RAM. After all, any one app's speed diminishes as the number of background processes increase or as more data is collected. The majority of top-of-the-line tablets now offer expanded memory. What about cameras and the amount of pixels? Most cameras inside tablets offer at least 8 megapixels, which helps ensure that scene evidence items and the entire scene itself can be adequately recorded, with high resolution.

Tablet Extensively Designed to Work Like Laser Scanning

In the years leading up to the year 2020, tablets have undergone enough design passes to qualify as a serious tool deserving of a place in any reconstruction expert's or crime scene investigator's toolbox. A tablet for forensic use at crime and crash scenes can now perform 3D capture of scenes in color that can be viewed right on the tablet, at the scene. This allows the tablet's operator to rotate and zoom within the scene, extract measurements, and begin performing line-of-sight analysis directly on the scene, all in a matter of minutes. Next, by downloading the resulting point cloud created on the tablet to post-processing software, more detailed line-of-sight analysis is possible along with scene reconstruction, and virtual walk-throughs. Similar to terrestrial LIDAR scanning, the entire scene and all of its evidence is preserved so that anyone can revisit it for further viewing and analysis at any time—a real benefit since the actual scene itself will have been cleared.

As with other scene reconstruction technologies, the tablet as a forensic tool is not offered by a large number of manufacturers. When first introduced, tablets were basic in functionality, but adequate for the consumer market. For more hardcore applications, such as those needed for the forensic field, the tablet would need to be totally redesigned, especially for use with crime and crash/collision scene reconstruction. One tablet maker that has consistently strived to build on its tablets aimed at this market is DT Research of San Jose, California. Since 2019, the company's 10.1-inch DT301X TR rugged tablet has met the stringent demands of forensic science applications. This tablet is loaded with an Intel Celeron processor, and offers a 2-in-1 configuration, water-resistant, detachable keyboard, internal hot-swappable battery, and hardware-software security. Earlier versions of tablets from various manufacturers, particularly for niche markets like law enforcement/crime scene investigation, were too thick and heavy, making them unsuitable for mobile, handheld usage. DT Research's DT301X TR measures 10.7 × 7.5 × 0.86 inches and weighs under 3 pounds. The tablet has a 1920 × 1200 resolution, and with front and rear cameras (Figures 11.1, 11.2, and 11.3).

Need for Specialized Software

The need for specialized software for use with the DT301X TR was not lost on DT Research, which is why it teamed up with Norwood, Massachusetts-based DotProduct 3D, to offer a fast and powerful 3D crime scene capture software package that works well for most crime and crash scenes. DotProduct is one of a few manufacturers of

Figure 11.1 The DTX302X TR rugged tablet meets the stringent demands of forensic science applications. It saves investigators significant time at crime scenes and allows them to send a scene to detectives rather than making them visit the scene. (Photos courtesy of DT Research, Inc.)

Figure 11.2 The DTX302X TR rugged tablet meets the stringent demands of forensic science applications. It saves investigators significant time at crime scenes and allows them to send a scene to detectives rather than making them visit the scene. (Photos courtesy of DT Research, Inc.)

kits aimed at the forensic and public safety markets. The company's model DPI-10, for example, is used not only by reconstructionists, but by detectives, forensic technicians, and criminologists as well. It is loaded with the company's Dot3D Pro, a full-function 3D capture and editing application that works with Intel (®) RealSense (™) Depth Camera, among others. The camera is well suited for high-accuracy

Figure 11.3 The DTX302X TR rugged tablet meets the stringent demands of forensic science applications. It saves investigators significant time at crime scenes and allows them to send a scene to detectives rather than making them visit the scene. (Photos courtesy of DT Research, Inc.)

applications such as 3D scanning, and offers unlimited HD photo capture during scanning.

Dot3D can export industry standard point cloud formats (i.e., PTS, PTX, PLY, PTG, E57, LAS, LAZ, and POD workflows), as well as with the company's own highly compressed DP file format. With these point cloud formats, scanning data will be imported directly into numerous point cloud, CAD, and meshing solutions, such as SketchUp, FARO Scene, Leica Cyclone, and Trimble RealWorks, to name just a few.

Works Alone, but Compatible with Other Mapping Technology

In some instances, the tablet can be used as a standalone tool for mapping and documenting scenes. But a more typical scenario is one in which other technologies are being used in conjunction with a tablet to record scene data. "We offer the tablet for photogrammetry and to allow the user to get control points," explained Mario Gosalvez, DT Research's manager of business development and sales. "Then we are able to take the tablet off the range pole and scan an incident where total stations can't because they are situated on a tripod." Likewise, there are times when a total station might be the best tool to use for a scene, and the tablet will communicate with the total station.

Tablets are well suited for crash scenes since they can help document such scenes quickly. As mandated by Congress, the Federal Highway Administration (FHA) has issued initiatives for tighter traffic incident management. The initiatives promote safe, quick clearance of traffic incident scenes, thereby restoring traffic flow. The benefits include more lives being saved, fewer secondary crashes, and reduced incident clearance time.[1]

According to Tom Greaves, chief marketing officer for DotProduct 3D, it is reasonable to expect that the tablet can cover 1,000–2,000 sq. ft of area at a scene. "Work flows show that the data gathered from this size of scene all fits together," Greaves said. "What is not feasible is to try using the tablet to capture a 200,000 square-foot scene. For that, you'd have to use drone technology, a tripod terrestrial scanner or total station." The tablet especially excels at recording tightly confined spaces for which other scene capture tools would be inadequate.

The promise of tablet technology is that it can be used by just about anyone, and the user does not need to be a survey specialist to get a useful deliverable.

Data files gained from a tablet are small compared to larger ones generated by laser scanning. "With a tablet," Greaves noted, "you can get into gigabytes of files very quickly. We have a very compressed file format—40 to 50 megabytes for a large scene. What that means is that, for instance, files can be transmitted from the field to the office over a cell phone network or with WiFi capabilities," Greaves continued. "This means investigators and detectives can look at this data from their devices (tablets) without ever having to visit the scene. So, we're sending the scene to detectives rather than making them visit the scene." In addition, the tablet's 8-megapixel camera captures images precisely and gives the user orientation for his scene. He knows where he is standing when taking photos with the tablet.

Oregon State Police Buys Tablets, Wants Multiple Apps, Sufficient RAM

Depending on how the DT301X TR is customized using the Dot3D software, its price can range between $6,000 and $10,000. This pricing, combined with how well tailored the tablet is for crime and crash scene capture, prompted the Oregon State Police (OSP) to buy five of the DT301 tablets. However, one of the absolute requirements OSP set forth with its purchase was that DT Research enable the DT301X TR to run with multiple software apps and sufficient RAM so that no slowdown in any of the software apps loaded on the tablet or crime/crash scene data capture ever occurs. Another component that would be essential for the tablet is its ability to operate with full GNSS data capture. DT Research handily met these requirements. What's more, OSP, now armed with the most powerful and versatile rugged tablet it could ask for, was able to start using an sUAS (small Unmanned Aircraft System) with the tablet to map and document scenes of any scope and size based on real-world coordinates, representing a major milestone for the agency's crash and crime reconstruction efforts.

The high level of thorough and accurate scene detail and 3D modeling achieved with OSP's rugged tablet and sUAS combination came about after four years of considerable experimentation through the efforts of Trooper William Bush, a District Lead Reconstructionist with the OSP's Collision Reconstruction Unit. Trooper Bush, in particular, had been seeking a way to more easily and quickly map what is predominantly collision and crash scenes on Oregon highways in his district. In 2016, the OSP invested in a number of robotic total stations using grant funding. Within that grant was an additional group of funding allocated for researching the possibility of integrating scene data captured by the Collision Reconstruction Unit with site data already captured for every highway in the state by the Oregon Department of Transportation (ODOT) (Figures 11.4 and 11.5).

Capturing "Context" of a Scene Critical

Crucial in Trooper Bush's view was not only capturing the evidence at a crash scene, but also the context—the actual, entire site—through which scene evidence is found and recorded. "This context helps the evidence make more sense," Bush explained. When looking at a crash scene on a highway, it's important to know, for example, if the highway was a three-lane, single-direction stretch of interstate,

Figure 11.4 Trooper William Bush, a District Lead Reconstruction Expert with the Oregon State Police Reconstruction Unit, scans a crushed vehicle using a DT301X TR rugged tablet. The tablet, which measures 10.7 × 7.5 × 0.86 inches and weighs under 3 pounds, is ideal for rapid mapping and documentation of crash and crime scenes. (Photos courtesy of Bob Galvin, RS Galvin & Assoc./ Writing Services, Lebanon, OR)

Figure 11.5 Trooper William Bush, a District Lead Reconstruction Expert with the Oregon State Police Reconstruction Unit, scans a crushed vehicle using a DT301X TR rugged tablet. The tablet, which measures 10.7 × 7.5 × 0.86 inches and weighs under 3 pounds, is ideal for rapid mapping and documentation of crash and crime scenes. (Photos courtesy of Bob Galvin, RS Galvin & Assoc./ Writing Services, Lebanon, OR)

or a two-lane, bi-directional highway on a curve with a grade. This context helps in making the evidence more sensible. "We can't understand the dynamics of what happened unless we understand the site in addition to the scene," Bush said. Because ODOT has already captured this site, as Bush continues explaining his premise, "We can eliminate this from our on-scene time. We can integrate our evidence data that we document with the site data that already exists."

Next, it's necessary to develop a workflow that makes sense for all stakeholders who will need to see it. This means there must be reliable control points for the scene. So, Bush argues, if he goes out to a scene with a robotic station to establish control points and then builds his scene for those points, other investigators or reconstruction experts could later capture these same points in real-world coordinates using a GNSS device. The two scenes then would be merged. "I would have the evidence mapped and documented, and they (ODOT) would have the site," Bush said. "Using these shared controls, we could determine whether or not the workflow was going to be sustainable." ODOT captured its data with a mobile laser scanner and stored this data on its servers. Bush used the robotic total station, yet was discovering that the extensive time and effort being absorbed with these combined systems was placing a huge workload on the DOT to capture control points at a scene they had previously documented as part of their mapping of all Oregon highways. Even more concerning, Bush said, was that the DOT personnel were exposing themselves to dangerous traffic to try to geo-locate one of his controls and then take their data to merge with his scene data. He added, "There's a lot of opportunity for error, as well."

GNSS—an Important Component

Where does the DT Research tablet fit into all of Trooper Bush's scene capture and post-processing efforts? Well, as Trooper Bush describes it, the road toward making the tablet a tool that will tie crash scene capture and post-processing together was winding, but successful. The Oregon DOT offered Bush a Lecia GS14 GNSS Smart Antenna that he could use to capture the control points at a scene. However, he wondered, if this tool could capture the control points, why could he not use it to capture all the points. So Bush did this, and it allowed him to abandon the robotic total station he had been using and just use the Leica GNSS system instead, which meant he could capture scene data along with control points, and then see any errors on each point at the same time. This approach worked well. As a result, Bush eliminated all of the total station setup time, and the data he captured became universally useful; Bush could now go out and capture any new points at a crash or crime scene without having to rely on locating the original control points.

Two years before these efforts by Trooper Bush, the Oregon DOT had been working on a project to provide some of its surveying supervisors with tablets, of which the first iteration was DT Research's DT391GS tablet that incorporated a GNSS board. A huge milestone, right? Not exactly, at least not for Trooper Bush who felt an even more powerful tablet with GNSS capability was still needed. He wanted to borrow one of these tablets and research whether or not it could be redesigned to capture more points as well as point controls using quality GNSS in addition to running all of the software required for typical day-to-day law enforcement operations. Bush asked DT Research to improve its tablet so it could be more valuable for public safety by incorporating multiple software apps and sufficient RAM to handle them. The apps included software for ongoing GNSS data capture for CAD, reporting, ticketing, among others. "I needed something in my hand that could handle all of my needs as a law enforcement officer in addition to being able to drop in a cradle on a rod and capture scene data," Bush said.

Powerful Tablet Replaced Other Tools, Joined a Drone

DT Research met this challenge with its DT301X TR tablet, allowing Bush to replace a $3,000 computer in his vehicle plus the Leica RTK device, and with less need for use of his robotic total station except to capture a few additional points at certain crash and crime scenes. Bush considers the DT301X TR tablet as the primary tool that he and his colleagues within the Oregon State Police Collision Reconstruction Unit can use for all of their collision and crime scenes. However, Bush also had long been planning to partner a UAS with the tablet so that additional, high-quality data could be captured for long and complex scenes. "The UAS is part and parcel of one system—one system that can adapt to every and any scene we need to capture," Bush said. The UAV saves time and captures data accurately. He added, "Our primary workflow is to get substantial data from the drone with large scenes and merge it with data captured through the tablet." He continued, "In the last two years—2017 and 2018—I've been called to crash scenes where investigators have been there for four or five hours and they're not done documenting these scenes." "I could now go into major scenes with a tablet and drone and be done in 30 minutes" (Figures 11.6, 11.7, 11.8, and 11.9).

The tablet cannot accomplish everything needed to capture a collision or crime scene. But what it enables Bush or anyone else who uses this scene documentation tool to do is get accurate, real-world coordinates and data points. On the back end, in post-processing, the reconstructionist can take data points gained from the tablet and any other tools, such as a UAS, and merge them seamlessly. And this is

Figure 11.6 The DT301x TR tablet displaying a point cloud of a crushed vehicle. (Photos courtesy of Trooper William Bush, Oregon State Police)

Figure 11.7 The DT301x TR tablet displaying a point cloud of a crushed vehicle. (Photos courtesy of Trooper William Bush, Oregon State Police)

all being done based upon GNSS control points, with consolidation; no longer will multiple technology tools need to be lugged around in the trunk of a car. "It could be just a tablet and drone," Bush offered. But this does not mean those other technology tools are being sidelined. For instance, said Bush, "I will never eliminate a total station

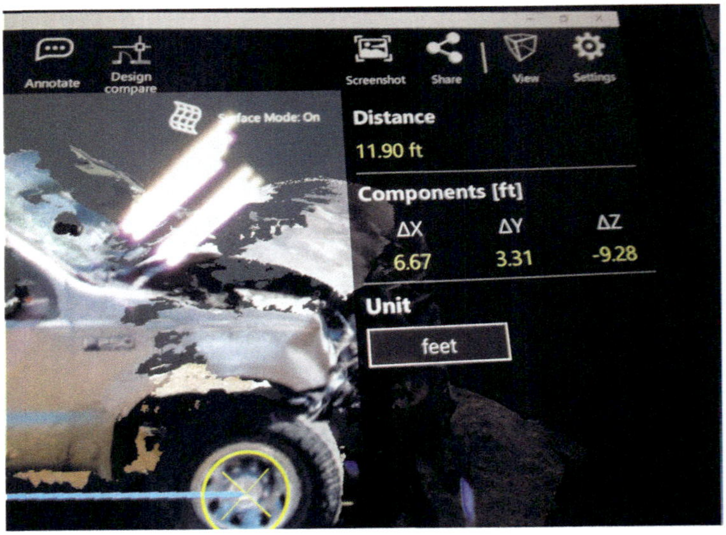

Figure 11.8 The DT301x TR tablet displaying a point cloud of a crushed vehicle. (Photos courtesy of Trooper William Bush, Oregon State Police)

from my inventory because there are scenes where a total station will function best of all tools, especially at scenes where you have no active correction signal. That correction signal can only come from a known location. We need a degree of precision when it comes to our controls" (Figure 11.10).

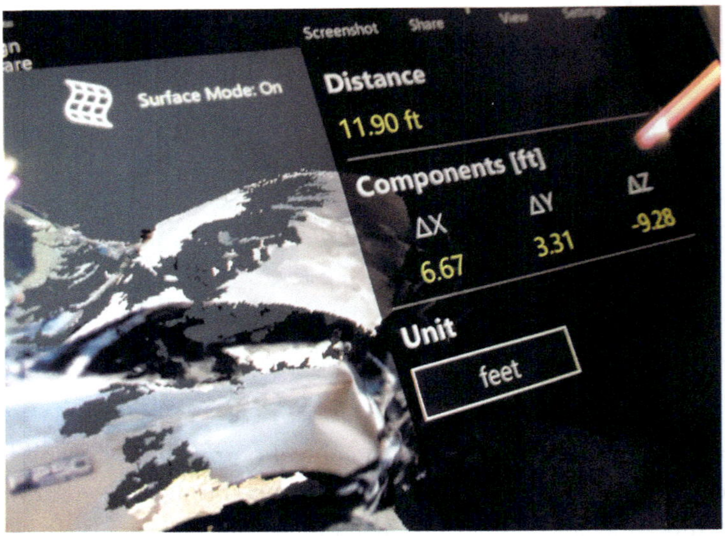

Figure 11.9 The DT301x TR tablet displaying a point cloud of a crushed vehicle. (Photos courtesy of Trooper William Bush, Oregon State Police)

Figure 11.10 Oregon State Police Trooper William Bush launches a drone for a test flight. This drone is used to map lengthy crash scenes that are also captured on the ground with the DT301x TR tablet. (Photo courtesy of Bob Galvin, RS Galvin & Assoc/Writing Services, Lebanon, OR)

Highly Valuable for Closed Cases

The tablet armed with GNSS technology will become particularly valuable for closed cases that are reopened and whereby the scene must be re-examined and measured again. It is probably the only way such a scene can be measured again. Trooper Bush cites a specific crash scene on one of the mileposts along an Oregon highway that stretches between Portland, Oregon, and the coast and that is notorious for multiple vehicle collisions or crashes. The scene, which has been visited by reconstruction experts many times, has a sharp S curve with a steep grade on the south side of the roadway and measures 150 ft. There is no engineering issue with the curve. Typical evidence to be captured includes vehicle location, tire marks, area of impact, and final rest location.

What proves valuable for Bush in using his tablet to map this scene is that he can set his controls and capture real-world coordinates based on GPS. If anything has changed in the scene from a prior mapping, he still has data he can tie back to. What's more is that the control points are always intact from one scene visit to another. "All I've had to do is go back to the original scene that I had stored on my tablet, reopen it, execute the new resection, and collect the data at the scene,"

Bush said. "The control is always there no matter if a case for any incident at this scene reopens or there's another crash at this exact same location." He added, "The key to this accurate scene mapping is GNSS which pinpoints where evidence is at the scene based on control points that it always retains. As a result, this capability makes the data not just valuable today but at any other time reconstructionists or others want to revisit it."

Tablet's Success Relies on Established Control Points

The tablet's key strength is that because it has the ability to establish and retain GNSS controls, data gathered from any other technology and merged with the tablet's own captured data can be processed with the software. "With the post-processing software, I tell it to work with data based on the control points I've established at the scene," Trooper Bush said. "So it processes everything and now every point in whatever point cloud I send it is based off of those real-world coordinates." These coordinates will be the same whether a point cloud is generated from a multi-station, depth camera, laser scanner, or UAS and photogrammetry. And, the tablet itself as a crime or crash/collision scene documentation tool has and will stand up to a Frye standard check in court because of the way data are captured and recorded.

This chapter has revealed how tablets are gaining acceptance as a reliable, comprehensive tool that can map crash and crime scenes, but that must be tied to GNSS. Tablets can only help if they are used with software apps that meet the needs of law enforcement.

In the following chapter, drones are analyzed for their ability to quickly map lengthy and, at times, hard-to-access crash and crime scenes, and whose data can easily be merged with laser scanners and other technology tools.

Note

1. "FHWA Strategic Plan – FY 2019-2022." 2020. www.safety.fhwa.dot.gov/proven.

12

How Drones Give Scene Reconstruction New Perspectives, Crucial Interrelationships of Evidence

More than any other technology applied to documenting crime and accident scenes, Unmanned Aerial Vehicles (UAVs) or drones have been adopted by law enforcement and crash reconstruction expert as a mapping tool with what seems at warp speed. Although UAVs have been with us for decades, mostly in military and surveillance applications, they have splintered off into law enforcement and forensic usage only during the last few years. A dozen U.S. police forces had applied for UAV permits by March 2013. Approximately 167 police and fire departments bought UAVs in the United States in 2016, which is double the number of UAVs purchased in 2015.[1]

More law enforcement agencies and crash reconstruction experts are now using UAVs as part of their toolbox for crime and crash scene documentation than ever before. Laser scanners, which have long prevailed as a tool that could handily capture most small-to-large scenes in their entirety, now are often accompanied by UAVs. Unlike laser scanners, UAVs can map lengthy, hard-to-record crash scenes, or murder scenes spanning several blocks, which means that a full and complete data set can now be achieved from the sky. And due to their mobile nature, UAVs can avoid shadowing from nearby objects. In addition to generating point clouds a UAV provides thousands of images that reveal far greater depth of information than is possible with laser scanning. The actual drone itself is of little value without the proper sensor to capture the aerial images. The Photogrammetry and 3D imaging software is already successfully being used to document accident scenes on the ground. But when this software can be partnered with a high-resolution camera having the recommended pixel count and it is connected to a drone, a crash scene can be captured completely and swiftly. The data from UAVs can be processed and imported into processing software that can create a detailed, useful 3D model (Figures 12.1, 12.2, and 12.3).[2]

Drones Give Better Overview of a Scene

What has made a UAV so valuable as a forensic tool is that it can be utilized to carry cameras, video cameras, and/or 3D laser scanners into areas not accessible by terrestrial scene capture tools. A UAV can fly over an incident area and collect data from otherwise inaccessible areas due to their location or height.

"Drones are one of the best tools for which we're getting a lot of acceptance," said Joe Lefevre, department chair for Appleton, Wisconsin-based Fox Valley Technical College's Public Safety Training Center. "Different parts of the country have adopted them early. The nice part is that you can map a crash scene on the ground,

Figure 12.1 On December 3, 2016, the morning after the devastating Ghost Ship warehouse fire in Oakland, Calif., which took 36 lives, a small DJI Phantom drone was flown using Pix4D photogrammetric mapping software to achieve a map of the debris. Shown here is a shot from the night of the fire. (Photo courtesy of www.visuallaw.com)

Figure 12.2 A screenshot showing the Pix4D generated drone 3D model of the warehouse fire. (Photo courtesy of www.visuallaw.com)

then put a drone up over the scene to get a good overview with photography and video," added Lefevre, who is a former Platteville, Wisconsin, police officer and fire marshal. He continued, "If it was an intersection crash, you can see how the intersections came into play. You could see where the skid marks and gouge marks are, where the debris field starts and stops, and where bodies in an ejection landed in relationship to the vehicles" (Figure 12.4).

UAVs are ideally suited for recording accident scenes since so many of these scenes can be long, complex, and involve curves, slopes,

Figure 12.3 The 3D point cloud of the Oakland, Calif., warehouse fire derived from the drone video footage. (Photo courtesy of www.visuallaw.com)

Figure 12.4 A typical commercial drone that many law enforcement agencies and reconstruction experts find ideal for mapping and recording mostly complex, lengthy crash scenes. (Photo courtesy of Robert Galvin, RS Galvin & Associates/Writing Services, Lebanon, OR)

embankments, and hard-to-access sections. Fort Collins, Colorado-based Petauro Systems, a UAV training company for U.S. law enforcement agencies, fire departments, and search and rescue teams, offers four reasons how UAVs will transform accident scene response. These include:

1) *UAVs can document accident scenes far quicker.* Clearing an accident scene as fast as possible is critical to preventing traffic buildup, secondary crashes, and precious lost time to commerce. The National Highway Safety Administration has weighed in on faster accident scene clearance and law enforcement personnel safety amid moving traffic with its own set of initiatives that need to be followed. Accident scenes typically have been documented with total stations, laser scanners, and photography, or by combining two or all of these methods to gather measurable data and generate a 3D point cloud of the scene. However, these methods, although reliable and accurate, require large chunks of time and trained experts who may not be available when an accident or crash occurs. But drones equipped with special cameras and photogrammetry systems can rapidly fly over accident scenes covering long distances and capturing a huge data set.

2) *By cutting time spent on roadways where accidents have occurred, human and financial costs are lowered significantly.* The methods for documenting accident scenes before drones were introduced left traffic crash

reconstructionists dangerously exposed to fast-moving traffic as they recorded scenes. The ability to quickly deploy UAVs to clear accidents reduces the time law enforcement and reconstructionists must spend to capture data and their exposure to traffic. Another benefit is that secondary collisions are reduced.

3) *UAVs capture measurable data that can be used to build a 3D diagram for presentation in court.*

   When a UAV is deployed it accomplishes two important tasks: 1) The UAV captures data points that, with photogrammetry software, allow the user to take measurements and rebuild the scene in 3D; and 2) Photos are taken by the UAV that can be used by themselves to show evidence or to connect a scaled, aerial diagram (Figure 12.5).

4) *UAVs can collect data more easily, requiring less training and offering greater accessibility.*

   Finely configured drone flight planning and photogrammetry software for UAVs mean that less time and specialization is required to accurately document an accident scene. This makes workflow more streamlined. As UAVs fly over scenes to acquire images, they are not as sensitive to obstacle occlusions or moving objects (i.e., cars, people) as laser scanners or total stations are. This allows UAVs to more easily capture and build a model. Also, UAVs can accept a wide range of cameras to reconstruct imagery in the photogrammetry software.[3]

Shows Interrelationships among Locations, Helps Jury's Understanding

Aerial photography of expansive crash or crime scenes from helicopters or airplanes was a routine approach until the introduction of UAVs. The chief benefit is that aerial photos can supplement normal crime scene photography because higher scene views can show interrelationships among different locations much more effectively. A jury also can understand these interrelationships more easily. In short,

Figure 12.5 A drone hovers above a crushed truck in a wrecking yard, mapping it for collision damage data. (Photo courtesy of Robert Galvin, RS Galvin & Associates/Writing Services, Lebanon, OR)

the aerial photograph provides a quicker synopsis of the overall scene (Figure 12.6).[4]

Once aerial photos of a crash or crime scene have been taken, how they are used is an important step in making them useful and relevant. Andrew Klane, managing partner with Forensic Mapping, Inc., Mashpee, Massachusetts, knows this challenge well. Before launching his crash reconstruction firm in 2017, Klane was a lieutenant with the Massachusetts State Police Collision Analysis and Reconstruction Section (CARS). In this job, he would take helicopter rides many times over crash scenes to take aerial photos. Eventually, Klane became responsible for the design and implementation of the UAS (unmanned aerial system) program for the state police that was used for the quick clearance of crash scenes.

Scene Mapping Time Slashed

The importance of UAS technology became even more impactful for Klane when he attended a reconstruction conference and learned about how the Pix4D image processing software could more

Figure 12.6 Trooper Brian Leventhal with the North Carolina Highway Patrol, who is a reconstruction expert and helicopter pilot, demonstrates the operation of a DJI Phantom 4 Pro drone via a Pix4Dcapture application. This solution is ideal for mapping and capturing long, complex vehicle collision scenes. (Photo courtesy of www.Pix4D.com)

effectively map and document crash scenes when combined with a UAV. About a month before he attended the conference, Thomas Clardy, a Massachusetts state trooper was killed on the Massachusetts Turnpike by a driver who had been using medical marijuana and swerved into the breakdown lane, striking Clardy's cruiser in the rear while he was conducting a traffic stop. At the reconstruction conference Klane was attending, he met with representatives for Pix4D, who upon hearing about Klane's aerial photos of the trooper's crash scene asked if they could see them. Klane gave the reps his thumb drive containing the photos; an hour later they had generated a 3D model of the crash site. Excited about this dramatic result produced by the Pix4D software, Klane introduced the software to the state police, with the idea of linking it with a UAV. At the department's direction, Klane created and implemented the use of UAVs to map collision scenes. As Klane was about to retire, this development spurred him to start his reconstruction consultancy. "The big push for this software and drone system is in the area of traffic incident management and time savings," Klane explained. He added, "We can now reduce an hour or hour and a half mapping time for a scene down to 20 minutes from beginning to end by using a drone with the software. The drone flight is just 12 to 15 minutes!"

Larger, outdoor scenes that cover a large area are ideal for UAVs, Klane said, and these include crime scenes, not just accident scenes.

A prime example would be a shooting on one block in a neighborhood after which the shooter drives five blocks down the street. "When you're in this kind of wide, open area, this application is ideal for the UAV," Klane said. Arson scenes are excellent for UAV mapping, too, because the UAV allows investigators into areas of the scene that they might otherwise be unable to physically access (Figure 12.7).

Klane emphasizes that photogrammetry software such as Pix4D needs to be used in conjunction with RTK GPA or GNSS to give the user ground control points (GCP's) so that the scene is locked down to these points, to ensure the measurements are accurate.

Combining Laser Scan, Drone Data Makes Sense for Lengthy Scenes

When there is a need to incorporate other mapping tools with the image recording software, a laser scanner, such as a Leica RTC360, is a very effective instrument. The scanner's resolution of scans is excellent. But if a user needs to scan, say, two miles or 2,500 ft of highway, "You're going to be there for a while with the scanner and you will have way too much data," Klane said. Klane provides a crash scenario where combining drone and scan data make sense. "Let's say I fly this

Figure 12.7 Shown is an arson scene that involved a murder, as well. The scene was mapped and recorded with a drone and rugged tablet. (Photo courtesy of Oregon State Police Trooper William Bush, OSP Collision Reconstruction Unit)

crash scene (using a UAV) that's an intersection or stretch of highway and I have the overall scene—lane markings, the approach, the grades, all of that," Klane explained. He added, "Now I laser scan (on the ground) the area of rest, point of impact—with two or three scans and get a lot of detail. I can take those scans and merge them into one with the UAV data that was captured and have some really high-end detail up close, plus I have my overall scene, as well. And, if I have total station measurements that someone took at the scene previously, I can pull all of this together in post-processing."

The Royal Canadian Mounted Police (RCMP) has had its share of challenging crash scenes to document, even when using laser scanners and photogrammetry. From 2009 to present, Sgt. Brian Nightingale, unit commander in charge of the agency's Vancouver Island district, has used the IWitness Pro ground-level photogrammetry program successfully 90 percent of the time to record crash scenes. But one challenge he's faced is that if a scene is too large, it means putting out too many road markers. For long crash scenes he and other reconstruction experts have had to take a large number of photographs. "This prompted us to consider having an aerial view of these scenes," Sgt. Nightingale said. The RCMP has used UAVs with photogrammetry to document major accident and crime scenes since 2012 when it acquired a DragonFly UAV with a Sony camera mounted to it. One aerial flight over a scene takes approximately ten minutes. "We often do a second flyover just to make sure we get the entire scene," Sgt. Nightingale said. "We're surveying the whole scene plus getting all the photographs we need in about 30 minutes."

Scene Perspectives Captured that Other Tools may Miss

The use of a UAV for a long scene is valuable because it can capture so much crucial detail and provide perspectives that could be challenging for other tools to accomplish. Nightingale recalls a fairly large scene in Courtenay, a city on the east coast of Vancouver Island, B.C., Canada, that involved a driver who suddenly drove her car on a sidewalk and later struck a pedestrian. The driver then moved back onto the street, and accelerated just a little over the speed limit, hitting five vehicles before her car came to a final rest. According to Nightingale, court

Figure 12.8 Drones have become highly effective at mapping and documenting long crash scenes, such as this collision involving two commercial vehicles that resulted in fatalities and blocked one direction of an interstate highway. The collision scene was captured by a Matrice 200V2 UAV with a Zenmuse XT2 camera, and tied to five control points captured with a DT 301T/RTK rugged tablet. (Photo courtesy of Oregon State Police Trooper William Bush, OSP Collision Reconstruction Unit)

records indicated the driver claimed she had blacked out due in part to a pre-existing medical condition. But she also had a blood alcohol level that exceeded the legal limit. The driver suspect was found guilty in the court hearing (Figures 12.8 and 12.9).

Due to the length of this scene, mapping it with photogrammetry was effective to a large extent. However, Nightingale decided to launch a UAV over the 500+ foot scene to capture it more completely, which revealed helpful details. "We had a lot of small pieces of physical evidence all the way down the road—the pedestrian's shoes, things he was carrying in his hand," Nightingale explained. "So there is all of this detail you can include in a diagram that you might not get from a terrestrial 3D laser scanner because the point cloud (from the scanner) has so many points." The scanner's point cloud, while providing phenomenal detail, can become difficult to work with, Nightingale added. By using the UAV in conjunction

Figure 12.9 Drones have become highly effective at mapping and documenting long crash scenes, such as this collision involving two commercial vehicles that resulted in fatalities and blocked one direction of an interstate highway. The collision scene was captured by a Matrice 200V2 UAV with a Zenmuse XT2 camera, and tied to five control points captured with a DT 301T/RTK rugged tablet. (Photo courtesy of Oregon State Police Trooper William Bush, OSP Collision Reconstruction Unit)

with photogrammetry and laser scanning, however, the aerial point cloud makes it easier to snap to a specific, desired measurement point. Thus, the reconstruction expert can zoom into an image that is under the point cloud to assist in identifying physical evidence, such as tire marks. "We actually see tire marks through aerial surveying with the UAV that we wouldn't normally see at ground level," Nightingale said. This is because the aerial photos pick up the tire marks. Also, Nightingale added, the aerial photos become especially invaluable if the reconstructionist misses marking a piece of evidence with an on-road marker.

UAV Data Allows for More Detailed Scene Diagrams

In addition to drastically cutting time needed for mapping scenes and capturing substantial imagery, UAVs enable scene diagrams to be more detailed. For instance, Nightingale stated, "You can put in the sidewalk line exactly the way it appeared at on the ground. A scanner might miss this depending on where you set up the scanner.

Aerial imaging basically eliminates all of this." British Columbia has 5-foot lanes with 8-foot gaps before another 5-foot lane comes along. These can be inaccurate when diagramming a roadway as the lanes and gaps do not always match up. "With the aerial scan created by the photogrammetry program, you can come in and create the broken line precisely with what you see in the image, instead of trying to use the CAD program that is estimating," Nightingale said. "So, if you're going to court and showing a piece of evidence by a line on the roadway, the line is actually there, it's drawn in, because of the more accurate aerial/photogrammetry imagery and measurements," Nightingale added.

Evidence plus key details of a crime or accident scene effectively captured from the air by a UAV can be powerful and persuasive in a courtroom, which is why this makes the UAV a valuable addition to any reconstruction expert's toolbox. Mark Johnson, CEO of Visual Law, a San Jose, California-based consultancy specializing in forensic scene visualization and documentation, is well-experienced with courtroom presentations focused on photogrammetric reconstruction of forensic scenes based on imagery recorded both on land and from the sky. Johnson, who has spent years as a dynamic plaintiff's trial lawyer, is now considered one of the leading experts in 3D forensic visualization and animation, as well as an authority in photogrammetric reconstruction technologies. Johnson said he has seen a big spike in UAV usage among law enforcement agencies. In fact, he noted, some large agencies are buying drones for every patrol unit assigned to accident scene reconstruction. Standard work products for reconstruction will more routinely include drone aerial imagery and drone photogrammetric mapping just as total stations became the mainstay tool years ago. Visual Law clients include law enforcement agencies, lawyers, and accident reconstruction engineers.

Drones Combined with Laser Scanners Help Prove Elements of a Crime

Visual Law is typically hired by the prosecution in a case to prove the elements of a crime. This has not changed for decades, but what *has* changed, Johnson said, is what Visual Law recommends be done to achieve results tied to authentication and verification of evidence that will be admissible in court. Johnson's work involving aerial photogrammetric reconstruction of crime scenes, as well as laser scanning, easily meets the Daubert standard when it is applied to a case he's working on. "Mainly, the object is to get crucial information in front of the jurors," Johnson said. This means presenting jurors with a 3D model of a crime scene built from data often captured with drone photogrammetry and terrestrial laser scanning. In many instances, Johnson needs to incorporate crime scene evidence and data already recorded as part of a case he's handling on behalf of a client.

A good example of such a case is one where a Dallas, Texas, police officer fatally shot a 21-year-old woman as she was seated with her boyfriend in her vehicle in the parking lot of an apartment complex. Six officers were on the scene at the time of the shooting, five of whom had activated body-worn cameras and who had surrounded the car. The body-worn cameras show officers yelling at the woman to vacate the car with her hands up. The woman instead tries to drive backwards and hits a squad car that had been moved up to her car. Next, the woman tries driving forward, hits a fence and then begins to slowly drive backwards again. One of the officers opens fire on the car, shooting 13 times. The woman's boyfriend finally gets out of the car after the shooting and upon repeated orders to do so from officers. The body cameras capture what happens. Although officers claimed they felt the driver might attempt to run them over, prompting the shooting from the one officer, a former assistant Dallas Police chief over the investigation unit handling the shooting argued that the video proved that officers violated the use of force policy. A weapon was found in the victim's car, but prior to the shooting officers did not know this. The officer who shot the victim was arrested and indicted for aggravated assault by a peace officer. The Dallas Police Department fired him.

Body Camera Views of Complex Scene Incorporated with Scanner, Drone Data

Texas Rangers were called by the Dallas prosecutor's office to laser scan the shooting scene, but they were not involved in the incident. Laser scanning of the scene was taken within a couple weeks of the shooting, and spray paint marks applied by the Dallas Police Department's CSI team to mark vehicle positions were part of the scanning effort. Visual

Law was hired to provide a reconstruction of the crime scene. "What was critical about the case was knowing the positions of the officers and the precise movements of the victim's vehicle to ascertain whether or not the shooting was justified," Johnson explained. To unravel and reconstruct the scene, it was necessary to scan it. The scene was scanned from the ground prior to Johnson's involvement in the case. "I came in and performed a full drone mapping of the scene and digitally recreated scene views recorded with the body cameras," Johnson continued. "This allowed us to show exactly frame-by-frame where everybody was (on the scene) and what was happening." Johnson also flew his UAV over the apartment complex at which the victim's car was parked to acquire a high-resolution orthographic image as well as geometry for the full complex. Johnson's laser scanning via the UAV was primarily used to confirm the accuracy of the Texas Rangers' laser scans and to calibrate and measure the lens distortion of the body cameras. All of the data (both terrestrial and UAV) were used to recreate the camera positions of the five officer-worn body cameras and vehicle positions. To build the 3D model of the shoot scenes, Johnson used AutoCAD, SCENE to rectify and combine the data sets, and FARO Zone 2D for quick reconstructions of the scene (Figures 12.10 and 12.11).

How accurate are data captured by a drone? Johnson claims that for 80–90 percent of accident reconstruction work where a drone is used, the drone's accuracy coupled with a photogrammetric mapping program is sufficient. However, Johnson cautioned, it is essential

Figure 12.10 A drone point cloud from the scene of the Dallas, Texas, officer-involved shooting. The 3D model created from the drone map is shown superimposed. (Photo courtesy of www.visual-law.com)

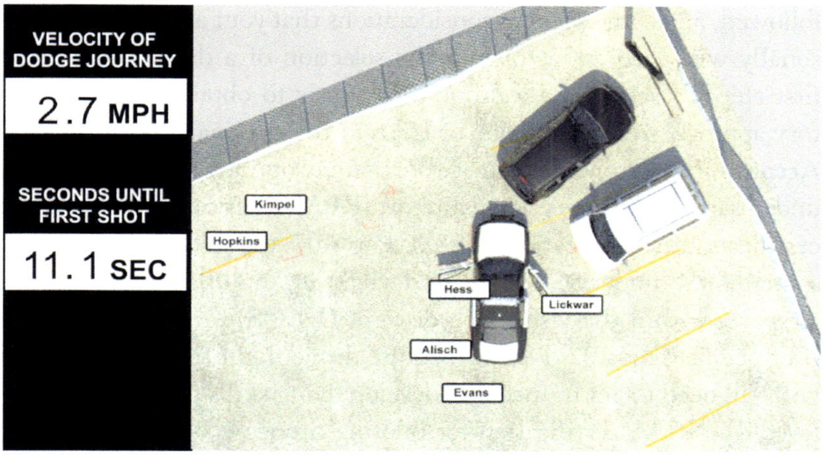

Figure 12.11 A frame from an animation introduced at trial that represented positions of the officers and velocity of the suspect's vehicle. (Photo courtesy of www.visuallaw.com)

to establish ground controls via three or four points within a scene. These points will be rectified by the photogrammetry software used for post-processing the scene. "RTK uses a network of satellites to verify and correct drone data to match terrestrial surveying accuracy," Johnson said. "The drone is collecting data and the system of processing after the drone lands allows the GPS to correct the data to the level of accuracy you need."

Merging drone data with data captured through other technologies, such as terrestrial laser scanners, is now quite routine. Johnson said this process is made easier with specialized software. One such type of software that Johnson uses is Arena4D Data Studio made by Veesus, which enables the user to combine multiple different data sets into a complete 3D document that can be shared. The program offers a free "View only" option allowing the user to open and view other people's projects, even if the user does not have a license. Arena4D Data Studio can visualize point clouds, imagery, panoramas, shape files, and GPS tracks and more in a single, contextual view. The software also includes a powerful animation package that generates HD quality movies.[5]

Gain Proper Approvals Before Selecting, Using a Drone

Whether you are employed with a public safety agency or work as a private reconstructionist, there are airspace regulations that must be followed, and some specific considerations that your agency or you personally will need to factor into the selection of a drone. One of the first steps in setting up a drone program is to obtain federal regulatory approval to fly the drone or UAS in the national airspace (NAS). According to Dronelife.com, two different options include operating under part 107 remote piloted aircraft (RPA) certification and or under certificate of authorization (COA). Part 107 allows an operator to fly a small UAS under 55 pounds in daylight up to 400 ft in unrestricted airspace, within the visual line of sight (VLOS) of a drone, and not over people. Part 107 does not require drone flight training, but pilots will still need to get trained and develop flying skills to a specific safety level. The COA certification for piloting drones is better for agencies needing to operate in more complex airspace (Classes B, C, D, or E) or who may need to fly more complicated missions. The COA requirements are more rigid than Part 107, and public safety agencies or individual pilots must submit a detailed plan for FAA approval.

Whichever of these categories of drone flight certification is chosen, it is best to get some support or training from a vendor partner. For more information on obtaining these certifications, one good resource is Fire Cam (www.firecam.com), an experienced vendor that provides a wide variety of drone models, but also expert training and counsel on drone flight certification resources.[6]

Determine Proper Payload for Drone

The type of drone you need will depend upon the payload you'll be using to accomplish your mission—crash or crime reconstruction in this case. The payload—a camera, thermal imaging tool, optical zoom lens—is a significant part of your investment. Next, determine your budget. A reliable drone vendor can guide you on your drone investment. Remember, if budget and affordability is a concern, the right drone of high-quality construction and operation will still enable you to upgrade to other payloads, such as thermal imaging, when funds are available. This will prove more cost-efficient versus, say, having to totally replace an inferior drone model should it break down or need extensive service or repairs.

Plan for how your drone will be maintained or repaired. Will this be handled by your agency or you personally? If not, be sure to choose a vendor whose service, repair, and support are reliable and reasonably fast. Many drones are made overseas, so customer service can be dicey.[7]

This chapter has detailed how UAVs have become an affordable, fast, and efficient way to document long and complicated crash and crime scenes. UAVs give better scene overviews, show interrelationships of locations and evidence, and work compatibly with other mapping tools.

In Chapter 13, active incident scenes, especially mass shootings at schools, are examined as to how challenging they can be to document; laser scanners have proven so far to be one of the most reliable tools to capture evidence at these difficult scenes.

Notes

1. Lunding, Leigh. "Eye in the Sky." 2013. www.Sleuthsayers.org.
2. "UAV Data Fits into the Scan to BIM Workflow." 2013. www.remote-aerialsurveys.co.uk.
3. Jurosky, Drew. "4 Reasons Drones Will Revolutionize Accident Scene Response." Petauro Systems, 2016. www.petaurosystems.com.
4. Robinson, Edward. "Crime Scene Photography." *Science Direct*, 2017, www.sciencedirect.com/book.
5. "Product Software – Veesus Arena 4D Data Studio." 2017. www.Or3d.co.uk.
6. McNabb, Miriam. "Public Safety Drones: Do You Need Part 107 or a COA?" Drone Life, 2017, www.dronelife.com.
7. McNabb Miriam. "3 Things Every Fire and Police Department Should Know Before Investing in a Drone." *Drone Life*, 2017, www.dronelife.com.

13

Laser Scanning a Strong Fit for Reconstructing Active Incident Scenes; Useful for Autopsies, Powerful Training Tool

On August 1, 1966, rifle shots began blasting from the outside observation deck on the 28th floor of the clock tower at the University of Texas in Austin. Before starting his shooting rampage, the sniper, Charles Joseph Whitman, a student at the university and ex-Marine, already had shot and killed three people whom he had confronted in the tower's stairwells on his way to the top floor. After that, he situated himself on the observation deck and began shooting indiscriminately onto the university campus and surrounding business district 231 ft below. Once the shooting spree ended, with 150 rounds fired by Whitman, 11 people lay dead and 31 others were wounded. The incident was one of the worst mass murders in a public area in the history of the United States. Even though some have called the University of Texas clock tower shooting the first mass murder in American history, there have been multiple other mass murders between the start of the 20th century and the clock tower rampage. Only weeks earlier, on July 12, 1966, Richard Speck brutally murdered eight female nursing students in a Chicago townhouse. The slain nurses' crime scene, like the clock tower shooting, was large as Speck stabbed and strangled each of the young women throughout various rooms of the townhouse (Figure 13.1).[1,2]

Mother Jones, an American magazine focusing on news, commentary, and investigative reporting, has posted a database of U.S. mass shootings that date from 1982 to 2019. The database, looking more like a scorecard

Figure 13.1 The Clock Tower, University of Texas at Austin, where, in 1966, a sniper fired 150 rounds with his rifle on the campus, killing 11 people and wounding 31 others. (Photo – Larry D. Moore, CC BY-SA 3.0 – https://commons.wikipedia.org/wiki:/File: The_Tower_University_of_Texas_at_Austin_ca_1980.jpg)

of the grisly carnage brought about by rampant mass shootings, lists each shooting case, location, date, and tally of fatalities and injured persons. Some of the locales of the butchery and numbers of people killed (shown below in parentheses) are painfully unforgettable to most of us: El Paso Walmart (22); Thousand Oaks, Calif., Nightclub (12); Texas First Baptist Church (26); Las Vegas Strip massacre (58); Orlando, Florida, Pulse nightclub (49); Parkland, Florida, school shooting (17); and Umpqua Community College, Roseburg, Oregon, shooting (9).[3]

Mass Shooter Scenes Are Large, Complex; First Responders Don't Know Building Layouts

These active shooter events show at least three clear, troubling facts: First, that active incidents can take only minutes to unfold, especially if they involve mass shooting events with multiple rounds rapidly fired—frequently with AR-15 assault rifles; second, these incidents can occur nearly anywhere, be it schools, shopping malls, restaurants, nightclubs, entertainment venues, or religious and government buildings; and third, that these shootings are all part of a trend that appears likely to continue unabated, as mass shootings are occurring with frightening, accelerated frequency. Many of the shootings are meticulously planned weeks, months or years in advance, yet other active shootings occur with little planning because the shooter has allowed his internal rage over some issue to boil over, after which he decides to unleash it by launching a shooting tirade on his target. Active shooter scenarios are extremely difficult to predict or to stop before human lives are taken. For law enforcement, it must feel like a no-win situation since the result—carnage—is the same. Compounding this situation is the fact that law enforcement and first responders typically do not know the floor plans of schools or buildings they are entering during an active shooter incident. Consequently, precious time slips away as the perpetrator gains more control of his environment with the intent of killing innocent people until he is arrested, thwarted, killed himself, or commits suicide. Mapping and documenting active incident crime scenes has never been more daunting given their sheer scope. Shooting scenes in particular are especially difficult because they can grow rapidly as an active shooter conducts his binge of violence and require large chunks of time to map and record.

3D Scanning Can Help Show Geometry of Shooting Events

Mass shooting scenes across the United States so far have been well suited for 3D laser scanning as a mapping tool given scanning's quick and very thorough capture of a scene. Once scenes are ready for reconstruction, laser scanners seem to be the predominant tool for most law enforcement agencies tasked with mapping and documenting evidence. There has been widespread adoption of laser scanning by law enforcement over the past several years, and for good reason. Scanning can help the reconstruction expert understand the geometry of a shooting: what happened during the incident, what the bullet trajectories were, and the location of the shooter from which particular shots were fired. Additionally, laser scanners can cover all parts of a scene, even if some of these parts seem unimportant at the time of mapping and recording. Whenever any scene is scanned it is important to include not just the immediate area where impacts are identified, but also the larger surrounding area in order to put the shooting scene in proper context. That could mean identifying a room in a house, school, or building. Also, the area outside the immediate shooting scene can contribute significantly to the investigation; for instance, revealing access points, witness vantage points, and path of egress.[4] Laser scanning may be the predominant method for capturing scenes, especially shooting scenes, yet, as this book has emphasized, it is not the only way these scenes can be documented given the wider range of scene mapping technology now available.

As the scores of mass shootings we have learned about so far have shown, the size of their scenes varies greatly from one scene to the next. On April 20, 1999, the Columbine High School shooting in Littleton, Colorado, for example, which ended with 13 people dead and more than 20 others wounded, produced an enormous scene. The perpetrators, Dylan Klebold and Eric Harris, began shooting fellow students outside the school on the day of their planned attack. The pair then moved inside the school, where they gunned down many of their victims in the library. The gunmen also had planted two duffel bags, each containing a 20-pound propane bomb inside the school cafeteria. But after the bombs failed to detonate, as Klebold and Harris waited near their parked cars, they began their shooting spree, first shooting students outside school buildings, then entering the school to continue their deadly attack. This crime scene involving both sprawling exterior and interior areas of the school no doubt took days to reconstruct (Figure 13.2).[5]

Oregon College Shoot Scene Scanned While Event Still Active

Fast forward 16 years later and another significant, large shooting scene emerged on October 1, 2015, at Umpqua Community College in Roseburg, Oregon, about 180 miles south of Portland. It is to date Oregon's worst mass shooting scene ever. Laser scanning proved highly valuable and effective for capturing the extensive college shooting scene. On that day, while classes were underway, a gunman opened fire in a classroom and killed nine people before dying in a

Figure 13.2 One of the diagrams made by the FBI's Investigative and Prosecutive Graphic Unit after the Columbine High School Massacre. Harris (red dot) and Klebold (blue dot) are shown leaving the school's library; green dots indicate witnesses of the event. (Photo – United States Federal Bureau of Investigation – Photo - https://commons.wikimedia.org/wiki/category:Columbine_High_School_massacre)

shootout with police. The killer, 26-year-old Chris Harper Mercer, parked his car in the campus parking lot, walked through one of the school's entrances to classrooms and entered a men's bathroom carrying a backpack containing ammunition, a semi-automatic rifle and several handguns to prepare for what appeared to be a long-drawn-out assault. Next, he entered a classroom just across from the bathroom, ordered students to huddle in the center of the room, and began shooting them at random, killing nine students and wounding seven others. After the shooting, the gunman ran outside, where he began firing at students fleeing the buildings, then was forced into a shootout with two sheriff's deputies as they approached him and began firing their guns. The gunman, who was struck by a bullet in his stomach, ran back into the classroom where he shot himself and died.

Crime Scene Covered Indoors and Outdoors

Officer Michael Klews, a seasoned crime scene reconstruction expert with the Eugene, Oregon, Police Department, 70 miles north of Roseburg, was one of a throng of law enforcement officers and first responders to race to the college campus; his job was to reconstruct the crime scene via 3D laser scanning. When Klews arrived, however, the college was on lockdown because the shooting incident was still active and buildings had not been cleared or confirmed to be secure. This was one of several challenges that Klews faced upon his arrival at the college. "The shooter was dead, but we didn't know if there was a secondary shooter, or if there were explosive devices set to go off. We just didn't know what to expect," Klews added. As the U.S. Marshal Service and personnel from other law enforcement agencies descended on the college campus, Klews was able to dive right into scanning the interior and exterior shooting scenes. A second challenge was just the sheer size of the crime scene, which included the classroom where the initial shooting had occurred, additional classrooms and hallways, as well as the sidewalk outside the college building entrance where the shooter entered earlier after parking his vehicle and then later would have a shootout with sheriff's deputies. The reconstruction expert pointed out that it was crucial to scan the shooter's parked car location, even though this area had no evidentiary value, so that it could be tied to the shooting scenes along with the sidewalk and classroom. In doing so, "We're also trying to give the overall scene and what occurred some context," Klews said. In total, 120 scans were taken by Klews throughout the college campus. The interior of the main classroom was scanned first, then the bathroom, and finally the shooter's car and sidewalk where the shooter and sheriff's deputies exchanged gunfire.

A third challenge was where Officer Klews could physically work after scanning the classroom where the shooting rampage was unleashed. Because he did not know what was in play with the still active incident, the officer decided to work in the women's bathroom so he could begin processing his scene scans. He set up his laptop computer on the bathroom's counter and was able to start processing the scans he had captured.

Scanner, Only Months in Use, Captured Total Scene Plus Blind Spots

Similar to most crime scenes, it was critical to record the entire crime scene (interior and exterior) at Umpqua Community College while it was still fresh and intact. Umpqua College's shooting scene was especially time-sensitive because the shooter's car was eventually towed away, and the portion of the college buildings where the shooting spree unfolded has now been torn down. Eugene Police Department had just acquired its laser scanner four months before the Umpqua Community College shooting occurred. Given this very short amount of time during which Klews and his reconstruction team had to become proficient with the scanner, particularly for lengthy and complex shooting scenes, "it showed how critical it was to capture everything at the college scene," Klews said. "If we had just scanned one room, it would not make sense if a court presentation needed to be made. You wouldn't understand the magnitude or totality of the scene." The reconstructed college shooting scene did not go to court since the shooter killed himself. Klews brought the raw data points collected from the many scans taken into FARO SCENE where they were rendered and colorized together, and then converted them to a point cloud.

Officer Klews took ten scans of the classroom where students had been gunned down. Why so many scans? As Klews explained, "The scanner is a line of sight piece of equipment, and there are blind spots in a scene it cannot see and pick up. So, to pick up everything you need as many views as possible." The classroom scene was chaotic, with bodies strewn across the floor and desks and chairs in disarray. Therefore, Klews decided it was important to achieve multiple scans, especially under desks. "We needed to memorialize this shooting scene," Klews said. By performing the ten scans of it, Klews could overlap the scans and stitch them together in his post-processing software. "It's a method to assure that we capture the entire scene," he said. For the

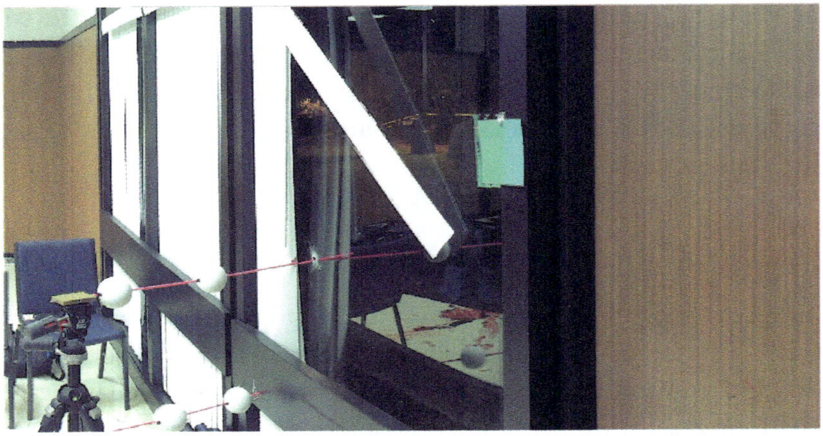

Figure 13.3 The classroom at Umpqua Community College, in Roseburg, Oregon, where in 2015 an active shooter gunned down nine students and wounded seven others. Shown are bullet trajectory rods with sphere targets used to trace the path of some of the shooter's bullets. In this scene, some bullets traveled through a classroom window as the shooter sprayed the room with gunfire. Eugene, Oregon, Police Detective Mike Klews made 10 scans of the classroom and its carnage, which allowed him to overlap the scans and stitch them together in post-processing software. (Photo courtesy of Eugene, Oregon, Police Department)

classroom scene evidence he would need, Klews wanted to make sure it was all captured in color. If the officer is called to another shooting scene that has both interior and exterior areas requiring documentation, he said he would use his laser scanner again, but also use a drone to capture the crime scene's exterior portion (Figure 13.3).

College Mass Shooting Prepared Reconstruction Technicians for Later Homicide Scene

Considering that the Umpqua Community College shooting scene was never presented in court, was it still necessary and valuable to reconstruct it via laser scanning? Officer Klews definitely thinks it was. Not long after mapping and recording the college shoot scene, the officer and his reconstruction team were tasked with reconstructing a multiple homicide scene that occurred in Springfield, Oregon, which is just over three miles east of Eugene. A male suspect had killed his father in the family house and severely attacked his mother, then stole the family car to drive to Eugene. During the drive, the suspect ran down a pedestrian in a Springfield parking lot and struck two additional pedestrians at an intersection in Eugene. The events all took place within about 20 minutes of each other. Officer Klews only had one laser scanner, but the reconstruction team also had a total station. Klews used the scanner to map the bodies at the house that had been set on fire in Springfield and the parking lot where the first pedestrian had been run over by the suspect's car. The other reconstruction team members mapped the scene of the pedestrian who had been run down in Eugene, although by the time of this scene mapping the body had been removed.

Fortunately, applying two different scene mapping technologies—the laser scanner and total station—was no problem; the separate data sets could be easily merged. "I later scanned the intersection in Eugene where the vehicle crash occurred after the suspect stuck a pedestrian and then took the data from the total station and laid it on top of the scan," Klews said. Officer Klews considered the practice he gained from scanning the Umpqua College scene not just helpful for scanning the Eugene-Springfield crime scenes—as the latter crime case went to court—but essential. The practice of continually scanning has been invaluable for Klews and he stresses the need to apply scanning, if this is what an agency is using for crime scene reconstruction, on as many scenes as possible.

Alina Burroughs, a former Senior Crime Scene Analyst and currently Senior Applications Engineer with FARO Technologies, would agree with Officer Klews' view that laser scanning practice must be a constant commitment, since it pays off hugely for vast crime scenes that are difficult to capture. Burroughs should know. She has had her share of investigating crime scenes, and one of her most unusual crime scenes involved participating in the identification and processing of victims following the Pulse Nightclub shooting in Orlando, Florida, in which 49 people were shot dead by a lone gunman. At the time of the nightclub massacre, Burroughs was part of a team called FEMORS (Florida Emergency Mortuary Operations Response System) that was called in June 2016, to assist with the identification and autopsy of the Pulse shooting victims. FEMORS, composed of a wide range of experts including crime scene investigators, DNA specialists, fingerprint experts, forensic toxicologists, autopsy technicians, and medical examiners, was instrumental in helping the medical examiner's department of Orange County, Florida, identify the Pulse victims as soon as possible after the shooting.

Special 3D Scanner Could Aid in Autopsies, Especially in Mass Shootings

Burroughs was not personally involved with the Pulse shooting scene itself, but she argues that even if the scene was not documented via laser scanning, this is not the last chance for laser scanners to make an impact. Scanning could have aided with the autopsies of shooting victims. For example, laser scanners could be utilized in the documentation of victims, including injuries sustained, resting positions, and fleeting evidence such as blood spatter, or lividity. Scanning a crime scene such as the Pulse shooting could have been helpful with showing the victim position at the time of gunfire, at what angles victims were shot, the shooter's position and distance determination. Scanning could recreate the shooting scene in its entirety and preserve it for what most likely would be many subsequent examinations of evidence. Locations of victims and suspect(s) at the time of the shooting as well as during the events can be of particular importance, considering how many people lost their lives in such a crowded and confined space. "The end game to all of this is court presentation," affirmed Burroughs who believes that presenting only 2D photographs in a court trial will not enable jurors to understand the spatial relationships among multiple items of evidence. Laser scanning is a way of providing these spatial relationships because an entire scene can be captured, shown, and shared, and key evidence items identified, and measurements provided. "When we can show jurors the entire scene and allow them to walk through that same scene that investigators have walked through, we can give them 100 percent of the information they need so that when they make a life or death decision they have all of the facts," Burroughs said.

Powerful Training Aspect

Laser scanning of the Pulse shooting scene would be tremendously valuable not just from a purely evidentiary level, but a helpful learning experience at the same time. After all, a scene of the mammoth scope of the Pulse shooting is an important one not just to map and document but to use as a golden training opportunity based on what scans of the scene would show. "The training aspect of this kind of scene can offer perspectives for different law enforcement personnel," Burroughs offered. "There is a tactical perspective for officers just arriving on scene—what did they learn about how they approached the scene, where they parked, what cover for responding officers was at the scene, what potential for cross-fire was there?" Knowing the answers to these questions could help law enforcement, investigators, S.W.A.T teams, and other first responders be better prepared for another similar shooting scene. By analyzing scans of a wide scene filled with all kinds of evidence, this can aid in building a compelling 3D model and be a kind of blueprint for knowing how to respond to and document similar scenes in the future (Figure 13.4).

The Pulse shooting scene as well as any major crime scene could benefit well from 3D laser scanning. "You can utilize more than one scanner simultaneously so someone can be inside the crime scene

Figure 13.4 Shown is the point cloud for the interior of a high school building that was laser scanned to display soft targets for a potential active incident. Such 3D visualizations can be helpful to first responders in possibly helping to intervene more quickly and effectively if and when active incidents occur at large public buildings like this one. (Photo courtesy of Clackamas County, Oregon, Sheriff's Office)

documenting and outside at the same time," Burroughs said. This would reduce the amount of time spent capturing the scene.

———

This chapter has explored the value of applying 3D laser scanning to active incident scenes for determining bullet trajectory, suspect/victim positions and perspectives, capturing critical scene evidence—especially in blind spots—and with providing a view of how quickly these types of scenes can move and expand. Laser scanning of active incident scenes provides some of the best training in scanner operation. Finally, scanners are also helpful for use in medical autopsies following active incidents.

Chapter 14 will detail how risk assessment and emergency planning between communities and law enforcement, and using 3D visualization tools for building virtual tours of buildings, can strengthen preplanning for active incidents overall.

Notes

1. Wallenfeldt, Jeff. "Texas Tower Shooting of 1966." *Encyclopedia Britannica*, 2017. www.britannica.com.
2. Lavergne, Gary. "University of Texas Tower Shooting." Handbook of Texas Online, Texas State Historical Association, 2017. www.tshonline.org.
3. Follman, Mark, et al. "U.S. Mass Shootings, 1982-2020. Data from Mother Jones' Investigation." *Mother Jones*, 2020. www.motherjones.com.
4. DeFranco, Charles, and Carlo Rosati. "A Practical Guide to Shooting Scene Preservation for Crime Scene Investigators." *Journal of the Association for Crime Scene Reconstruction*, 2009. www.crime-scene-investigator.net.
5. History.com. "Columbine High School Shooting: Victims & Killers." History, A&E Television Networks, 2016. www.history.com.

14

Risk Assessment, Security Planning Critical for Future Active Incidents; How Technology can AID

Hostile events take many forms, whether they involve active shootings, armed assaults, deployment of deadly weapons, or vehicle attacks. In the past few years, these have become almost weekly events as they fan out across the United States. Most of them have taken the form of mass shootings in schools, factories, churches, entertainment venues, and other settings. Besides shootings, knifings and explosions have also become part of a wide-ranging mix of lethal acts. Post-Columbine (1999), law enforcement has changed its response paradigm to one where officers first arriving on a scene aim to neutralize the incident. Unfortunately, most of these incidents are over in less than five minutes, which usually means that their actions often are not in time to prevent loss of life. More frustrating, upon arriving at an incident scene and entering a building, first responders don't know where to go to stop the perpetrator. This presents a real dilemma not just for first responders, but also for the victims, the management of these locales, and the communities.

Getting in front of these events to prevent tragic outcomes obviously would be the ultimate win. A more realistic situation, however, calls for ongoing and dedicated risk assessment and security planning. *Technology solutions may have an effective role in this solution*, as well. Of course, technology will not be a panacea because its effectiveness will depend on how quickly the information it offers about buildings where active events occur can be used by S.W.A.T. operators and first responders.

Preplanning Needed for Incidents at Schools

After a blizzard of mass shootings at schools and other venues, especially during the last decade, it has become clear that planning and preparation are key in helping to bring about an effective response by law enforcement. Security experts uniformly agree that schools in particular must have a strong emergency plan firmly in place. The most important element of this plan is *Planning,* and that is essential for all personnel who will have a role in response and recovery *(MJ Fagel, Principles of Emergency Management, Chapter 3 – "Developing a Planning Team – CRC Press 2010).* Also needed is a threat assessment of facilities where people come to meet or work, yet who are vulnerable in the event of a life-threatening incident. "We can do this by having better preplanning and seeing how relationships between law enforcement and their communities can be forged, to learn about the needs of the community and what their fears are so we can plan better for incidents," said Steve Albano, an expert consultant in physical security risk and vulnerability assessment. Threat assessment, he explained, involves going into a building, walking through it, and identifying vulnerabilities as a way of providing better access control, and ingress/egress. This is needed not just for active shooter incidents at, say, schools, but for natural disasters, as well. Therefore, risk assessment means communities and law enforcement must undergo training exercises and preplan for incidents. "We need to be familiar with our surroundings and our community because we've got to think on a larger scale, not just what's going to happen with our schools but what affects them, how something in the surrounding area can pose a problem for us," said Albano, who is a former senior special agent with the United States Secret Service. An example is a factory with deadly, flammable chemicals in the vicinity of a school and for which there should be an evacuation plan for both it and the school in case of an emergency or disaster.

Proactive Emergency Planning Must Involve Communities, Police

Risk assessment can be a balancing act between communities and law enforcement that need to work together to make schools and public areas safer, but without making them feel and operate like a prison.

Communication is another key component, Albano said, whereby one of the strongest tools, social media, can help identify problems with potential perpetrators of active incidents by studying their behaviors before the individuals spiral out of control. "This is not just a police function," Albano emphasized. "It's all the things prior to an incident." Some schools have resource officers stationed in schools, which Albano recommends highly. These officers can get to know school kids, hear what is going on, and perhaps deal with problems as they occur because they are onsite and able to be more embedded in the daily environment of a school.

Like Albano, Michael Fagel is a private consultant in risk assessment and emergency planning, and is working with numerous facilities to help both their managers and employees better understand how to protect themselves during active incidents as they unfold and before law enforcement can arrive on the scene. Fagel is well experienced with major incidents, especially those that are terrorist-based. A former paramedic, firefighter, and police officer, Fagel was recruited by FEMA (Federal Emergency Management Agency) in 1995. His first FEMA mission was investigating and aiding people after the April 19, 1995, Oklahoma City bombing. In 2001, he worked at the site of the New York City World Trade Center terrorist attack for 100 days, assigned to the New York City Fire Department as a team member from the Office of State & Local Domestic Preparedness of the U.S. Department of Justice. Fagel also has written textbooks on crisis management and emergency planning. When Fagel enters a facility, he looks at it from a holistic point of view---from people to manufacturing to every door and angle. His goal is to expose threats in any facility. The upshot of his emergency planning approach is, first, to help clients understand how to empower themselves when an incident begins to unfold. Secondly, it is key for people in a facility to grasp how to interface with public safety response agencies. This is especially important because agencies do not know the buildings or schools that they must enter when an incident occurs.

"Run, Hide, Fight" a Popular Methodology

What makes active incidents so hard to respond to in time before human life is jeopardized is the short time during which they happen.

Most events are over in 4–6 mins, Fagel said. "The Columbine syndrome where they spent hours assembling S.W.A.T. has disappeared," he emphasized. "The Marjorie Stone Douglas High School shooting was the same situation." Today, officers will charge into a building during an active shooter event; they no longer have the time to strategize. As law enforcement is responding to an active incident within a building, there is a critical role for victims to embrace and take seriously in Fagel's view. Victims, he said, must prepare themselves for how to become empowered and take charge of their situation during an incident until law enforcement can rescue them. Many schools and institutions are encouraged to adopt an approach similar to the Federally endorsed "Run, Hide, Fight" concept promoted by the Department of Homeland Security (DHS) in preparation for active violence incidents. This concept involves instructing trainees first: "run if you can", then "hide if you must", and finally to "fight if you have to."[1] This is at the heart of classes Fagel teaches through a Department of Homeland Security (DHS)-certified course on emergency planning as it pertains to an active shooter scenario. In one DHS training class he taught in New Mexico during 2019, Fagel fired a realistic blank pistol so attendees recognize it in potential real active shooter situations. His course simulates the environment with chilling effect---the building is secured, police and fire departments are alerted, a uniformed police officer is onsite, and 911 has been notified. The blank gun was fired outside of a secured area, such as a hallway. "We want people (the class students) to know what a gunshot sounds like," Fagel said. The course is aimed at school teachers, K–12, and college professors. Many schools already are conducting their own security training for both teachers and students. And, Fagel noted, multiple states have even enacted laws requiring students to participate in active shooter drills. "This training is a great tool to get students and teachers engaged and realize they can do something (in active shooter events) and not become a victim," Fagel said.

Currently, many schools are increasing their preparedness for hostile events, such as active shooting incidents. Part of this problem, aside from absent emergency plans and risk assessment, stems from the lack of complete, updated, and, preferably, digital floor plans that can be shared with the people who use schools (teachers, administrators, and students), as well as law enforcement and first responders.

The other part of schools' unpreparedness for active incidents points to poor access control. A worrisome example of weak access control is the February 14, 2018, shooting at Marjory Stoneman Douglas High School in Parkland, Florida. As the shooter arrived on the school's campus, numerous critical access failures gave him easy access to the school. The shooter was dropped off outside a perimeter fence. The fence had a gate that was open and left unstaffed. The shooter took advantage of this and entered the campus. As he entered Building 12 where the shooting spree unfolded, the shooter exploited another critical safety failure as the door was left unlocked and accessible to anyone. According to the Marjory Stoneman Douglas Public Safety Commission, "the overall lack of uniform and mandated physical site security requirements resulted in voids that allowed the shooter initial access to MSDHS and is a system failure"[2] (Figure 14.1).

Building's Hot Spots, Interior Visibility Are Major Focal Points

An obvious, though perhaps overlooked solution to the rampant active shooter dilemma has been to look at how high school and university buildings are actually designed and built, to see how well they help prevent or deter a threat from materializing and how future construction of these structures could make them less vulnerable during active incidents. It is possible to run simulations of building floorplans to

Figure 14.1 A close-up of a school building captured with a laser scanner. The technology captures comprehensive, high-accuracy scans and impressive full-color HDR imagery in less than 2 mins, even in low-light conditions. (Photo courtesy of Clint Norris, New Mexico State Police)

see how the layout of the building impacts people's ability to execute Run, Hide, Fight as recommended by DHS. Such simulations can point to hotspots within the building that will increase awareness among first responders to the site. Building visibility analysis can aid in measuring such variables as egress, evacuation, and building logic. If a building's layout does not flow smoothly and logically, it may be difficult to understand how to quickly navigate evacuation routes when victims of an incident are under duress. In existing buildings, the posting of enhanced maps of floorplans plus signage might strengthen wayfinding. Clearly, law enforcement and first responders need well-researched hotspot analyses on the floor plans of campus buildings. Additionally, architects and designers must take a closer look at how spaces are configured, to identify hotspots in buildings which may create opportunities for active shooters. Updating building codes is another recommendation because these codes are aimed at improving design measures for prevention and deterrence steps against active shooting, through modifying existing buildings and for planning safer new buildings.[3]

Although knowing the floor plans of schools or public buildings may not enable first responders to immediately stop or thwart an active incident suspect, it still might aid in the rescue of victims and in stopping the event more quickly. Some technology tools already are being used to address the question of how first responders might improve their response to active incidents with a detailed digital floorplan. The tools have already been discussed in this book: 3D laser scanning and 3D imaging via tablets and panoramic cameras, both of which can render panoramic visualizations of all kinds of important areas within a building, from one area and floor to the next.

Digital Floorplans Can Help if Quickly Deployable

The notion that by having a digital layout for a school or public building can be helpful to first responders as they arrive on scene during an active incident, such as a mass shooting, is debatable. While some professionals in the law enforcement community think this is a valid and worthwhile way to help them reach and neutralize an active shooter, for example, others feel it would be useless because there is no time to reference it. Yet it is probable that so few agencies have actually tested the use of digital floor plans to help them intervene an active incident, this solution has not been given a fair and thorough test. Bryon O'Neil, a deputy and certified crime and crash scene reconstructionist with the Clackamas County, Oregon, Sheriff's Office, considers digital floor plans as valid and has actually scanned a school to produce a digital floor plan. Without the floor plan, first responders heading into a building where an active incident is underway is too risky. "If we're going to a school or public building where there's an active shooter, and there's a team already in the building before additional first responders arrive, and they're hunting, and they tell us they are in Room 103, that doesn't mean anything to us if we don't have a layout that shows us where that room is," O'Neil said. "Having a digital floor plan would be better for the S.W.A.T. team because they can strategize their building entry ahead of time."

Mike Fagel, the risk assessment and emergency planning expert, agrees with O'Neil about the value of having a digital floor plan, but with a caveat. "It's much more valuable than just having a line drawing (of a building's interior and exterior floor plan and indicators of key features, such as doors, hallways, common areas, various floors, etc.)," Fagel said. "It is important to know what's there. But the digital floor plan has got to be deployable quickly and be available in an instant."

S.W.A.T. Commander Found Digital Floorplans Helpful

O'Neil already has laser scanned the complete floor plans of several local schools in Clackamas County. He converted the 2D floor plans into a pdf and these all reside on his laptop computer that he uses in his police cruiser. Whenever O'Neil needs to access a floor plan, he brings it up and then can print it off on the ticket writer printer that also is in his cruiser. This makes it easy for him to reference a particular school's floor plan and print it off while he is driving to that school. "I can then reference quickly whatever room at school responders say the shooter is in," O'Neil said. However, he added, "We still want a 3D view of a school's interior floor plan if a shooter is locked down in a certain classroom. Our S.W.A.T. team needs to know what the path into that classroom looks like." O'Neil continued, "This is where our 3D fly-throughs come in" (Figures 14.2 and 14.3).

Figure 14.2 Digital floor plans of public buildings that could be targets for active incidents, like this Oregon high school, can be useful to first responders and S.W.A.T. teams. These responders could use the floor plans to help strategize their building entry ahead of time. (Photos courtesy of Clackamas County, Oregon, Sheriff's Office)

Figure 14.3 Digital floor plans of public buildings that could be targets for active incidents, like this Oregon high school, can be useful to first responders and S.W.A.T. teams. These responders could use the floor plans to help strategize their building entry ahead of time. (Photos courtesy of Clackamas County, Oregon, Sheriff's Office)

Still, to risk management expert Fagel's point that floor plans must be quick and easy to use, how could these digital floor plans be placed into a format that is useful to S.W.A.T. operators? After all, scanning a school's floor plans generated giant data files for O'Neil that would have been too difficult to store on a computer. O'Neil himself would not disagree with this point. But he was able to condense his scanner-generated floor plans down to a 3" × 5" format that could be easily printed off and distributed. When O'Neil asked his agency's S.W.A.T. commander if these floor plans would be helpful, the commander said they would. The floor plans, in both 2D and 3D formats, were created in FARO SCENE, software specifically designed for all FARO FOCUS 3D laser scanners and third-party laser scanners. The software is able to process and manage scan data efficiently and easily by using real-time, on-site registration, automatic object recognition, scan registration, and positioning. In addition, SCENE offers a Virtual Reality View, allowing users to experience and evaluate captured data in the VR environment.[4] Using SCENE enables O'Neil to go into a point cloud and remove roofing of all the structures so that interiors can be seen. This also means a fly-through to be accomplished. The fly-through allows a user to get the 3D view of the school so he or she can see its physical features. The video used in this process is a standard MP4 format that doesn't consume much space but packs a lot of data. This was helpful when O'Neil needed to show such detail with a school that had 30 rooms plus a main floor and two upper floors. "We can show and hide data as needed," O'Neil said. He added, "S.W.A.T. liked this, and they can bring the fly-through and floor plan on a computer terminal as they are enroute to an active shooter incident. In this way, everyone can generally know what to expect when they enter the building."

Because O'Neil has compressed all of this data into a couple of megabytes, the Clackamas County S.W.A.T. team can easily store the floor plans on their computers and activate fly-throughs without needing any special software. "They can play the video of the fly-throughs, which is a minute and a half long," O'Neil said. Also, this video can be paused at any time to study some aspect of the floor plan more closely, such as a room that is a focal point of search to see what's in it.

Although Electronic Floorplans Have Faults, Information Still Valued

While the laser-scanned floor plans are both impressive and useful, O'Neil admits the whole process has some drawbacks, acknowledging that a project of this scope is a matter of time and data load.

It took O'Neil two days to scan a 65,000 square-foot school with over 140 scans, then three or four days to post-process the scanning data to produce a composite 3D point cloud. What's more, O'Neil had to find time to scan the school's floor plans when the school was not open. "These digital layouts and fly-throughs aren't going to prevent anything; they will only limit the scope of the evolving event, if used," O'Neil said. However, O'Neil argues that if S.W.A.T. had the digital floor plans for a school experiencing an active shooter incident, they may well find it useful for clearing the school building once they arrived on scene.

When asked if school buildings should still be laser scanned, O'Neil's response was quick and emphatic. "Yes, because the more information you have about these schools, the better. Information is power."

When it comes to school security, this need is really about a "culture of security," according to Kelly Watt, president and CEO of Visual Plan, a facility management, campus and building security software program that was discussed in this book's chapter regarding documentation of active incident scenes. This culture of security involves performing regular drills, setting and pursuing emergency planning objectives, training a building's occupants to respond to incidents effectively and safely so that when an event happens everyone can lunge into action and prevent loss of life. Watt said his software is designed to help with incident victims' response and to increase and maintain security (Figures 14.4 and 14.5).

Uncovering Building's Risks, Safety Challenges is Goal

At the heart of Visual Plan's solution is the capture of critical building information so others can browse through it and uncover risks and safety challenges and address them before an incident happens. By using the software, a school, for example, can document an immense amount of visual data from which a security plan can be built. Compared to the time required for O'Neil's 3D scanned school, the Visual Plan capture time would be four hours, produce 1,500 pano-images and be processed overnight for next day viewing. Also, a 2D or 3D diagram can be created from only the images and video capture. The speed and ease of use to complete large projects is key,

Figure 14.4 The Doug Mitchell Thunderbird Sports Center, University of British Columbia, Vancouver, B.C., has been mapped with the Visual Plan 360° facility management mapping system. The software program helps aid incident victims' response and increases and maintains security. Shown is Visual Plan's mapping of the sports center's imagery and detailed floorplan, which can expose blind spots and hiding spots---critical to the active incident neutralization efforts of first responders. (Photos courtesy of www.VisualPlan.com)

Figure 14.5 The Doug Mitchell Thunderbird Sports Center, University of British Columbia, Vancouver, B.C., has been mapped with the Visual Plan 360° facility management mapping system. The software program helps first responders more effectively respond to victims of incidents, and increases and maintains security. Shown is Visual Plan's mapping of the sports center's imagery and detailed floorplan, which can expose blind spots and hiding spots---critical to the active incident neutralization efforts of first responders. (Photos courtesy of www.VisualPlan.com)

as no tripods are needed and a user can walk the site at a regular pace collecting the imagery and video. An additional upshot of using this kind of 3D visualization solution is that it can expose blind spots and hiding spots from the detailed imagery—both aspects of any active incident scene that would be critical to the neutralization efforts of first responders.

Visual Plan has been planned for use at the Todd Beamer High School in Federal Way, Washington, which on April 19, 2007, had a gun scare when a student brought three guns to school three days after the Virginia Tech Massacre. The school was put on lockdown the same day. Watt, Visual Plan's CEO, said he captured all school buildings at Todd Beamer in roughly eight hours on August 16, 2018, measuring over 160,000 sq. ft. In the software, he said, "I can add things---arrows, objects from the object library, images, such as a wall." Watt is also able to move objects around and place them in his floor plan of the school's buildings, add annotations, digital forms, photos, documents, video, and links that can direct a user from the software to a webpage. "Much like a crime scene, I can place evidence markers on the ground within this software program, as well," Watt said.

Universities More Vulnerable; Students Can Scan Their Buildings

The special facility management and security software are also being aimed at universities because Watt said they are so much larger and vulnerable to active incidents than high schools or elementary and middle schools. Speed of capture, simplicity of use, and the ability for multiple users to capture at the same time with low-cost cameras are essential to scaling large campus projects. An example, is one of Watt's customers, the University of British Columbia in Vancouver, British Columbia, Canada. The sprawling campus, devoted mainly to research, has 180 buildings and many venues for large events. The Visual Plan mapping system was used for one of these venues, a newly built area with a 7,200-person seating capacity. Visual Plan captured the arena's entire space in cooperation with Xpera Risk, contracted by University of British Columbia to provide a risk assessment of the facility in February 2020. The project was virtually shared among facilities, risk managers, and security director Ali Mojdehi. Jack Schmidt, a risk consultant from Xpera, who contracted Visual Plan for the Digital Twin capture at University of British Columbia, said, "Visualization during the UBC project was very valuable for identifying egress, sitelines, blind spots, vulnerabilities and even maintenance issues that can elevate risk via potential active incidents."

Richard Borger, a professor in the Building and Construction Sciences building at Mohawk College in Hamilton, Ontario,

Canada, has developed an applied research program focused on 3D technology. Through this program, students scan various buildings, including the main college campus using 3D lidar and 360 capture for various applications. Borger has been using Visual Plan on these projects and noted it is a faster and more efficient way to capture the layouts of large facilities, and added that the software's collaboration tools are excellent. These tools are for annotating and markup, helping to visually reference documents, images, weblinks and other media, tagging assets for identification, referencing maintenance, and other tasks. "Not only do our industry partners gain an invaluable tool with Visual Plan for managing their facilities to increase efficiency and safety, and reduce costs, but law enforcement and fire and emergency management personnel can gain a no-cost digital twin for security planning, pre-incident training and critical response," Borger said. "Protecting our campus was not the original purpose of this program, but it has resulted in a very valuable investment in 360 capture."

Sgt. Matt Hewko, with the Hamilton Police Force, and whose agency supports Mohawk College with policing services, said, "Visual Plan provides such valuable intelligence for first responders to prepare for active incidents. In law enforcement, we rely heavily on onsite training for these incidents, but it's impossible for all first responders to gain first-hand experience at every facility prior to an incident." With virtual digital twins, it is not possible to offer an effective way for law enforcement personnel to train at multiple facilities, even in the same afternoon.

Cornell University in Utica, New York, also is proceeding with a large capture of floor plans for its facilities on campus. For facility manager Keith W. Barton, the challenge is that Cornell has more than 600 buildings on just the main campus. Now, however, "Based on the ease of use and speed of capture when deploying Visual Plan, we are looking to having our employee summer session students capture the campus facilities' layouts as a cost-effective and quick method to achieving this goal," Barton said. "Additionally," said Watt, "With the number of semesters and students at this university, now there is a very practical way to scan the entire Cornell campus. And by having the entire set of campus buildings documented with Visual Plan, Cornell will have lower to costs update its buildings' floor plans."

Brian Billings, director for campus security services at Carleton University in Ottawa, Canada, is equally supportive of the mapping system. "Visual Plan is something that we are considering in our emergency management plans for the campus," Billings said. "The opportunities that it gives for virtual table-top exercise in preparation for the response to real-life incidents is remarkable. It is almost like being there!"

Fagel, the risk assessment consultant, considers Visual Plan the right kind of technology for starting to deal with active incidents at schools. "You can immediately bring this up onscreen with a computer and let your S.W.A.T. team and other first responders know what's behind a building's exterior," Fagel said. "It's much more valuable than having a line drawing. You can see stairways, doors, hallways and classrooms, plus other rooms and areas."

Virtual Walk-through of Buildings Could Help First Responders In Real Incidents

By using a 3D visualization product that allows the user to capture important features of a building as he is walking through it, this imagery can be invaluable, and especially to first responders for an active incident. Albano, the former Secret Service agent and current risk assessment consultant, is a strong proponent of the technology. Armed with a 3D digital floor plan for a school that later has a mass shooting incident, a first responder who is arriving at the school would know the floor plan from having viewed the virtual floor plan, Albano concludes. He said, "Even if first responders didn't have time to train for incidents in that school in which they will enter and walk around, they have actually walked through it virtually." He added, "By doing that, when first responders enter and they are alerted that there is a shooting incident in the east wing of the school, they will know that area because they've actually been there (using the virtual floor plan created with the 3D visualization system)." "So, this technology can certainly help with situational awareness and with preplanning." Laser scanning can accomplish a similar result, but Albano feels this technology is better for mapping crime and crash scenes for which precise measurements are needed. For a large building, such as a school, the data sets produced by 3D laser scanning would be way too large, he said. The 3D visualization system is better suited for building not just a digital floor plan but one that is virtual, as well. "The 3D photography is much easier to share," Albano added. "A command post could be set up at a building with an active incident and supervisors can pull up the virtual layout and be walking through the building at the same time the responders are going through it."

He continued, "Virtual 3D visualization products like Visual Plan are a tool, not the solution to stop active shooter scenarios; it's a way to have a plan in place for an event whether it's an active shooter, natural disaster, fire or something else."

Mapping System Built Expressly for Schools, Law Enforcement

In the wake of so many school mass shootings nationwide, the Anaheim Union High School District in 2018 decided that a major preventive measure to protect its own schools from similar events was needed. Thus, the school district contracted with The Sobel Group, Inc., of San Diego, California, to have a unique digital mapping system developed for the district so all of its schools could be mapped. Schools today are already highly proactive about trying to do whatever it takes to mitigate or prevent serious incidents, according to David Sobel, CEO and founder of The Sobel Group and a former law enforcement officer. A key aspect of the proactive work of these school districts is how they are working with local law enforcement agencies on situational awareness for school buildings. When Sobel collaborates with a school district regarding his services, he includes local law enforcement agencies to ensure that the district and agencies within the jurisdiction are involved in the mapping solution. Although there is a cost to any school district to develop the mapping solution, first responders have access to it free of charge and with free training.

The solution Sobel offers is called TSG 360°, which includes high-resolution, immersive panoramic photography and digital mapping services. The solution enables school districts to offer their staff and first responders a virtual view of every physical feature of a school's exterior and interior floor plan, and, in particular, shows egress and ingress points that will help a first responder find any floor and room on it with a simple search tool. The whole process for the production of the TSG 360° solution includes taking thousands of high-resolution

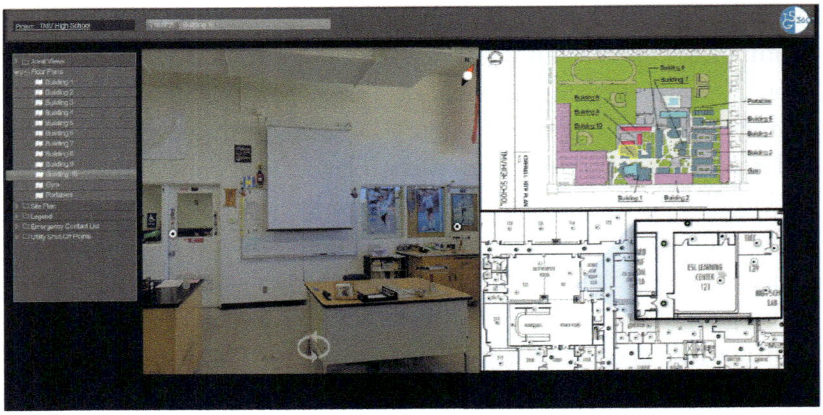

Figure 14.6 Shown is a photo of a school classroom and matching floor plan created with TSG 360°, an immersive panoramic photograph and digital mapping program. The solution enables school districts to offer their staff and first responders a virtual view of every physical feature of a school's exterior and interior floor plan, including egress and ingress points. When dispatchers and responders view the capture locations on their computer screen or other devices, they appear as side-by-side images, one showing the floor plan and the other of 360-by-360 images. (Photo courtesy of The Sobel Group, Inc., San Diego, CA)

images that are stitched together to create "capture locations," as Sobel describes it. The images are linked to the proper floor plans or site plans. When dispatchers and responders view the capture locations on their computer screen or other device, they appear as side-by-side images, one showing the floor plan and the other of 360-by-360 images. This whole approach is highly welcome since first responders typically have no previous views of a building they're about to enter during an active incident. "These responders often are going into buildings during an active incident essentially blindfolded," Sobel said. "Our system can be accessed by dispatchers, watch commanders and other responding officers, to help guide officers that are on-scene to have intelligence about the location of the active incident" (Figure 14.6).

Responders Have Full View of Building Interior Before Entry

When Sobel works with a school district that will use TSG 360°, his team conducts a security assessment of the entire facility, after which a detailed walk-through is conducted with the law enforcement tactical team. Each school's TSG 360° solution from Sobel is tailored to the specific needs of the law enforcement agency and its jurisdiction.

One version of the mapping service is developed for the school district and another one with additional features is prepared for law enforcement and is always available for viewing by first responders on mobile dispatch computers and mobile devices such as tablets. "The law enforcement version has some intelligence and detailed response information that would be proprietary to first responders," Sobel said. "It may have tactical or response information that law enforcement does not want anyone else to see."

Once an active incident at a school is over, whether this means that the suspect has been neutralized or has moved to a different location and who possibly can be contained, all rooms need to be cleared. "This is another area where the mapping system becomes invaluable because responders can see how (with the mapping system) it is going to look inside the rooms before entering them," Sobel said. Responding officers can also access live video feeds from the location, which are linked in the TSG 360° system. In addition, the mapping system is capable of performing photogrammetry to create point cloud 3D models. Measurements can be taken of a door, window, or room, which is valuable for first responder entry teams at a location of an active incident prior to a deployment.

Aids in Courtroom Presentations

In addition to giving a comprehensive view of building interiors, the imagery created with TSG 360° can be useful in courtroom presentations of scene reconstructions, as well. Sobel said his clients have found the images produced by his mapping system for crime scene reconstructions to be more valuable for juries than diagrams. This is because anyone using the system can move around within them and zoom into particular aspects such as evidence. "The floor plan (screen in the mapping system) also shows the location from which the person is viewing along with their orientation as to which direction the person is looking," Sobel said. The mapping system shows viewers the building they are in, and the floor plan is identified. Compass direction is part of the floor plan, too, and in any panoramic image being viewed.

Above all, given the extensive navigation and preplanning capabilities of Sobel's TSG 360° mapping system, Sobel cautions, "We make it very clear that this is not something to prevent an event from occurring. This is a solution for giving responding agencies more information, which can reduce response time."

Preplanning for active incidents at schools and other facilities and the urgent need for risk assessment and emergency planning have been the core of this chapter's content. Virtual walk-throughs of buildings and quickly deployable digital floorplans can aid first responders who enter active incident scenes.

The use of 3D laser scanning to help explain events at officer-involved shooting scenes will be covered in the next chapter.

Notes

1. Kellom, Kristy, and Linda Nubani. "One Step Ahead of Active Shooters: Are Our University Buildings Ready?" 2018. www.mdpi.com.
2. "Keeping Our Schools Safe: A Plan For Preventing Mass Shootings and Ending All Gun Violence in American Schools." 2020. www.everytownresearch.org.
3. Kellom, Kristy, and Linda Nubani. "One Step Ahead of Active Shooters: Are Our University Buildings Ready?" 2018, www.mdpi.com.
4. McKay, Jim. "Immersive Digital Mapping Service Gives First Responders Unique Visuals and Information." 2018. www.govtech.com.

15

Scene Perspectives at the Core of Reconstructing Officer-Involved Shootings; Video Evidence a Big Factor

Officer-involved shooting scenes can be among the most challenging and complex crime scenes to map and record. The events leading up to these scenes and the actual shootings themselves can unfold very rapidly, with considerable tension and chaos, and the outcome is usually deadly. Crime scene reconstruction experts must not only be meticulous and careful about how to document these scenes, but also use the right technology and tools to ensure scene evidence is fully and accurately recorded. The cases for officer-involved shooting scenes frequently head for court; juries need to ascertain the course of events and be presented with a scene depiction that they can collectively grasp.

Laser Scanning Can Pick Up Key Pieces of Evidence

For most law enforcement agencies and private reconstruction experts, 3D laser scanning has been the most effective tool in capturing officer-involved shooting scenes. This is because the scanner can capture the entire scene and show the scene as it actually appeared. Data gathered by the scanner, as a point cloud, can be used with special processing software to give numerous scene perspectives. These perspectives are valuable because they can help show the likely course of events and be used to corroborate or dispel the accounts given by various participants in the scene—from law enforcement, victims, and suspects. Officer-involved shooting scenes must be recorded with extraordinary care due to the increased pressure and scrutiny involved in cases tied to them. In today's world of 24-hour news and social media coverage, every officer-involved shooting can instantly become a high-profile case.

The difficulty with investigating these shooting cases stems from the wide variety of evidence that may have spread over a large area during the shooting event. Shootings can occur inside buildings or on streets. The shooting itself can be confined to a relatively small area, but the movements of the suspect and police might cover a much larger area. All of this must be properly and thoroughly mapped and documented. The events leading up to a shooting incident are vitally important to understand, not so much the actual shooting itself. Although the evidence at these scenes is perishable, much of it can be immediately captured and can include blood, bullet shell casings, bodies, vehicles, and weapons, but also any video footage of the scene's people and their actions. Capturing this evidence is imperative to understanding how events and movements may have unfolded.

These circumstances help explain why laser scanning is one of the best ways to document an officer-involved shooting scene. Most critical is that the scanned scene can be digitally visited at any time after it is reconstructed to re-examine scene details, take accurate measurements, scrutinize witness testimony, and examine different scene perspectives. Forensic investigators and scientists can use scanned scenes and their point clouds to analyze line of sight, blood patterns, bullet trajectories, and suspect height approximations derived from video surveillance footage (Figure 15.1).

Detective Matt Archuleta with the Arvada, Colorado, Police Department is well experienced in the use of 3D laser scanning and has found it to be a specially helpful technology for mapping and recording officer-involved shooting scenes. He recalled one incident in particular that involved a homeless man living in his pickup truck in front of a convenience store. The store's manager called Arvada PD to investigate the car's owner who, it turns out, had several outstanding arrest warrants. Officers arrived at the scene and approached the car to try speaking and negotiating with the man in his vehicle. But after a long standoff this attempt failed and so Arvada PD's

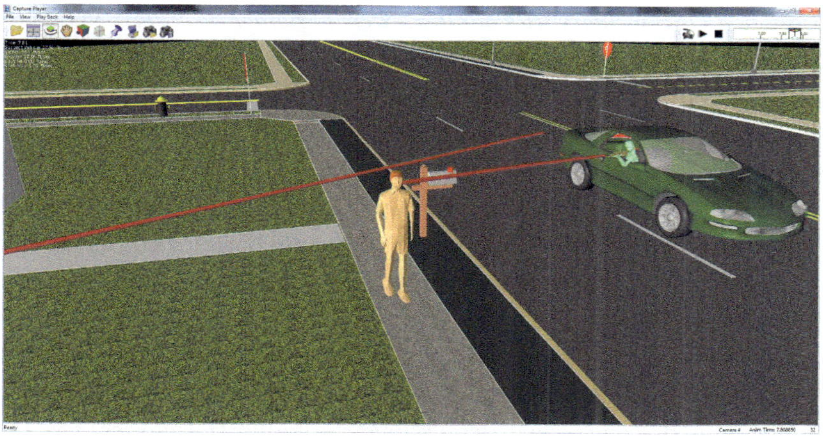

Figure 15.1 Data from a laser scanner can be imported into CAD software to create a 3D model of a crime scene. If the crime incident was a shooting, as shown in the scene here, the 3D model can have bullet trajectory rods inserted to show the direction and angles of gun shots fired. This kind of scene representation is compelling for a jury and will help it better understand the likely sequence of events at the crime scene. (Photo courtesy of Evidence Technology Magazine/November-December 2015, www.EvidenceMagazine.com)

S.W.A.T. team was called to the scene. Upon S.W.A.T.'s arrival, the homeless man had become anxious, then pointed a gun at S.W.A.T. operators. The S.W.A.T. team fired, with one bullet hitting the man and killing him.

Determining What Could Be Seen in Shooting Through Scanning Became Crucial

Upon learning about the case, the district attorney had to decide whether the homicide was justifiable. Det. Archuleta noted that laser scanners were used to map and record the shooting scene. "We created bullet trajectory holes through the pickup truck," Det. Archuleta said, which was accomplished by towing the truck from the scene to a police department yard so that it could be laser scanned inside and out. Trajectory rods were inserted into the locations of several bullet holes. Three laser scanners were used at the scene, and once the scene was scanned, the point clouds were loaded into FARO SCENE 2go to show the different viewpoints of the fired bullets and their trajectory. *SCENE 2go is an application for transferring and viewing laser scans to a USB memory stick or other external storage medium.* "We made this part of our PowerPoint presentation to the DA," Det. Archuleta said. Statements were gathered from the S.W.A.T. team's members. Det. Archuleta had to document a point of view in the scanned crime scene to either corroborate or refute the positions where S.W.A.T. members claimed they were standing during the shooting incident. This documentation was critical "to confirm what they could or could not have seen and if they were in danger from the position they were at," Det. Archuleta said.

"This was really a homicide," added Det. Archuleta, referring to the shooting incident. Ultimately, based on how the 3D model showed the laser-scanned scene's clear details plus the bullet trajectories, the DA ruled the Arvada PD's shooting was justified. The DA's decision underscored not only how valuable laser scanning is for capturing complicated scene details, but also the power of software specifically designed to show accurate bullet trajectory. Det. Archuleta adds that his reconstruction team had received bullet trajectory analysis training from Eugene Liscio, a 3D forensic analyst at ai2-3D, Toronto, Ontario, Canada. The firm specializes in 3D forensic measurement, analysis, and visualizations.

Officer/Suspect Vantage Points, Aided by Audio and Video, Are Key Factors

Liscio, who has served as an expert witness for many officer-involved shooting case trials, emphasizes that because these cases are so high profile, officers need to receive intense training on when and when not to fire their guns. "If an incident goes to trial, everybody wants to know what happened, what were the sequence of events, and where people were located (at the scene)," Liscio said. He confirms that laser scanning still seems to be the best way to measure and document officer-involved shooting scenes; Liscio has himself scanned several such scenes.

Every officer-involved shooting scene is different, and many aspects of a shooting scene can change over a period of time. "If you have the physical geometry of the room or area of the scene, you can recreate certain aspects based on photographs, video, hand measurements and other instruments, such as total stations," Liscio said, "you can bring all of these elements into a reconstruction and tie them in with your laser scan data, even at a future date." For any crime scene, the goal is always to try establishing a sequence of events before the officer arrives on scene, to determine his actions before he shoots his weapon, where he was located, and what happened at the scene once he arrives. Therefore, it's important to study audio communication between officers and different people, and any video that might be available showing where people were in the scene. If the video contains audio, it is important to synchronize these two components so others can understand the sequence of events. "Where the laser scanner comes into play is helping to show *where* people were in the scene," Liscio said, "you can actually measure the distances and you can move out of different perspectives and look at what could be seen from one position versus another." What the officer was able to see and what the victim or suspect was able to see when shots were fired, all play an integral role in reconstructing the events when using the audio, video, and 3D environment of the shooting scene, Liscio added.

Contrasted to decades during which any 3D representations, and especially animations, of a crime scene were highly scrutinized in a courtroom, today judges appreciate and welcome it. As for the juries, "They just get it," Liscio said. As laser scanning evolved as an accepted and adopted crime scene–recording tool, Liscio has found it necessary to educate the judge and jury on what this technology is all about, what it does, how it helps, and then to walk them through the reconstruction process tied to laser scanning. Three-dimensional scanning is most helpful in officer-involved shooting cases, where the position of the officer and the suspect or the victim is important. At the core of this analysis is what the officer was able to see. "It really helps to lock down the perspective of people," said Liscio, who stresses that scanning can be extremely useful with pinpointing bullet trajectories which can help lock down the possibilities of where someone was in the scene. He added, "When you start running scenarios with a bullet trajectory, any of them that you can start to exclude as not being possible, you're limiting your analysis to what is most important."

Bullet Trajectory Analysis of Explosive Shootout at the Heart of Reconstruction

A major officer-involved shooting that occurred during 2017 in Boring, Oregon, a rural suburb southeast of Portland, began when

Clackamas County, Oregon, sheriff's deputies were searching for 44-year-old Nathaniel Fritz Macalevy for a restraining order violation at around 11:30 p.m. on a Monday. A woman at the property, which has a farm and extensive acreage, alerted police that Macalevy was heavily armed and wore a helmet and vest. A S.W.A.T. team was called for back-up. The S.W.A.T. operators swept the farm's property for several hours, but it appeared that Macalevy had slipped into nearby woods to hide. The woman who called the police was transported to safety. Then around 4:30 a.m. the next day, Tuesday, police spotted Macalevy as he was driving his work van in an attempt to escape, and pursued him. The chase eventually ended not far from the suspect's property. Sheriff's deputies said Macalevy was wearing a helmet and vest when he exited the car and started firing shots at the deputies, striking their cars several times. During the shootout, Macalevy managed to hide behind his van, but one of the bullets fired from the deputies hit Macalevy's ankle, and another bullet struck his head, killing him instantly.

The shooting scene, which was laser scanned, was broken up into two areas. Officers from the Clackamas County Sheriff's Office's Criminal Reconstruction and Forensic Technicians (CRAFT) unit used a 3D laser scanner to map and connect the two portions of the vast shooting scene via a line of sight with the scanner, even though scanning shots were being made 150 yards away. Attempting to accomplish this same measurement with a total station would require moving it numerous times and would have substantially increased time on the scene. Also, it was important with this shooting to map bullet trajectory. Although the suspect who was firing bullets at sheriff's deputies when they arrived on the scene was 150 yards away from the laser scanner's position, one of the deputies using the laser scanner actually scanned another 20 yards beyond this point. Keep in mind that the scene involved a 300-square yard area that needed to be scanned. The aim of the scanning was to eventually create bullet trajectory analysis, which would include location of all shell casings, vehicles, locations of people on the scene, and any evidence on buildings (i.e., bullet holes). "Because the scanner picks up everything within its view, it yields a more robust picture, the entire scene, which is vital," a CRAFT reconstructionist said. As for what was being sought with the shooting scene's scans, it was necessary to back up accounts of what happened

Figure 15.2 A point cloud showing the scene of an officer-involved shooting at a large farm in Boring, Oregon. Red bullet trajectory lines indicate gunfire exchanged between the assailant and Clackamas County, Oregon, Sheriff's deputies before the assailant was shot and killed. A laser scanner proved effective for mapping and connecting the two portions of the vast shooting scene as it appears here, even though scans of the whole scene were made from 150 yards away. (Photo courtesy of Clackamas County, Oregon, Sheriff's Office)

as described by S.W.A.T. operators and sheriff's deputies. This could be determined, in part, because the scanner shows where people in the scene were positioned (Figure 15.2).

Establishing Sight Lines, "Stacking Evidence" Were Goals

For the scene to be scanned, all police cars were left in place and all shell casings marked. "We started scanning, and built the bullet trajectories which showed all of the bullets fired from Macalevy's rifle, and bullets fired by officers into the barn where Macalevy was hiding, and tied these trajectories back to the two officers who were firing at him," the CRAFT reconstructionist said. In post-processing of the scene, it was possible to see that one of the rounds of gunfire discharged at Macalevy hit the rear differential of his van, causing fluid to leak onto the snow-covered ground. "There was a clear marking where the fluid was dripping, so by using this drip as a starting point plus the surveillance video footage from within the police cars, I was able to put a copy of that van back into the shooting location," the reconstructionist added. "This helped us to see sight lines" (Figures 15.3 and 15.4).

To make a scanned scene more powerful, informative, and convincing, the CRAFT reconstructionist said it is important to "stack evidence." This means a crime scene reconstructionist needs to laser scan, take photographs, and get video footage of the scene. It is best not to put hopes on just one type of scene documentation. "If we lose

Figure 15.3 Shown is one of the Clackamas County Sheriff's cars struck with bullets by the assailant. The white sphere targets indicate the location and angles of bullets that struck the vehicle. (Photo courtesy of Clackamas County, Oregon, Sheriff's Office)

one of these items, we can rely on the others," the CRAFT reconstructionist said. "It's redundancy."

Merging Photogrammetry and Video—a Compelling Trend

The use of video in conjunction with laser scanning for analysis of an officer-involved shooting scene warrants a closer look. Over the

Figure 15.4 Shown is one of the Clackamas County Sheriff's cars struck with bullets by the assailant. The white sphere targets indicate the location and angles of bullets that struck the vehicle. (Photo courtesy of Clackamas County, Oregon, Sheriff's Office)

past few years, we have seen an increase in officer-involved shootings that have been captured on video by police dash cameras, body cameras, and cell phones used by civilian witnesses. Angelos Leiloglou, founder/president and 3D forensic analyst with Forensic Viz, San Antonio, Texas, argues that proper videogrammetric analysis of these videos is central to reconstructing officer-involved shooting scenes. For a brief definition, videogrammetry is the science of determining precise and reliable three-dimensional measurements of objects seen in a video. These measurements are frequently used to determine the size of an object, how far one object is from another one, or to ascertain the path of an object and/or how fast it is moving.

Videogrammetry is well-suited for use with officer-involved shootings captured on video, especially those captured by moving cameras. The first step in applying videogrammetry is to use 3D laser scanning to capture a point cloud of the shooting scene. The next step is to use a videogrammetric process called "matchmoving" to solve for, or "calibrate", a virtual camera that matches the position, orientation, focal length, and lens distortion of the physical camera used to record the video footage. The process is performed using special matchmoving software to identify two-dimensional points or "features" that are tracked through multiple frames of the video. Each of these features represents a specific 3D point on the surface of a fixed object within the shooting scene. The object could be a fence post, road marking, the corner of a roof, or window, etc. Each tracked feature is then assigned and constrained to its corresponding 3D coordinates (x,y,z) as shown by the shooting scene point cloud. The software then mathematically solves for and creates a virtual camera that emulates the real-world camera originally used to record the video footage. In the use of a body-worn camera or police cruiser dashcam, the path and speed of the officer or cruiser correlate to the path and speed of the virtual camera. Furthermore, by viewing the 3D shooting scene through the virtual camera, objects seen in the video footage can be tracked and measured over time in three-dimensional space.

"We take the video and use a process called matchmoving, which is the application of photogrammetry on the frames of a video," Leiloglou said. "This process is used to calibrate a virtual camera that matches the movement of the real-world camera that captured video." Therefore, if a police officer has activated a body-worn camera during an incident, matchmoving can be applied to determine the movement of that officer within a scene by tracking the movement of the body-worn camera. Additionally, any suspects, other officers, or vehicles seen in the body-worn camera footage can then be tracked to determine their position and movement in the scene, as well. Forensic Viz is one of the first videogrammetry consulting firms to use this process for forensic applications.

Leiloglou has used matchmoving for several officer-involved shooting scenes where it was proven to be invaluable for understanding actual scene events and the movement of people in the scene that otherwise would be impossible to capture. In one incident, in 2016, three police officers responded to a domestic violence call at an apartment building in Kentucky. The first officer on the scene had an activated body-worn camera and was in the parking lot speaking with two females, when the male suspect, who was carrying a tree-pruning saw, emerges from the front door of a nearby apartment. At about the same time, the two other responding officers arrived on the scene in their police cruiser, which was equipped with an activated video dashcam. The officer driving the cruiser also had an activated body camera. As the cruiser came to a stop, the dashcam captures the first officer as he begins walking toward the apartment while drawing his firearm. The other two officers exited their cruiser, drew their firearms, and quickly followed the first officer. After the suspect refused to drop the saw when ordered to do so, two of the officers fired multiple shots, killing him.

Matchmoving Applied to Aid Jury's Decision of Excessive Use of Force

According to Leiloglou, using point cloud data of the shooting scene and applying matchmoving on the video footage from the cruiser dashcam and two of the officers' body-worn cameras made it possible to track the movement of all three of the officers and the suspect. "The dashcam didn't capture the actual shooting, but one of the body-worn cameras did," Leiloglou said. "So, by triangulating between the body cameras and the information we can see up to a point from the dashcam, we could track the movement of officers and determine their path in 3D virtual space. We could then calculate their speed because we know the distance and the time and could determine if the officer was walking or running," Leiloglou added.

A key question that was raised during the analysis of the body-worn camera footage was where the officers were positioned relative to the victim when they used deadly force. In this case, the victim was an elderly man—a handyman—who came out of his apartment with a tree pruning saw in one of his hands. "Analyzing the bodycam footage frame by frame, we determined that the victim did not raise the pruning saw above his head or in any threatening way, as the officers claimed," Leiloglou said.

The use of matchmoving was instrumental in the plaintiff's presentation of the shooting scene reconstruction and helped lead to the jury's conclusion that there was excessive use of force by the officers and no effort by them to render aid to the victim once he was shot. As a result, the victim's family was awarded $1.25 million.

Combining Video and Laser Scanning Best Verifies Officer-Involved Shooting Details

Jason Fries, owner of San Francisco, California-based 3D-Forensic, Inc., a firm specializing in forensic video analysis, 3D laser scanning, and photogrammetry, contends that capturing officer-involved shooting scenes with video is now the standard for understanding these scenes with the highest confidence and accuracy. "It's an unbiased piece of evidence," Fries said about the value of video taken of crime scenes. "When it comes to evidence from a crime scene, the video may be the most important evidence you get." And because video will usually include audio, and in the audio it is possible to hear the shots fired from a gun, the video tends to be more important as an evidentiary tool. Furthermore, video cameras can be used to not only capture a lie, but also to capture what someone says is truthful, Fries said.

Fries argues that the combination of using 3D laser scanning and video analysis (of body-worn camera and/or dashcam video footage) is more important than anything for reconstructing an officer-involved shooting scene. He added, "You can demonstrate and show things to a jury that would not be possible without using both of these technologies together."

In 2017, a high-profile court case focused on three Chicago police officers who were indicted on felony charges alleging they conspired to cover up the fatal shooting of black teenager Laquan McDonald by a white officer. A Cook County special grand jury voted in favor of the three-count indictment, and the special prosecutor claimed the indicted officers "did more than merely obey an unofficial code of silence; they "lied" to prevent investigators "from learning the truth."

The three officers were each charged with conspiracy, official misconduct, and obstruction of justice. Body-worn video and dashcam video released as part of the case's court trial showed that white officer Jason Van Dyke shot McDonald 16 times.[1]

3D-Forensic, Inc., was hired by the legal defense team representing Van Dyke. The objective was to analyze footage from several dash cameras from various patrol cars that arrived at the shooting scene, and a security camera from a local restaurant. The video analysis firm also studied laser-scanned diagrams of the shooting scene to ascertain the most accurate unfolding of events. The case was complicated because it initially was uncertain if the victim was a threat to the officers since he had a knife and was coming towards the officers or walking away. Officer Van Dyck and his squad were told that they should look for spring-loaded switch blades that are designed to shoot out the blade like a bullet or arrow from a bow. Van Dyke was concerned that the knife McDonald had on him was one of these knives, and felt threatened, but when the knife was inspected later, it was found to be a normal knife.

Fries explained that when McDonald was shot by Van Dyke, he spun around and then fell to the ground. While McDonald is on the ground, Van Dyke continues to fire his gun on him, discharging 17 bullets. The dashcam video from one of the responding patrol cars shows that Van Dyke starts to open fire on McDonald. Then the dash cam moves and Van Dyke is no longer visible, but it is clear he is still shooting based on how McDonald's body reacts to being shot while on the ground. While McDonald is standing, it is known that Van Dyke shot six times into McDonald's body, at which point the victim drops to the ground. Van Dyke keeps shooting at McDonald, but now the evidence shows he is shooting at McDonald's hand that is still holding the knife. There is no audio in the dashcam, so it is not known if Van Dyke verbally commanded McDonald to drop the knife. When Van Dyke has emptied his firearm, his partner uses the pause in firing to walk over—with gun drawn—to kick the knife out of McDonald's hand.

McDonald died of his injuries, and medical examiners for both the prosecution and defense concluded that a bullet shot that went through McDonald's right lung would have killed him, which turned out to be true. Another bullet went into the victim's neck. According to Fries, Officer Van Dyke argued that McDonald kept the knife—a spring-loaded switchblade—in his hand and would not drop it when commanded to do so. The officer was concerned that McDonald could release the switchblade at any moment and began shooting. An ambulance came to transport McDonald who ultimately died of his injuries.

Determining If Victim Was a Threat—a Key Case Element

As a forensic video analyst representing Officer Van Dyke, Fries was asked to determine if McDonald was actually walking away from the officers during the confrontation, or toward them. By laser scanning the shooting incident area, Fries could map that portion of the actual shooting that was caught in the dashcam videos. Fries explained how the scene was able to be reconstructed to show critical details. "We could take the 3D point cloud from laser scanning the scene and match it to the 2D scene that was captured from the dashcam video camera and recreate the video footage three-dimensionally," Fries said. "So, combining the scanning and video allowed us to create a 3D video, in a sense." Next, by using measurements gained through the laser scans of the scene, Fries was able to perform camera matching or camera tracking. "In doing so," he continued, "we knew exactly where this one camera (the dashcam) in a police cruiser was at the time it captured the incident." He further added, "The camera is moving because it's a dashcam inside the patrol cruiser that was at the scene and is following the incident. We could calculate the place of that camera frame by frame. The 2D camera was showing what was happening in a real 3D world."

Bullet Trajectory Showed When the Victim Died; Scanning Pinpointed Bullets

This process allowed Fries to show where the victim, McDonald, was and the location of the officers at the scene. Bullet trajectory analysis also was performed. The analysis provided by Fries in the case showed that either the first or second shot fired by Officer Van Dyke was the fatal shot out of the 17 shots fired; 5 or 6 shots the officer fired had lined up with the bullet trajectory. The challenge of analyzing the bullet trajectory, Fries explained, was to determine the exact moment that each bullet entered McDonald's body. This determination was key because it would allow Fries to see the order of each shot fired. By doing so, it would be possible to determine when the fatal shot (chest or neck) occurred. "So, we were able to demonstrate that McDonald was killed either with the first shot or the second shot," Fries said. By tracking McDonald's movements, frame by frame, "We could see when McDonald's right chest was facing Van Dyke at an angle that matched the trajectory or when McDonald's neck lined up with Van Dyke," Fries explained. Because there was only one instance when McDonald's neck and chest were aligned, defining the order of shots was possible. "Only by camera matching the exact movement of McDonald (combining video footage with laser scanning) were we able to pinpoint the order of wounds on the suspect's body," Fries said.

Additionally, "We were able to establish that McDonald was walking closer to the officers (during the incident)," Fries said. However, "When you look at the video, it looks as though McDonald was walking away from the officers; the video demonstrated he was actually walking closer to them." Finally, Fries continued, the video does not show the bullets going into McDonald. "The only way to see this kind of detail was to look at the laser-scanned scene," he said.

The growing role of 3D laser scanning to pinpoint pivotal details of officer-involved shooting scenes has been the central point of this chapter. Particularly germane in this discussion is how videogrammetry can verify essential shooting scene aspects, such as positions of suspects and officers, and bullet trajectory analysis, when used with laser scanning to reconstruct an officer-involved shooting scene.

In Chapter 16, the unique ways that laser scanning can provide evidentiary clues in blood pattern analysis will be examined.

Note

1. "3 Chicago Police Officers Indicted in Laquan McDonald Case." Policeone.com, Associated Press, 2017. www.policeone.com.

16

Scanning for Bloodstain Pattern Analysis Helps Identify Vital Clues at Crime Scenes

Crime scenes, especially those involving shooting incidents, almost always have some type of bloodstain pattern evidence. This type of evidence is some of the most important to *collect* from a scene as it can offer clues about how a vicious crime, such as a shooting, stabbing, or some kind of blunt force trauma event may have happened. Bloodstain pattern evidence will be especially essential to include in a homicide case that goes before a jury. The idea that bloodstain patterns will adhere to certain laws of physics enables examination of blood at the scene of a violent crime or on items of evidence at the scene to offer possible insights into the likely course of events. By successfully interpreting bloodstain patterns that are left at a scene, the crime scene reconstruction technician not only can extract clues as to the nature of the offense, but also ascertain possible sequence of events, any disturbance to the scene, and even the positions of individuals and objects as the incident unfolded. Equally powerful is analyzing bloodstains as it may help refute or corroborate eyewitness accounts.[1]

The job of the crime scene reconstruction expert when performing blood pattern analysis (BPA) is to map and record the scene based on events of an alleged incident that could have produced the stain patterns present at the crime scene. This documentation will depend on items of physical evidence recovered from the scene and what blood evidence exists on numerous surfaces and on items of clothing that were found. Equally important for the investigation is not only where blood is present, but where it is also absent. In some crime investigations, it is not possible for BPA experts to access the crime scene firsthand to document bloodstain evidence. Therefore, it may be necessary to conduct bloodstain pattern analysis by using photographs and whatever investigative reports from the scene are available.

Crucial to the analysis of bloodstains are the sizes of the individual stains creating a pattern, their shapes, and their distribution in relationship to one another. Unlocking this information can reveal how a particular stain or pattern may have been produced. BPA can determine what actions or sequence of actions could have created the bloodstains and/or patterns visible at the crime scene. The BPA can include vital clues such as the position of people at the crime scene when the blood was dispersed (i.e., sitting, standing, lying, curled up, etc.), how these people and their positions are interrelated, the type of weapon possibly used, and how bloodstaining might have spread over a surface.

There are different types of bloodstain patterns. These include:

- ***Drip Pattern***: A nonlinear blood spatter comprised of circular or elliptical stains in a random distribution. The drip pattern occurs when blood has dripped into a pool on, say, a floor, causing droplets to be released from the pool. It includes a volume accumulation in the *parent stain* and random spatter stains around the margin.
- ***Cast-Off Pattern***: A Cast-off blood pattern is created when blood drops are sprayed or released from an object in motion, as with a weapon being used to strike someone. The motion of the object that creates the cast-off blood pattern can be from right to left, for example. This type of pattern is characterized by a general linear configuration and a progressive change in observed impact angles.
- ***Impact Pattern***: The Impact Pattern can occur whenever an object strikes a blood source. It is hard to determine whether or not they can be accurately analyzed. Usually, it's ideal to look for upward moving stains on a vertical surface such as a wall. However, it's possible to have impact pattern in the middle of a parking lot (i.e., someone is struck low to the ground) and the bloodstains radiate outwards with no walls to hit.[2]

Blood Behavior and Tracking—the Area of Origin

Critical to the reconstruction of an incident scene having blood evidence is establishing the area of origin of the impact pattern based on directionality and angle of impact. By examining certain bloodstains, it is possible to determine the blood's trajectory as it impacted the target.[3] Determining this trajectory often has been accomplished by the so-called stringing method, which involves running strings from the rear edges of the bloodstains upward at the appropriate angles to find where they roughly meet—*the area of origin*. But this method only yields an approximation and is primarily used to establish whether a victim was seated, standing, or lying down when a violent event involving the use of a gun, knife, or blunt force object occurred. The presence or absence of blood on other surfaces can also aid in this analysis. One of the benefits of this method is that it gives you a visual perspective at the crime scene, but the downside is that it takes substantial time to perform depending on the number of stains to include. In the past few years, bloodstain pattern analysts have used computer programs to enable them to store bloodstain and spatter data, calculate values such as impact angle, and then display information about bloodstain patterns in 3D renderings[4] (Figure 16.1).

Crime scene investigators use BPA to work backward from traces of blood and bloodstains that are present at a crime scene. This approach

Figure 16.1 An example of a laser-scanned bloodstain pattern area of origin. (Photo courtesy of Eugene Liscio, ai2-3d Forensics)

allows them to reconstruct the locations and actions of people and weapons involved in the crime that has been committed. Blood traces can include drips, smears, and spatters. These traces occur when drops of blood radiate from the impact of a bullet or blunt instrument. From the standpoint of physics, BPA reconstruction is a complicated issue associated with fluid mechanics that involves tracing the behavior of blood under varied forces and ambient conditions. The issue is compounded because blood is a complex fluid that contains both liquid (the plasma) and solid (the blood cells) components. Blood is classified as a non-Newtonian fluid. A non-Newtonian fluid is a fluid whose rate of flow is not proportional to the stress applied. Its viscosity varies and may increase or decrease with stress, time, or a combination of both.[5]

When properly used, BPA can yield helpful clues toward an understanding about the circumstances of a shooting, for instance. Using this shooting example, drops of blood that strike a floor at an angle will create a set of elliptical stains whose width-to-length ratio gives the impact angle. BPA experts have been trained to draw straight-line trajectories that follow the long dimension of each ellipse at this impact angle. Eventually, these trajectory paths meet in what's known as an area of convergence. However, although this process correctly gives the projection onto the floor for the location of a gunshot wound, the straight-line trajectories method overestimates the height of the wound. This is because the true paths are parabolas, or U-shaped curves, modified by aerodynamic drag. The error as part of the overestimated height is often large enough to incorrectly place a victim as standing rather than sitting[6] (Figures 16.2 and 16.3).

BPA Can Help Build a Plausible Storyline of Where and How a Crime Unfolded

At the end of a crime scene investigator's examination of a scene that shows bloodstain patterns, and with his analysis completed, the goal is clear: define what could have happened at the scene and, more importantly, what could not have occurred based on the bloodstain evidence available (in concert with all other available evidence). This is the conclusion of Sergeant Daniel DellaSala, Bloodstain Pattern Analyst and Technical Review Supervisor, Crime Scene Unit, Harris

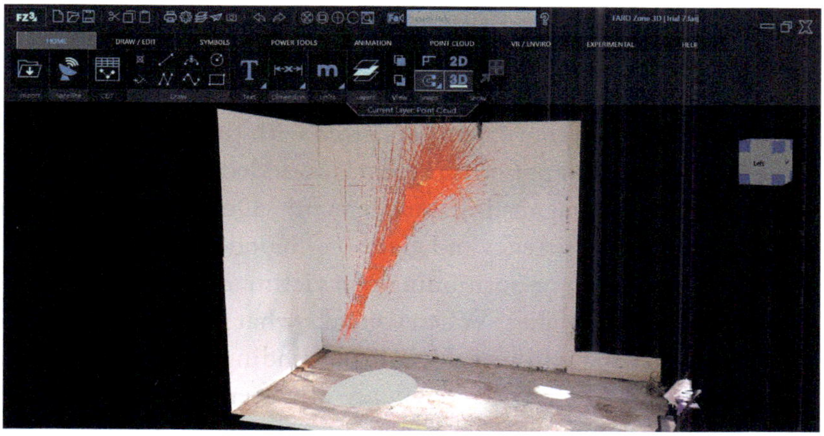

Figure 16.2 These are images of cast-off stains showing bloodstain backtracked trajectories on a wall, also laser scanned. (Photos courtesy of Eugene, Liscio, ai2-3d Forensics)

County Sheriff's Office in Houston, Texas. As Technical Review Supervisor over BPA at crime scenes, Sgt. DellaSala emphasizes that he is making sure his investigators stay objective when performing blood pattern analysis. "I want the (bloodstain) evidence to speak to them so they can make their own conclusions," DellaSala said. "The driving factor that supports BPA in general is that blood is a fluid and it will react predictably." It is this predictability that allows analysts to look at the relationships among different blood patterns that are found at a crime scene and to the nature of a blood-letting

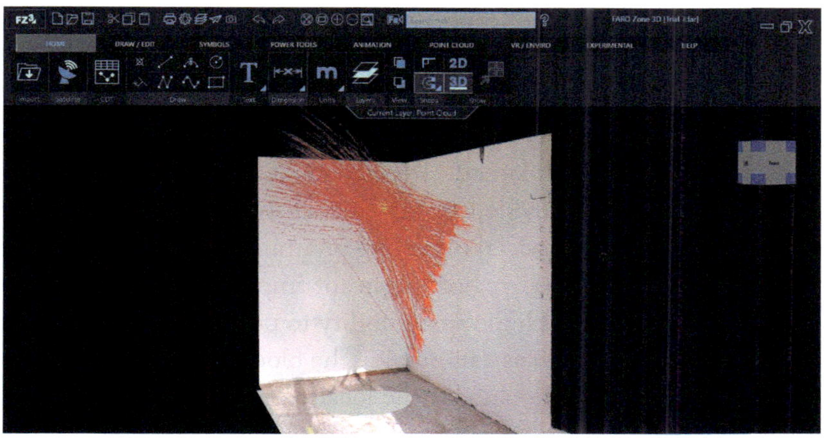

Figure 16.3 These are images of cast-off stains showing bloodstain backtracked trajectories on a wall, also laser scanned. (Photos courtesy of Eugene, Liscio, ai2-3d Forensics)

event at a crime scene because physics as applied to blood pattern analysis never changes, DellaSala continued. "It (BPA) can aid in the determination of the location of the crime and where it originated, what kinds of movements occurred with the victim or suspect based upon the blood patterns present," he added. "Do we see blood going along a wall suggesting a movement?" DellaSala posed. "Do we see a certain consistency in height—of blood on walls that show maybe the posturing or positioning of a victim at the time he or she was struck, shot or beaten? When you take what you gather from the blood evidence that will reveal what your findings are, and then you couple that with the physical evidence at a scene—a broken chair, a gun—and combine this with witness statements, suspect statements, complainant statements, then you start to get one consistent storyline," DellaSala said.

Terrestrial laser scanners can capture millions of data points in minutes. Laser scanners can either capture up-close HDR detailed scans or bloodstains located within a scene, or high-resolution photos can be merged with the scan data for analysis.

Harris County Sheriff's Office uses a laser scanner for many of its crime scenes, and has found it particularly beneficial for BPA, DellaSala affirms. The laser scanner not only electronically maps crime scenes but is also able to capture up-close HDR detailed scans of bloodstains located within a scene. Sgt. DellaSala has found the laser scanner is particularly helpful for capturing bloodstain patterns that are present at a crime scene. And, he added, the scanner can show specifically and accurately what the bloodstain patterns look like in a room, and that his 3D modeling software enables a jury to enter the scene in 3D capacity and understand better what blood evidence is being shown and explained. The 3D model produced also allows jurors to see how the evidence was located within the crime scene. Also used in BPA are special modeling programs, such as HemoSpat, which can calculate the area of origin for impact patterns of bloodstains at crime scenes. HemoSpat's ability to perform this directional analysis of impact patterns can provide the bloodstain pattern analyst with essential information about the location and posture of an individual at a bloodletting scene.[7]

As forensic science evolves and adapts to technology for crime scene mapping and documentation, such as 3D laser scanning, software programs such as Hemospat can be imported into laser scanner software like FARO Zone Advanced or Leica Map360 to allow merging of datasets and to create more informative and illustrative point cloud models.

Shooting Scenes Well Suited for BPA

Shooting events tend to serve as one of the best examples of studying blood patterns since blood evidence frequently is present at the scene. Although crime scenes involving the use of firearms present unique challenges for the crime scene investigator, it is still possible to reconstruct events that give some indication as to what occurred during the actual discharge of a weapon. More specifically, it can be determined what the actual path or trajectory of bullets was, and, using this information, the location of the shooter may be pinpointed. Several factors must be considered, including the position of cartridge casings ejected from automatic and semi-automatic weapons. Exact position of casings once ejected must be marked and documented before any other investigative procedures are launched.

The crime scene must be photographed, especially if it has bloodstain pattern evidence. Photos should be taken of the overall scene along with medium distance and close-up photos. Next, a diagram should be made of the scene and location of each bullet casing in the scene delineated. Naturally, many law enforcement agencies use a 3D laser scanner to capture crime scene evidence, with focused attention on bloodstain patterns, and, thus, can build 3D models to show these specific patterns as well as bullet trajectories.[8] (Figures 16.4 and 16.5).

"Stringing" a Typical Method with Uncertain Accuracy

Determining bullet trajectory is at the core of crime scenes where it is clear that a shooting occurred. For decades, the "stringing" method has been used to determine the source of bloodstains and spatter as well as the path of bullets fired. The crime scene investigator usually must provide scene documentation to support his conclusions. As indicated earlier in this chapter, the stringing method involves using a series of strings to trace the source of multiple elliptical bloodstains back to an intersection, or *Area of Origin (AO).* This method is

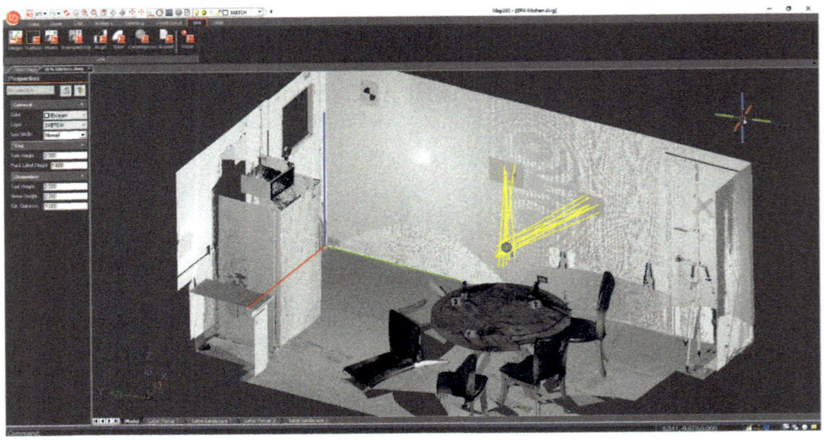

Figure 16.4 While software exist that can perform calculations and analyze bloodstain patterns captured with 3D laser scanning, workflows are often cumbersome. Importing and exporting the data and creating reports can require multiple steps. Newer approaches streamline the process by allowing you to integrate scan data with high-resolution photographs and create area-of-origin calculations in a 3D dataset directly within your scene mapping software, such as Map360, as part of a BPA-validated workflow.

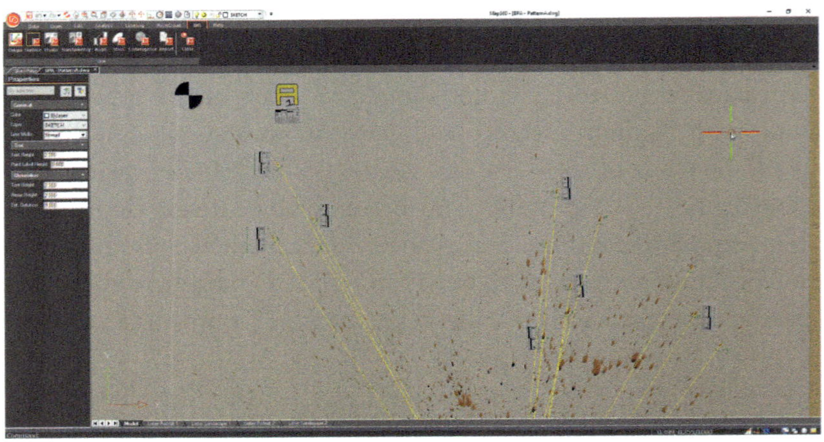

Figure 16.5 While software exist that can perform calculations and analyze bloodstain patterns captured with 3D laser scanning, workflows are often cumbersome. Importing and exporting the data and creating reports can require multiple steps. Newer approaches streamline the process by allowing you to integrate scan data with high-resolution photographs and create area-of-origin calculations in a 3D dataset directly within your scene mapping software, such as Map360, as part of a BPA-validated workflow.

tedious, and accuracy cannot be entirely reliable because it assumes that droplets travel in straight lines. Because of the parabolic nature of blood travel, due to air resistance and gravity, convergence is typically viewed in a 2D, top-down manner. Yet gravity and air resistance will be factors in making the droplets take a curved, parabolic path. Also, string is susceptible to droop or sagging unless strong nylon or other synthetic string is used versus cotton string. For this reason, virtual stringing methods such as those offered in programs like BackTrack and HemoSpat prove quicker and more accurate. And 3D laser scanning greatly reduces time on scene and preserves the entire crime scene, including whatever bloodstain evidence may be present. While laser scanning creates a comprehensive map of the scene, this does not mean BPA work has changed. Individual bloodstains must still be measured for entry into programs like HemoSpat.

Photos Overlaid Onto Scanned Scenes Yield Measurements—Details on Bloodstains

Laser scanning a homicide scene with bloodstain patterns can yield certain benefits for the reconstructionist. But before scanning a crime scene that has bloodstains it is crucial to first photograph all blood pattern evidence, as blood may be on walls, doors, floors, in hallways, and on furniture, light switches, picture frames, and many other places. The photos are essential because they will be used with a laser scanner to build a 3D model of the scene and determine key bloodstain aspects. So, it's important to take multiple photos of the crime scene (overall, midrange, close-up, and macro, with scale). Once the photos are taken and the crime scene has been laser scanned, the photos can be imported into special 3D documentation software such as FARO Zone Advanced or Leica MAP360. The software processes and manages the scan data by using real-time, on-site registration, automatic object recognition, scan registration, and positioning. When the user uploads his photos from the crime scene into this software, the software can skew the photos onto the scanned scene accurately and take measurements. In other words, once photos are brought into the software, the user can use the software's tools to overlay them on the scan itself. To do this, the user picks points on a photo, such as the corner of a light switch or maybe a door frame, and then the software will layer that photograph—to scale—over the top of the scan. This produces a very high–quality image of a wall that may have bloodstains on it in three-dimensional space. Once the photo is brought into the software and overlaid onto the scan of the bloodstained wall, this changes how a person will see the scene. Although the wall from the crime scene is part of the point cloud from the scan, it will not have details. This is why the photo must be imported on top of the scan; doing so will reveal the minute details of each bloodstain. And, because bloodstains can be extremely small, it is crucial to have very high-quality photographs. The software is able to use the photograph to show its details and make bloodstain pattern analysis possible.[9]

Manufacturers of laser scan data processing software today typically have a special bloodstain pattern module that is sold with the main software. With it, the reconstructionist can determine the origin of bloodstains at a crime scene, to determine the approximate location of where the event occurred. Again, by uploading photos of bloodstain patterns from a crime scene into the software it is possible to map out individual blood droplets that have struck a surface, such as a wall. The special BPA tool is used to map the origin, which can give a look, in 3D, of where the event happened. More importantly, the 3D visualization of the scene is one into which jurors can be brought to see all of these details tied to the murder scene and to the bloodstain evidence.

Laser Scanning Shows Credible Scene Perspectives Helpful to Jury

As mentioned earlier in this chapter, the stringing method is one of the oldest methods for determining a space in which bloodletting occurred based on bloodstains present at a crime scene. But this method is tedious, time-consuming, and may not give precise results. Equally concerning is that this method could also lead to scene contamination as the reconstructionist stretches strings directly from locations of bloodstains on a wall or some other kind of surface. More important, showing a crime scene with strings coming from bloodstains on a wall may not be clear to a jury. As Eugene Liscio, 3D Forensic Analyst with ai2-3D, Toronto, Ontario, Canada, said regarding the string method, "You're limited to tape measuring, basically, and to your rough judgment about where these lines (represented by strings) converge." A laser scanner is a more reliable method because it gives actual points that can be measured. He added, "From a visualization standpoint, this method is much clearer to a juror because the forensic analyst showing this kind of presentation can move around within the crime scene, get different angles and perspectives," "and if you were to do an area of origin analysis, you can see the analysis within a processing software program within the context of the crime scene."

Violent crimes committed by the use of a firearm, resulting in evidence of bloodstains, can offer some hypothetical yet plausible arguments as to guilt or innocence when the scene is reconstructed through 3D laser scanning. This is what Liscio discovered when he was hired to document a high-profile crime scene involving the case of David Camm, an Indiana state trooper who was tried three times for the murders in 2000 of his wife and two children, and acquitted after the third trial. Camm became a suspect for the murders because of bloodstain patterns found on his clothing, and due to numerous leads and evidence items that ultimately proved unreliable or false. Camm's acquittal came after his third trial when another suspect was identified as the actual shooter and convicted of the crime.

Bullet Trajectories Showed Locations of Shooter and Victims

On the day of the homicide, Camm had returned to his house after playing basketball with some friends and found his wife and two children murdered inside the family's Bronco in the garage. The wife was shot as she was standing by the Bronco's passenger door and her body was found on the garage floor next to it. The two children, sitting in the rear passenger and driver side seats were also shot. Using a laser scanner, Liscio was able to perform different scanning scenarios of the shooting to show what was likely and not. "I was able to take a scan of the Bronco and then set up the bullet trajectories and put 3D character models back in and show some different positions of the shooter and victims," Liscio said. The jury found it helpful during the Camm trial to see Liscio's trajectory scans because experts for the prosecution were verbally trying to describe the shooting scene and used a mannequin with rods through it to show bullet entry and exit trajectories. The jury's ability to see the trajectory scans most likely helped it

Figure 16.6 Trajectory rods and laser scans of the Bronco vehicle where three members of the family of David Camm, a former Indiana State Police trooper, were murdered helped reconstruct the different positions of the shooter and the victims. This reconstruction, coupled with blood spatter evidence on Camm's shirt, ultimately showed that Camm was not in a position to fire the shots as was argued at his trial. (Photos courtesy of *Evidence Technology Magazine*, 2008, www.evidencemagazine.com)

understand what happened or may not have happened (Figures 16.6, 16.7, 16.8, and 16.9).

The high point of the trial came when it was shown that Camm had some bloodstains on the lower left side of his shirt that the prosecution claimed were his. However, according to Liscio, "Had Camm fired on the side of the Bronco closest to the victim, he should have had blood on his clothes, but didn't. Everything else in the vehicle did have blood. 'Blood was all over the place,'" Liscio continued. Camm's shirt, it turns out, had only a small amount of blood from his daughter—eight droplets in the lower left area of his shirt. It was determined to be most unlikely that David Camm could have fired the gun inside the vehicle and from the outer passenger door since the side most exposed to blood droplets would have been on his right side. As the case was dissected in court, it was found that the prosecution had misrepresented the shooting scene's details.

Case Hinged on Details Found in Laser Scan Data

Liscio's role as expert witness in the Camm case expanded. "On the stand, I was talking about bloodstains, body position, and bullet

Figure 16.7 Trajectory rods and laser scans of the Bronco vehicle where three members of the family of David Camm, a former Indiana State Police trooper, were murdered helped reconstruct the different positions of the shooter and the victims. This reconstruction, coupled with blood spatter evidence on Camm's shirt, ultimately showed that Camm was not in a position to fire the shots as was argued at his trial. (Photos courtesy of *Evidence Technology Magazine*, 2008, www.evidencemagazine.com)

Figure 16.8 Trajectory rods and laser scans of the Bronco vehicle where three members of the family of David Camm, a former Indiana State Police trooper, were murdered helped reconstruct the different positions of the shooter and the victims. This reconstruction, coupled with blood spatter evidence on Camm's shirt, ultimately showed that Camm was not in a position to fire the shots as was argued at his trial. (Photos courtesy of *Evidence Technology Magazine*, 2008, www.evidencemagazine.com)

Figure 16.9 Trajectory rods and laser scans of the Bronco vehicle where three members of the family of David Camm, a former Indiana State Police trooper, were murdered helped reconstruct the different positions of the shooter and the victims. This reconstruction, coupled with blood spatter evidence on Camm's shirt, ultimately showed that Camm was not in a position to fire the shots as was argued at his trial. (Photos courtesy of *Evidence Technology Magazine*, 2008, www.evidencemagazine.com)

trajectories," he explained. "The whole case really was more a blood pattern analysis case than a bullet trajectory case." By using laser scan data processing software, Liscio was able to create and show the jury a 3D model with which he could rotate around the homicide scene in his courtroom presentation. It was the ability to show the Bronco in 3D with multiple scene perspectives that became pivotal in the presentation. Also, 10 years after this incident occurred, and with access to the original Bronco from the crime scene, it was still possible to document the bullet impact points on the windshield and through the back seat and into the trunk liner, according to Liscio. And there was still some evidence of bloodstains from the children's injuries. All of this intact evidence could be documented later and reconstructed to show where the bullet trajectories came from. "The laser scans show that Camm probably was not at the scene when the shots were fired," Liscio said. One more interesting note offered by Liscio is that the David Camm case was the first ever for which a FARO laser scanner had been brought into a courtroom and demonstrated for a jury during a trial.[10]

The value of analyzing bloodstain patterns at crime scenes as a way to learn how crimes occurred, and the positions and actions of victims and suspects at crime scenes, has been the aim of this chapter. Three-dimensional laser scanning aids this analysis by revealing core aspects crucial to a case involving BPA, such as bullet trajectory and bloodletting point or origin.

The next chapter explores issues tied to vehicle collisions and the value of 3D laser scanning in uncovering how and where collision damage occurred.

Notes

1. "Bloodstain Pattern Analysis." About Forensics, 2011. www.aboutforensics.co.uk.
2. "Bloodstain Pattern Analysis." Minnesota Department of Public Safety, www.dps.mn.gov.
3. "Bloodstain Pattern Analysis." About Forensics, 2011. www.aboutforensics.co.uk.
4. Freeman, Shanna, and Nicholas Gerbis. "How Bloodstain Pattern Analysis Works." *How Stuff Works*, 2018. www.science.howstuffworks.com.
5. Grutzmacher, Dave. "Industrial Mixing Basics: Newtonian vs. Non-Newtonian Fluids." *Proquip*, 2018. www.proquip.com.
6. Perkowitz, Sidney. "The Physics of Blood Spatter." *Physics World*, 2019. www.physicsworld.com
7. "Hemospat: Bloodstain Pattern Analysis Software." *Hemospat*, FORident Software, Inc. www.hemospat.com.
8. Penven, Don. "Recommended Procedures for Documenting Bullet Trajectory." *Crime Scene Investigator Network*, 2018. www.csitechblog.com.
9. Penven, Don. "Recommended Procedures for Documenting Bullet Trajectory." *Crime Scene Investigator Network*, 2018. www.csitechblog.com.
10. Liscio, Eugene. "3d Technologies for the Investigation of Shooting Incidents." 2008. www.evidencemagazine.com.

17

Vehicle Collision Damage "Autopsies" Yield Crucial Details with 3D Laser Technology

For decades, mapping and recording collision scenes was a slow, tedious, and inexact process, as most strikingly seen with the early methods of using tape measures and measuring wheels. These methods, of course, paved the way for total stations which, although still in use today, require substantial time at crash scenes and are viewed by many reconstruction experts as inadequate for picking up ample scene evidence that can be most meaningful to a jury. Regardless, total stations are still in use and can usually meet the needs of those reconstruction experts who deploy them. They should never be abandoned completely. In fact, total stations remain hard at work for crash scene documentation, and have even enjoyed a resurgence by being used in tandem with other technologies.

In the new millennium, 3D laser scanning and drones have catapulted to the top of the technology hierarchy for crash scene reconstruction. And while they do not replace other existing scene documentation tools, laser scanning and drones are viewed as the new centurions of the technology pack particularly because they can map and record a crash scene with one primary asset that reconstructionists treasure dearly: speed. Typically, a laser scanner's capabilities are so powerful, fast, and wide-ranging that crash scenes can be processed more efficiently and in a fraction of the time required by the total station. The net result is an ability to create more detailed, clearer 3D representations of crash scenes that will enable juries to fully and immediately understand a scene's likely chain of events (Figures 17.1 and 17.2).

Figure 17.1 Point clouds of a crushed vehicle that will allow a detailed analysis of the extent of deformation, types of damage, and the circumstances tied to this collision. (Photos courtesy of Eugene Liscio, ai2/3d Forensics)

Figure 17.2 Point clouds of a crushed vehicle that will allow a detailed analysis of the extent of deformation, types of damage, and the circumstances tied to this collision. (Photos courtesy of Eugene Liscio, ai2/3d Forensics)

What Took Hours to Collect Minimal Data Is Now Eclipsed by Laser Scanning

These advantages became clearly evident to investigator Weston Hadley, of the Santa Ana, California, Police Department's Collision Investigations Unit, as he has responded to multiple collision scenes along highways and extremely busy intersections. Like so many crash reconstruction experts, Hadley and his fellow collision investigators for years used a theodolite which, although it took accurate measurements at crash scenes, required the user to choose those measurements he felt were needed. And it could take up to five hours to collect just 200–400 points. At the time, the police department's budget did not allow for the purchase of a 3D laser scanner. By 2018, however, the department had acquired and began using a laser scanner that could grab millions of very accurate data points, in less than 30 minutes, and pre-register point cloud data in the field automatically. This translated to substantial time-savings for post-processing back in the office.

Securing the laser scanner has proven critical considering that the Santa Ana PD Collision Team responds to so many fatal vehicle collisions each year. At one point, Hadley said, his team had mapped its 12th collision scene by June 2019, after only acquiring the scanner in December 2018. Again, the speed of crash scene documentation is paramount for the collision team, and the laser scanner frees up patrol officers to more timely respond to calls for service. The scanner enables an investigator to map a crash scene in less than 30 mins, while reducing strain on personnel. "It provides a better service for the community because we can put our resources to better use than blocking roadways," Hadley said. Without the scanner, as Hadley has witnessed, severe collisions, especially at high-traffic intersections, can back up traffic for thousands of people who may not be able to get through such an intersection and be late to work. Equally important is how the laser scanner protects officers by decreasing their time spent on collision scenes with steadily moving traffic in which, at times, distracted or impaired drivers will plow through active scenes.

Jury Can Make Better Informed Decisions

One of the laser scanner's biggest advantages is its ability to capture such complete scene evidence, with millimeter accuracy, so that returning to the scene may never again be necessary. Because total stations only capture evidence that the user chooses, it's not uncommon to discover after leaving a scene that some critical evidence was missed, forcing the investigator to return to the scene and capture more data points.

A court's jury is the chief beneficiary of the laser scanner's end product—usually a 3D scene reconstruction into which jurors can be placed and walk around and see all kinds of evidence, plus at different angles and perspectives. Such information enables jurors to make better informed decisions on collision cases compared to two-dimensional illustrations that may require extensive explanation supplemented with scene photos. "With a 2D drawing," said Hadley, "You can talk about two cars colliding at 40 miles an hour. In concept, they (jurors) really don't know what it looks like when a violent collision occurs—the crushed vehicles, the debris field—it can be overwhelming."[1]

Scanning Shows What a Driver Most Likely Saw Before Crash

Beyond the laser scanner's ability to capture a crash scene in its entirety is the opportunity for a reconstructed scene to be built that reveals important details about vehicle damage and probable course of events during the collision. Mapping crash scenes is much different than mapping crime scenes, according to Sergeant Drew Bolzer, crash team coordinator with the Lancaster County, Nebraska, Sheriff's Office. He concludes that it is not necessarily always apparent what has happened at a collision scene. Although crash scenes are the result of collisions, the crashes may go unwitnessed, especially if they occur in rural areas. But even if there are witnesses to a crash, their testimony may not be reliable, which makes laser scanning and creation of an interactive 3D scene diagram pivotal for determining crash events. "I've had cars going in four different directions based on testimony from three different witnesses in some crash cases," Bolzer explained. "It's really hard to validate their statements in this instance." However, through interactive 3D diagrams created with special drawing software, "You can put the line of sight right inside a car where the driver was and rotate it left and right, and see exactly what the driver saw," Bolzer continued. "There might be obstructions in the crash scene that the driver was not aware of."

The Lancaster County Sheriff's Office Crash Team, operating since the 1970s and which is summoned to respond exclusively to fatal vehicle crashes, also uses laser scanners. They can process and manage 3D scan data efficiently and quickly by using real-time, on-site registration, automatic object recognition, scan registration, and positioning. The scanner was purchased in 2015 and has been instrumental in capturing many crash scenes; between 12 and 15 crashes are mapped and recorded a year.

Multiple Ways to Study Collision Damage

Although crush analysis has long been considered a more comprehensive way to determine damage to a vehicle involved in a collision, it is not necessarily the de facto method for analyzing this damage. Bolzer points out that because of technology advances, crush analysis is not essential for many of the collisions his team documents. "We have other ways of determining this," he said. "There is dashcam video, airbag control modules, and onboard telemetrics" in most new newer vehicles, Bolzer noted. In fact, a vehicle's EDR (event data recorder), or "black box," yield's a wealth of information about what happens to a car minutes or seconds during the crash itself. The EDR is similar to a vehicle's Airbag Control Module (ACM), which is a source of recoverable data. Even though the ACM's primary function is to operate the vehicle's airbags and other restraints, with the help of the PCM (powertrain control module), it also is constantly monitoring the vehicle's operation including the speed and changes in speed, braking operations, engine speed, throttle position, seat belt engagement, seat belt pretensioner activation, and other data. During a vehicle's operation, the ACM saves the flow of data to a temporary file. When an "event" such as a collision occurs, the ACM is programmed to capture and save the data for a preset period of time.[2]

Crash Vehicle "Autopsies" Yield Valuable Details

Bolzer performs what he calls vehicle "autopsies" on every car involved in a crash that he believes is going to be a chargeable offense. Collision vehicles are laser scanned at the scene, then, as part of his vehicle autopsies, Bolzer photographs damaged cars extensively using cameras with 12 megapixels and scans them again. "When a car is brought back to a garage (for an autopsy), it gives reconstruction experts a chance to scan inside the car," Bolzer said. "This might give us views of occupant seating positions, damage to the interior that may show direction of force. This may also help us learn where the vehicle was headed." A key motivation for performing the autopsies, Bolzer continued, is that they can give exculpatory evidence. This method can answer a lot of questions: Was the crash the result of mechanical failure? Was the crash's cause a roadway problem? Was the driver distracted, on his or her phone? Was the driver operating an infotainment system? Or was the driver in the middle of a texting conversation when the crash occurred? The reconstruction team removes a vehicle's tires, measures the depth of brake pads, looks to see if the rotors were functioning properly, and determines what percentage of braking efficiency the wheels had.

And it looks for whether or not a seatbelt was being used and for vision obstructions (Figures 17.3, 17.4, and 17.5).

The scanner's role in the autopsies is critically important because the Lancaster County Sheriff's crash reconstruction team does not have a lot of time at crash scenes to document evidence. "We are basically documenting a vehicle with four scans at the scene," Bolzer revealed. But back at the team's vehicle bay, reconstruction experts can take eight scans—left and right at the front and back, every corner, and usually overhead scans and under the car depending on where

Figure 17.3 Laser scanning point clouds of cars involved in a three-vehicle collision. One of the cars drove through a stop sign eastbound across a four-lane state highway and collided with a northbound SUV which then collided with a westbound car stopped on the east end of the intersection waiting to turn north. No one was killed in the collision, but a passenger in one of the cars was in critical condition. Sgt. Drew Bolzer, Crash Team Coordinator for the Lancaster County, Nebraska, Sheriff's Office, performs laser scanning "autopsies" that might reveal views of occupant seating positions, damage to the interior that may show the direction of force. This kind of analysis can help reconstruction experts learn where a vehicle involved in a collision such as this one was headed. (Images courtesy of Lancaster County, Nebraska, Sheriff's Office Crash Team)

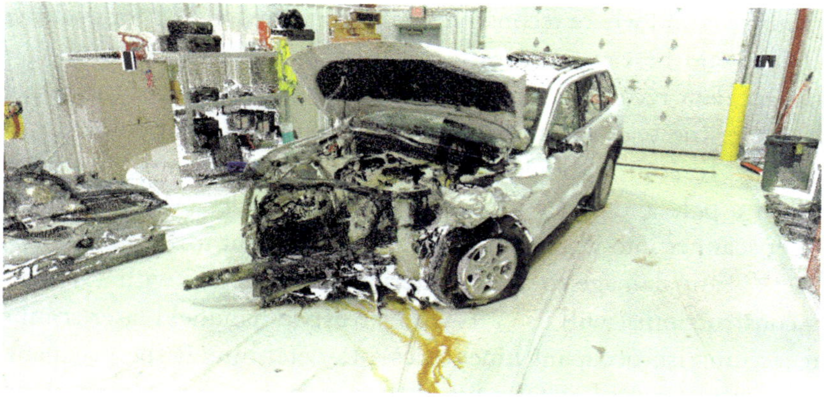

Figure 17.4 Laser scanning point clouds of cars involved in a three-vehicle collision. One of the cars drove through a stop sign eastbound across a four-lane state highway and collided with a northbound SUV which then collided with a westbound car stopped on the east end of the intersection waiting to turn north. No one was killed in the collision, but a passenger in one of the cars was in critical condition. Sgt. Drew Bolzer, Crash Team Coordinator for the Lancaster County, Nebraska, Sheriff's Office, performs laser scanning "autopsies" that might reveal views of occupant seating positions, damage to the interior that may show the direction of force. This kind of analysis can help reconstruction experts learn where a vehicle involved in a collision such as this one was headed. (Images courtesy of Lancaster County, Nebraska, Sheriff's Office Crash Team)

Figure 17.5 Laser scanning point clouds of cars involved in a three-vehicle collision. One of the cars drove through a stop sign eastbound across a four-lane state highway and collided with a northbound SUV which then collided with a westbound car stopped on the east end of the intersection waiting to turn north. No one was killed in the collision, but a passenger in one of the cars was in critical condition. Sgt. Drew Bolzer, Crash Team Coordinator for the Lancaster County, Nebraska, Sheriff's Office, performs laser scanning "autopsies" that might reveal views of occupant seating positions, damage to the interior that may show the direction of force. This kind of analysis can help reconstruction experts learn where a vehicle involved in a collision such as this one was headed. (Images courtesy of Lancaster County, Nebraska, Sheriff's Office Crash Team)

damage is and where reconstruction experts are looking for evidence. Bolzer said he can even hang his laser scanner from the ceiling of his accident reconstruction bay to get top-down scans of the vehicle damage; the scanner is mounted to a tripod and then bolted to the ceiling. To scan a vehicle's undercarriage, Bolzer hangs the scanner off of a pole and slides it underneath the vehicle. "We can put the laser scanner into just about any position we want to," Bolzer said. If there is any damage to a car's interior in connection with a death, a reconstructionist will use a FARO Freestyle handheld laser scanner to accomplish occupant kinematics—to determine if the occupant's head went forward, what it hit, if there is hair evidence in the windshield, and if there is something in the vehicle occupant's area that needs to be documented. Such thorough documentation from terrestrial and handheld scanning gives a better overall representation of vehicle damage for a diagram.

Showing Crash's Impact on Vehicle Interior Aids Jurors

The extensive scanning that Lancaster County's reconstruction team accomplishes pays off when it's time to present a 3D model of a crash scene whose case heads to court. Prosecutors in particular cherish these models because they help them to explain more easily and understandably what occurred at a crash scene. "We give jurors a 3D model that they can manipulate, move around in, and see different views," added Bolzer. "We can also perform different what-if scenarios by moving cars around to see what possible impacts or effects this would have." One of the most striking and revealing capabilities that scanning and the subsequent 3D models for a collision scene offers is a view of a vehicle's interior. "We can show inside a car, at the driver's level, what that driver could or could not see," Bolzer offered. "That makes a huge difference in a jury's mind as to whether or not the driver could see another driver or pedestrian, or was able to legally leave an intersection before checking to see if the roadway was clear. Or, if the car was going so fast it did not have enough response time to avoid a collision."

The ability to return to a crash scene and collect additional measurements is another prized capability with scanning. The scanner usually captures the totality of a crash scene, but if some evidence is overlooked and cannot be identified, it is easy to return to the scene, within the diagram, and measure key scene items that would not be so certain by using a total station. Although total stations are still relied upon by many reconstruction experts, "You only have the points you took with a total station," Bolzer said. "You can miss certain things—roadway evidence, distances, critical measurements—because you didn't know it was important at the time. With a scanner, you can actually go back and measure that point and know what it is," he added.

Before the Reconstruction Team Arrives, First Responders Protect the Scene and Gather Evidence

Although a laser scanner is highly effective at capturing a crash scene once the scanner is activated, it is essential that the scene remains intact as much as possible *before scanning begins*, according to Officer Scott Kofoid of the Salem, Oregon, Police Department, who is a trained crash reconstruction expert. Until Kofoid can arrive at a collision scene to document it, he and other reconstruction experts rely on first responders who typically can obtain information that otherwise would not be available. "Many items of evidence are very fragile (i.e., tire marks, debris, evidence positions) and these initial responders are often able to provide us with a better overall picture once we, as reconstruction technicians, arrive on scene," Kofoid said. In addition to providing this key information, the first responders also photograph a crime or collision scene exhaustively. It is typical to have 400–500 photographs of a scene between what the first responders and Kofoid or his fellow reconstruction experts capture with a camera. Video evidence is also included.

When it is time to actually map and document a crash scene, Kofoid prefers to use a laser scanner every time. "If I can, I document every crash scene with a scanner that is on the highest quality setting for color, and then I fly the scene with a drone," he said. "I will use the drone over a crash scene to get some scans in black-and-white using Ground Control Points (GCP). A day or two later, when I'm serving a warrant on the crash vehicle from the scene for inspection, I perform a thorough color scan of the car because I don't have time constraints," Kofoid continued. With this approach, the officer can generate a complete 3D model of the damaged vehicle since lighting and color are good, and he can take as many scans as needed. "This allows me to find an exemplar vehicle, thoroughly scan that vehicle and perform crush analysis, and create a compelling 3D model for court," Kofoid added. A drone will help minimize the reconstruction expert's time and maximize the end result—the scanned scene in totality.

The Salem Police Department is extensively using drones for documenting crash scenes. Yet, drones are usually used in conjunction with laser scanners.

Nighttime Crash Scenes—a Particular Challenge to Document

Kofoid uses a laser scanner for nearly all of the crash scenes he is called to map and record. He scans both nighttime and daytime crash scenes. "I often scan nighttime collision scenes in black and white, as color mode is very limited when it is dark," Kofoid said. "Scanning in color will cause the scan data in the area of the direct light to become washed out. You have to be very careful how close and where you place auxiliary scene lighting, as items of evidence can be lost or difficult to locate in these washed out areas." And, Kofoid added, if evidence items at a crash scene being scanned at night (i.e., tire marks, scuffs, very small pieces of evidence, etc.) are not marked, they can sometimes be very difficult to locate in the completed scan data/point cloud. Scanning from each position at a scene can be completed in about 4 mins. "We have two scanners, so we can move through an entire scene regardless of lighting much faster," Kofoid added.

Drones are often used for nighttime crash scenes because they can effectively supplement evidence data that are captured with a laser scanner. Kofoid and his crash reconstruction team place ground control position (GCP) placards in a crash scene that has resulted at nighttime, then scan the scene in black-and-white to capture the same GCP locations along with the entire scene. "This helps to augment the data that the drone does not pick up as effectively (i.e., sides of the vehicle, detailed damage, detail of small items within the scene), and it allows for the collection of GCP positions to assist with the accuracy of the final map created from the drone data," Kofoid said. The drones are equipped with Pix4D drone mapping and photogrammetry software which can export the final mosaic or point cloud to

FARO Zone that allows investigators to move easily between 2D and 3D environments and improve the quality of their incident reconstructions and analysis for courtroom presentations.

The integrated scanner and drone data are entered into a completed product using a third-party software called Cloud Compare, a 3D point cloud processing software program. Once the scanner and drone point clouds are merged in this software, they can be exported as a combined map into FAROZone. Kofoid noted that his reconstruction team also joins total station data with laser scanning data to demonstrate locations of evidence at crash scenes, as well. The team also generates video fly-throughs of documented crash scenes from software that supports their laser scanner.

Crush Analysis Through Laser Scanning Helps Explain Interaction Between Vehicles

Some vehicle collisions can be complex enough that it may be warranted to examine vehicle crush. The crush of a vehicle involved in a serious collision will reveal the severity of the event. Wes Grimes, a certified crash reconstruction expert and owner of Collision Engineering Associates (CEA), Inc., in Mesa, Arizona, performs a considerable amount of crush analysis. "We frequently extract crush information from our scans of vehicles involved in major collisions," he said. "A scanner gives both high resolution and many measurements that you can use in equations and line up the damage of one vehicle with damage on the other vehicle to understand how both cars interacted," Grimes continued. The reconstructionist and his team seldom return from a crash scene with less than 15 or 20 scans (including scans of the scene and vehicles involved), and they always scan from multiple positions. The team routinely tries to scan at least four corners of any vehicle, and then document damage (Figures 17.6 and 17.7).

CEA deals with many heavy truck crashes, and the scenes for these particular crashes may be several hundred feet in length. Grimes will fly these types of scenes with drones to capture overall dimensions and context of the evidence, and if 3D portions of the scenes could aid in the reconstruction, this area will be scanned to capture these 3D depictions. Items such as guard rails, bridge railings, and culverts do

Figure 17.6 These images show point clouds from a scan of two vehicles from two different wrecking yards. The point clouds were used to return the wrecked vehicles to the original crash scene and place them at maximum engagement based on damage profiles documented within the point clouds. (Photos courtesy of Wes Grimes, reconstruction expert, owner of Collision Engineering Associates (CEA), Inc., Mesa, Arizona)

Figure 17.7 These images show point clouds from a scan of two vehicles from two different wrecking yards. The point clouds were used to return the wrecked vehicles to the original crash scene and place them at maximum engagement based on damage profiles documented within the point clouds. (Photos courtesy of Wes Grimes, reconstruction expert, owner of Collision Engineering Associates (CEA), Inc., Mesa, Arizona)

not show up well with only aerial drone photos. So, scanning, when necessary, and combining scan data with drone data yields the most complete three-dimensional data set, Grimes said. Ground control points help to maintain accuracy in drone imagery and aid in registering data gathered with different technology, he added. CEA regularly aims to scan an entire vehicle involved in a collision because many times a surface that does not have damage is just as important because it helps the reconstruction experts eliminate possible contact. "We try to use photos and scans to understand the interactions (between vehicles) that occurred," Grimes said. "Sometimes, it is not just about figuring out what happened at a crash scene, but equally important is understanding what pieces of a crash scene might be missing and how to account for this in the scene reconstruction."

Point Cloud Segmentation Is Like an "MRI"; Shows Important Vehicle Crush Perspectives

An impressive method for analyzing collision damage with a laser scanner is point cloud segmentation, and Grimes and his team apply it often for vehicles involved in highly complex crashes where crush analysis can present vital clues about a chain of events and movements of drivers. Crushed vehicles and their matching exemplar vehicles can be laser scanned and the resulting point clouds are segmented to produce more detailed crush data. Segmentation involves making narrow slices of the point cloud, much like an MRI or CAT Scan, to exhibit perspectives of damage that the point cloud alone may not reveal. The end result of segmentation using laser scanning, 3D drawing software and computer graphics is a treasure trove of vehicle crush features or data. Specifically, the segmentation method enables the user to better answer questions about how a car moved during a crash while also producing a more complete crush profile.

One crash case that Grimes was tapped to investigate proved to be ideal for the segmentation method. It involved an SUV that was struck twice by separate vehicles on a highway, causing it to rotate and go airborne before crashing into a concrete wall. The vehicle was a Ford Explorer that initially was struck on its rear bumper by a pickup truck, which pushed the Explorer forward. With this impact, the SUV rotated around, then was side-swiped by an oncoming vehicle, causing additional structural damage. As the SUV continued down the roadway, it rotated counter-clockwise and the right-rear side was struck by another oncoming SUV. That collision broke the SUV's right rear wheel and prompted the SUV to rotate once more, in the other direction, and then go airborne, after which it landed on a large retaining wall. The back-rear portion of the Explorer ended up hanging up on the retaining wall 3–4 ft off of the ground after striking the retaining wall. A young lady driving the Explorer was ejected and died.

Type of Crush Damage, Direction of Forces Revealed

Grimes worked with a team of biomechanics who needed to determine when the Explorer's driver was ejected, and if wearing a seatbelt would have made a difference in the crash's outcome. The case's most difficult challenge was trying to distinguish among the numerous vehicle damage patterns. "We were not able to completely isolate them, but we were able to understand how the crash events occurred," Grimes said. Grimes scanned a Ford Explorer exemplar vehicle and then lined up compatible reference points between the two vehicles (the exemplar and one of the other damaged vehicles). At that point, by laser scanning the vehicles, "We could slice through the scan and look at different elevations and what components in each car were damaged at that elevation," Grimes explained. This helped him to accurately determine what type of crush damage had actually occurred as well as the direction of forces involved. The interior of the Ford Explorer also was laser scanned to help the biomechanic expert understand how the driver would have moved as she was ejected from the vehicle's right front side window.

To start his reconstruction of the crash, Grimes obtained an exemplar, undamaged Ford Explorer model identical to the one involved in the crash. With this exemplar vehicle he was able to line up the left front tire and fender and doors with those of the damaged vehicle. Using the 3D model he created from scanning the exemplar Ford Explorer, Grimes removed the vehicle's roof to study how the damage occurred. "The right rear corner shows how that whole side of the car is crushed because the lines of the exemplar vehicle show how this should look undamaged," Grimes said. "The whole back left side and left two-thirds of the vehicle's back are crushed in because the lines in the 3D model tells us where it should be."

Extent of Damage and Type of Crush Offered Through Slicing

Determining the shape of the Ford Explorer's crush patterns was greatly simplified by slicing the point cloud produced from scanning the vehicle. "You have hundreds of thousands of points and so you can just slice through them," Grimes observed. "The slicing simplifies the point cloud so that it's easier to focus on a particular feature. With a top-down view through this method, you can see how the vehicles interacted with each other," Grimes said. For example, slicing showed Grimes how much the Ford Explorer's roof had moved during the various collisions with other cars. Slicing gave a view of how much damage had occurred in the SUV that was in the crash compared with the exemplar Ford Explorer.

A key point that Grime emphasizes is that crush analysis will reveal the severity of a crash. He frequently extracts this kind of information from scanning vehicles that were in crashes. More specifically, Grimes said, "A laser scanner gives both high resolution and multiple measurements that you can use in equations and line up the damage with damage on another vehicle (an exemplar vehicle) to understand how the vehicles interacted."

Several Crash-Recording Tools Were Used, But Drones Played the Key Role

To perform his analysis, Grimes generated a point cloud by scanning the original Ford Explorer from this collision and its exemplar Ford Explorer, using a laser scanner. FARO SCENE software was used to process the point cloud data along with another unique software program called CloudCompare. CloudCompare is a 3D point cloud and triangular mesh processing tool that performs a comparison between 3D point clouds. Also used was rhino3D, a versatile 3D modeler software program that can create, analyze, edit, animate, and render polygon meshes, point clouds, solids, surfaces, and NURBS curves (Non-uniform Rational B-spline—NURBS—is a mathematical model typically used in computer graphics to create and represent curves and surfaces. Source: en.wikipedia.org/wiki/Non-uniform_rational_B-spline).

Collision Engineering Associates currently uses three DJI Mavic 2 Pro drones and sees clear benefits with them in conjunction with its other mapping tools. With a drone, "I can scan right around the area of impact at a crash scene, and then I'll fly the drone over the entire scene," Grimes said. "We can cover the same area as a laser scanner with the drone much faster, but not with the same resolution and accuracy that the scanner gives." When using a drone for major crash scenes, it is essential to take multiple photos and passes over the scene to capture as much unobstructed area as possible. "But it's never a guarantee," Grimes added. This explains why Grimes considers the drone a useful mapping tool to cover large areas quickly and safely. "The scanner is still the preference, if 3D data is going to be part of the analysis of a crash scene reconstruction," Grimes said. In order to generate three-dimensional data from a drone, it is necessary to get as low or as high as possible at a scene. "You need to get multiple elevation views so that the software can extract three-dimensional data," Grimes said. However, he added, "For most reconstruction cases where the 3D component in reconstruction is not crucial, nothing beats a drone for documenting a crash scene."

Although several lawsuits were filed in this crash case, it eventually was settled out of court.

This chapter has detailed how laser scanning has greatly improved safety for crash reconstructionists and yielded significant time-savings with mapping crash scenes, and how it has strengthened the analysis of vehicle collision damage, especially for crush. The use of point cloud segmentation as a means to dissect vehicle crash damage detail was a particular focus in this chapter.

In the next chapter, the advantages that laser scanning offers for analyzing suspect height approximation in tandem with video are examined.

Notes

1. Lyons, Wendy. *Mapping Crashes and Collisions at Record Speed.* Hexagon/ Leica Geosystems. https:www.leica-geosystems.com.
2. Bushway, Todd. *Black Box Key to Vehicle Crash Analysis.* 2015. https:www.bizjournals.com/buffalo/news.

18

Scanning for Height Approximation Proves Invaluable in Helping to Target Prime Suspects

Determining the height of a suspect who has committed a crime, such as a robbery or murder, and whose actions were captured on a surveillance video is a process that has gained increased value and relevance in recent years. Today, it plays a key role in forensic science and is often part of criminal court cases. Height approximation had some rudimentary beginnings. Perhaps the first truly scientific attempt to identify criminals occurred in 1860, when a Belgian prison warden named Stevens began taking measurements of criminals' head, ears, feet, body lengths, etc. Stevens' imperfect method was eventually abandoned, although its intent was not. By 1882, a Frenchman, Alphonse Bertillion (1853–1914), had developed an elaborate anthropometrical system that required tabulating height, sitting height, length of outstretched arms, length and breadth of head, length of right ear, among other measurements. Bertillion enhanced his method with such additional data as scars and eye color, as well as full-faced and profile photographs.[1]

Fast-forward to the 21st century and the process of accurately determining the height of a criminal suspect seen in security surveillance video footage is highly refined. Exacting, detailed measurements and digitally enriched still-frames of video footage from different camera angles can be used to create a 3D model of a crime scene. Then, with special processing software plus photogrammetry, it is possible to compare this to the actual recorded surveillance video evidence to study height estimation of a suspect at the scene. Of particular value is the use of 3D laser scanning with this entire process. This is because images available from video surveillance cameras cannot alone be used to measure distances. Yet, when these images are combined with laser scans of the video footage, they indeed can be measured. Accuracy of the measurements is within millimeters. The user selects common points between the point cloud generated by the laser scanner and the image so that the picture can be aligned over the scan to determine a suspect's height.[2]

Agency Used Height Estimation Software to Help Identify Prime Suspect

Drew Bolzer, a reconstruction expert for Lancaster County, Nebraska, Sheriff's Office, used a 3D laser scanner as part of a case several years ago to scan surveillance video footage of a Lincoln, Nebraska, convenience store shooting. The aim was to identify the prime suspect by accomplishing suspect height approximation. Bolzer used still photos from the convenience store's surveillance video footage to laser scan and align common points to determine the suspect's height.

The shooter had gunned down an employee in the convenience store. Bolzer and the other members of his agency's collision reconstruction team were the only law enforcement professionals who had been trained at this time to use a laser scanner. Some of the crime investigators with the Lincoln Police Department wanted Bolzer to visit the convenience store and scan the shooting scene as part of their investigation. The investigators concluded that having a good, clear diagram of what happened at the scene would help with their investigation. So Bolzer scanned the shooting scene. It was not until a week or two later that Lincoln PD investigators had a suspect identified. However, it turned out they had three possible suspects. "Those suspects were pretty significant different ranges in height," Bolzer recalled. "They (the Lincoln PD investigators) were trying to eliminate the other two people after believing they had the prime suspect, and asked me if I could get a measurement off of the surveillance videotaped suspect's height through laser scanning." Bolzer believed he could accomplish this since one of the forensic applications that Lancaster County Sheriff's Office purchased with its laser scanner was a suspect height identification tool. "This tool," Bolzer said, "would allow me to get within pretty close proximity of the suspect's height."

The Sheriff's office chose laser scanning after realizing that crime and crash scenes clearly were not well documented with a total station. The agency purchased a laser scanner in 2016, feeling that higher quality and more detailed information could be captured at scenes, and that scenes could be documented in their entirety. At the time the Sheriff's office purchased its scanner, it also acquired software for various forensic applications, including suspect height analysis, bullet shot trajectory, and blood pattern analysis. It was fortuitous that Lancaster County Sheriff's Office purchased special software applications with its laser scanner. The convenience store shooting would tap into the suspect height analysis software program at just the right moment. "In fact," said Bolzer, "we had no idea we would use the suspect height analysis tool first." The convenience store shooting case grew complicated as it evolved. And then a twist to the case occurred. "We found out who the suspect was, and then we learned he had died in another state in reference to another homicide," Bolzer said. With this development in the case, Lincoln PD investigators wanted to get specific measurements off of the suspect's body to absolutely confirm that this person was the right suspect. "But we never got those measurements," Bolzer said (Figures 18.1 and 18.2).

At the time Bolzer had performed the suspect height analysis for the case, there were three suspects, but he did not know for sure which one had committed the convenience store homicide. "But investigators knew these suspects were different enough in height that they could narrow it down to the probable suspect," Bolzer explained. "That's what I did." In measuring the prime suspect shown in the surveillance video, "Once I came within two-tenths of an inch of what the suspect's actual height was, investigators wanted to further follow up with a body analysis in Georgia where the prime suspect was conjectured to have died. This autopsy would disclose what the body's measurements were." As a result, investigators wanted Bolzer to comb through the video to measure tip of the finger to elbow, elbow to shoulder, etc., to find out if this suspect was the right one. But Bolzer did not perform these measurements because he and his

Figure 18.1 Shown are screenshots of video surveillance footage of a convenience store robbery. Based on this footage, and by laser scanning specific measurement points for the suspect's height (see image with balloon measurement indicators), it was possible to focus on this suspect for the crime and eliminate other suspects from consideration. More specifically, it was possible to take still frames from the video and align common points within it in a 3D diagram produced with laser scanning post-processing software. (Images courtesy of Lancaster County, Nebraska, Sheriff's Office)

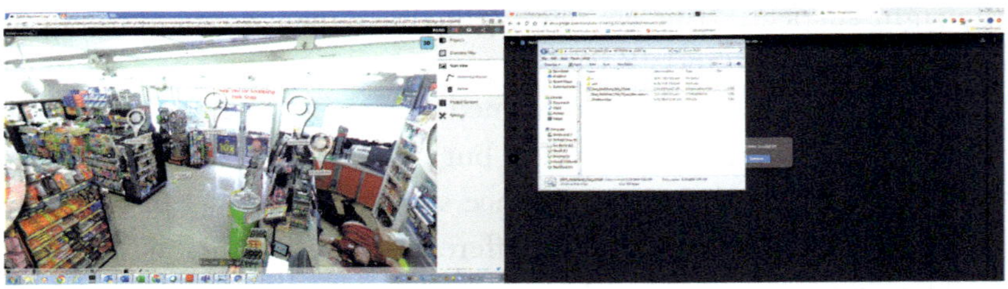

Figure 18.2 Shown are screenshots of video surveillance footage of a convenience store robbery. Based on this footage, and by laser scanning specific measurement points for the suspect's height (see image with balloon measurement indicators), it was possible to focus on this suspect for the crime and eliminate other suspects from consideration. More specifically, it was possible to take still frames from the video and align common points within it in a 3D diagram produced with laser scanning post-processing software. (Images courtesy of Lancaster County, Nebraska, Sheriff's Office)

reconstruction team learned from the suspect's father that the suspect had been in Lincoln, Nebraska, at the time of his death and, furthermore, was in Omaha hours before the homicide. Also, the suspect was wearing the same clothes as he had on during the convenience store shooting.

Scanning Crucial in Narrowing Down List of Suspects Based on Heights

It appeared that at this juncture the laser scanner was able to play a pivotal role in the case. "I think the laser scanner was vital because it allowed investigators who were focusing on the other two suspects—besides the prime suspect—to now focus all of their efforts in proving that this prime suspect was the guy who probably committed the convenience store homicide," Bolzer said. The biggest factor in accurately estimating a crime suspect's height is the quality and resolution of the video footage taken of him. In the Lincoln, Nebraska, convenience store shooting case, Bolzer found that the video was better than average and that it looked as though the surveillance camera it came from had been installed fairly recently. Working with suspect height approximation leaves very little margin for error. The agency in Georgia that examined still-frames from the convenience store video applied photogrammetry for height approximation. "Their measurements were close," Bolzer said, "but there was a lot more margin of error in the video expert's estimation of height."

Scanner Can Measure a Suspect in a Surveillance Video Scene

Just how does laser scanning work with surveillance video to achieve an accurate approximation of height for a criminal suspect? First, Bolzer explains, it is important to laser scan the facility or area in which you will try to generate height approximation—the area in which the person of interest is standing and moving around. "If the facility (convenience store, for example) has a surveillance video camera and you know roughly where that person is located in that camera's video of him, you have to scan the video footage to get a good 3D representation of what this environment is," Bolzer said. "Next, the video must be viewed to find out exactly where the suspect is, whether," Bolzer continued, "at a pretty good gait, so that the suspect is standing up and down as opposed to mid-stride. A mid-stride step won't give a real accurate height, but if the person is standing, with knees locked into position, you take that still-shot from the video and superimpose it—with at least eight common points—into that frame on the laser scan itself." At that point, measurement tools in the laser scanner can be used to actually take a measurement of that person inside the scene, Bolzer said. Once the laser scan's point cloud of the video with the suspect's measurements is processed and uploaded into a CAD modeling software program, "The 3D diagram should show what the surveillance camera saw at the time," Bolzer added. "You can take the still from the video and align the common points from within the video in the 3D diagram and it will scale it to within 10,000th of an inch." What is key to ensuring accuracy in this entire process, Bolzer said, is the quality of video from the start. "If you have some really high-definition video and it has quite a few pixels in it, this allows you to have a lot sharper image to superimpose into that 3D diagram," he concluded (Figures 18.3 and 18.4).

Baffling Crime Cases Prompt UK Investigator to Apply Height Approximation

When Daniel Sharp joined the UK's West Yorkshire Police (WYP) as a crime scene surveying supervisor, he had some specific ideas about forensic technology applications using CCTV in combination with 3D laser scanning technology. He put those ideas into creative practice, particularly after his WYP colleagues approached him with some baffling, live cases where CCTV footage was available but missing

Figure 18.3 Factual height measurements taken from laser scan data helped the York Regional Police achieve a conviction in a double homicide that occurred at a café in Woodbridge, Ontario, Canada, in 2015. "That's one of the greatest advantages to using a 3D scanner," said Detective Sergeant Brad Joice, commander of the Forensic Identification Unit. "You can capture data that isn't significant at the time but becomes important later." (Images courtesy of Joice/Leica Geosystems)

Figure 18.4 Factual height measurements taken from laser scan data helped the York Regional Police achieve a conviction in a double homicide that occurred at a café in Woodbridge Ontario, Canada, in 2015. "That's one of the greatest advantages to using a 3D scanner," said Detective Sergeant Brad Joice, commander of the Forensic Identification Unit. "You can capture data that isn't significant at the time but becomes important later." (Images courtesy of Joice/Leica Geosystems)

evidentiary significance. Each case was different and challenging. In one case, Sharp was asked if a quick burst of outdoor CCTV footage could be studied to determine the speed of a pedestrian. In a second case, he was asked if the footage could be helpful in corroborating or eliminating suspects in robbery cases. In yet another case, he was asked if, based on the known locations of two bullet holes, the location of where the shooter was standing could be established and if his gun had been aimed at police officers. Sharp was perplexed, but he was willing to answer these questions, given his ability to stitch digital images into his 3D scans.

Sharp addressed these questions by adopting three techniques using 3D point cloud models of scan data merged with still photos taken from CCTV footage. The techniques include:

- Suspect height analysis
- Speed analysis
- Bullet trajectory analysis

These methods have been successfully used in court and have in many cases contributed to convictions. Specifically, the West Yorkshire

Police has won convictions for numerous serious crimes through Sharp's techniques. Sharp's suspect height analysis technique was particularly welcome by the WYP because the agency had been using an external consultant to apply photogrammetry for analyzing suspects' images from crime scenes. This approach was slow, however, and could only produce 2D models, with a 2" margin of error. So Sharp decided to stitch laser scans and CCTV footage/images together, using some basic trigonometry methods, which enabled him to ascertain a suspect's height more accurately. This move sharply reduced the margin of error and helped to eliminate or corroborate evidence connected to suspects.

Height Analysis Tool Aided in Case of Multiple Robberies by Similar Suspects

The suspect height analysis tool was especially timely after a string of five armed robberies occurred at restaurants and bars in Leeds, a local government district of West Yorkshire. Three suspects repeatedly were seen on the CCTV footage from the locations of the robberies, but their covered faces and the lack of footprints or fingerprints made identification difficult. And even though mobile phone data records showed the suspects were in the vicinity of the robberies, the records were inconclusive. Sharp's technique found that the three suspects should measure 5'4", 5'11", and 6'5". The suspects' heights were the same at every robbery, Sharp's probe found, which made it likely they were the same males involved in each of the several robberies. Although the suspects initially refused to be measured, once Sharp's evidence led to their arrests, the suspects' heights were measured while in custody. It was determined they were very close to the heights that Sharp had calculated.[3]

Reverse-Engineering a Suspect's Height Seen in Video

Forensic video reconstruction expert Jason Fries has spent years refining the study and application of suspect height analysis for numerous criminal cases. Fries, who is CEO of San Francisco, California-based 3D Forensic, said he is the first person, along with his brother, to use 3D laser scanning in a forensic capacity in 1999, for a two-vehicle crash in Hawaii. Today, Fries and his brother have been able to harness the power of laser scanning to design a protocol to reverse-engineer the height of a person shown in a video or still image of a criminal act. 3D Forensic's process is called "Laser Based Photogrammetry," which uses fundamental principles of photogrammetry (extracting measurements from a photograph) and overlaying a 3D environment over them to address questions at a much higher fidelity.

To illustrate this concept, Fries poses the following example. Imagine if you had a video of a robbery suspect entering a convenience store and he's standing on top of a bullseye painted on the floor. The suspect is standing straight and pointing a gun at the store clerk. The police department who is investigating the incident wants to know how tall the suspect holding the gun is. They have brought in ten different people, each with differing heights, and asked them to stand on the convenience store floor's bullseye so they can presumably identify a suspect on the same security camera that captured the suspected robber. Using a computer, the police could overlay each of the ten videotaped suspects over the actual robber video so that whichever of these suspects had a height that matched the robber's height could be identified. "Of course, there are many challenges in using this method to determine how tall the real suspect was in the original video," Fries explained.

Laser-based Photogrammetry Can Override Challenges

Often, there is not a bullseye painted on the floor, the suspect is rarely standing up straight, it is unknown which range of height the ten stand-in suspects should be, and none of these suspects may be the same height. This becomes even more challenging if the original security camera has been moved or has been replaced with an entirely different surveillance system. "Laser-based photogrammetry can override these challenges because it is all done with a 3D model environment based on the laser scan data," Fries said. "By recreating the scene from the laser scan data, it is possible to recreate the crime scene with almost any 3D modeling software and to begin analyzing the video in three dimension." Even if the camera location is not known, Fries continued, it is still possible to calculate the camera location based on the 3D video image. Fries then asks, "Where in this 3D environment must the camera be located so the 3D laser scan data aligns with the 2D video?" Once that location is matched, 3D Forensic uses a Least Square algorithm as it is designed to create a regression analysis (*Least squares regression is used to predict the behavior of dependent variables*) to mathematically calculate the 3D location of the camera that captured the original robbery (Figures 18.5 and 18.6).

"Once you can create a camera in your 3D computer-generated world that matches the real world, you can, in essence, recreate the experiment of placing people to stand on the bullseye on the floor at different heights," Fries continued. However, "In the digital world, you have limitless heights you can try and which don't require a mark on the floor, because all you must do is place your digital person's feet on the floor in the same location as, in this scenario, the robber's feet," Fries said. Finally, whether or not the robber in our convenience store example is standing tall or has feet spread apart, it's possible to take a digital suspect and position him in the same position. Once he and the actual robber are matched, you can go into whatever 3D software is preferred and measure this suspect's legs, torso, neck, head, etc., and calculate his height as if he were standing tall. This method even works when you have a video of original video footage, Fries said.

Figure 18.5 An "officer height" image showing a laser scan with officers placed into the 3D scene and positioned to align with what a body-worn camera shows.

Figure 18.6 This "officer height and video used" image shows the image from the body-worn camera in this case. Once the camera has been tracked using photogrammetry, 3d-Forensic, a San Francisco, California, forensic technology firm, fine-tuned the positions of the officers and determined the height of each person at the scene (this is shown in the right-hand side of this image). (Photos courtesy of www.3D-Forensic.com)

Suspect Height Method Worked Even with "Video of a Video" in a California Store Robbery

In an actual case for which Fries' expertise was tapped, a robbery had occurred at a convenience store in Ventura, California, and was captured on video. However, when police arrived at the store, the clerk did not know how to make a copy of the security footage that recorded the event. The responding police officer used his cell phone to videotape the monitor replaying the footage of the robbery. Based on this footage, the officer felt he knew the suspect's identity and then went to his house to arrest him for the robbery. As a result, 3D Forensic was hired by the Ventura County public defender's office and asked to analyze the video to see if it could reverse-engineer the height of the person shown in the video as captured by the officer's cell phone, to determine the height of the suspect.

Fries went to the crime scene and used a laser scanner to scan the environment captured on the video. When he arrived at the scene, Fries noticed there were two video surveillance cameras in the same general location. The store clerk could not tell him which of these cameras was working on the night of the robbery. Once Fries completed scanning the store's interior, he returned to his lab to begin reverse engineering the exact 3D location of the camera that originally captured the robbery. The analysis developed by Forensic 3D confirmed that the security camera closest to the store's front door was indeed the camera that recorded the robbery. Fries placed a 3D digital camera inside the same exact location of the camera that captured the robbery. Because the original video camera could see the 3D location of the suspect's feet, it was easy for Fries to place a 3D model showing the suspect's feet in the same location.

Approximate Height of Convenience Store Robber Matched Digital Model

Next, this 3D model was enlarged until it matched the height of the 3D model of the person in the video. Again, the 3D model is being viewed from the same exact location as the actual video of the robbery; in essence, it was possible to overlay the two worlds—original suspect and 3D model—so that would match perfectly. They did. This process can be performed many times as, in the original video, the suspect walks in and out of sight. Fries concluded that the 3D model of the suspect should be able to follow the original suspect throughout the store, with their heights always remaining the same. "This process allows us to rely on our 3D model (the digital suspect) because he should be the same height when he kneels down," Fries said. He added, "This allows us to reconfirm our estimated height is correct over and over again," and "this process allows us to create a simple error analysis; if our 3D model matches the suspect in the video, we can start to make our 3D model taller and shorter and see if the heights of the model and original suspect still match."

Fries uses an example to explain this method a bit further. If a 5'10″ digital model suspect matches the original videotape suspect, does a 5'9″ height also seem to match? What about a 5'11″ model height? "By performing error analysis," Fries said, "we are able to find the threshold of where changing the height no longer gives us an accurate answer—letting us know what an acceptable error analysis range is for this video." Fries said he is often able to get within 0.5″ once the regression analysis is completed. "Often, the plus or minus comes from the types of shoes or hair styles that a suspect has, which can cause an error rate of up to one inch," Fries said.

In the case of the Ventura convenience store robbery, Fries was able to reverse-engineer the camera location and compensate for the fact that the camera footage analyzed was a video of a video. This led him to determine that the suspect was 5'5″ tall after measuring his position in six different locations throughout the convenience store. Fries gave this information to the Ventura County public defender's office which asked the county jail to measure their client. The suspect, it turned out, was much taller—at 5'9″. "I purposely tell my clients to never tell me the height of their suspect before my firm performs its work on a case, so that we cannot be accused of shooting for a target height," Fries said. "In many instances, we find attorneys do not know the height of their client when they contact us for help, which is perfect."

The valuable and expanding use of height approximation to aid with identifying one or multiple suspects in a crime has been the thrust of this chapter's discussion. Of particular note is the impact that 3D laser scanning has had when used with surveillance video to record measurements and movements of suspects. The upshot is that when laser scanning is combined with innovative methods such as reverse projection, this can help to narrow down a group of suspects targeted in a crime scene and aid in the presentation of evidence in court trials.

In Chapter 19, the benefits of using several technology tools to help solve crime scene reconstruction problems will be probed.

Notes

1. Nickell, Joe. *Camera Clues: A Handbook for Photographic Investigation*. The University Press of Kentucky, 2012. muse.jhu.edu.
2. "3D Suspect Measurement." Geo3d, www.geo3d.hr/software/delfl-forensics.
3. Skicko, Mike. *How a UK Agency is Combining 3d Laser Scanning with CCTV Tech to Solve Cases*. 2019. www.policeone.com/crime-scene-investigations/articles.

19

Integrating Technology Tools Help Solve Crime/Crash Scene Reconstruction Challenges, Clarify Probable Events

Throughout much of this book, 3D laser scanning has been examined for the many ways in which it can address specific needs of crime scene reconstruction depending on the incident. Up to this point, reconstruction experts have been able to successfully apply scanning for analysis of bullet trajectory, vehicle collision damage, blood patterns, and suspect height approximation, among some major applications. However, laser scanning also has been used for pre-planning buildings that may become targets of active incidents. Although this technology has been widely hailed by many reconstruction professionals as the most powerful and comprehensive for crime scene reconstruction, laser scanning should never be viewed as the only way to document crime and crash scenes. In fact, law enforcement agencies and reconstruction experts are seeing clear benefits to *integrating* one or more mapping technologies with laser scanning. Why? A chief argument is that by joining scanning with one or more additional technology tools, complex scenes can be reconstructed more thoroughly, giving multiple scene perspectives, more complete evidence, and major time-savings.

Laser Scanner Ideal for Many Scenes, but only Captures What it Sees

Vehicle collisions are a good example of scenes that can become complex very quickly. Their complexity depends on the number of cars, severity of the collision, injuries and fatalities, weather, eye witness accounts, and other factors. Crash scenes also can be extremely diverse in size and length of debris field and in number of gouges and tread marks, as well as with road surface and debris. When a crash scene involves multiple vehicles and perhaps several fatalities, and displays a large field of evidence, mapping the scene can take hours and cause traffic backup and potential secondary accidents. The safety of the reconstruction expert in this situation is also a great concern. So, this type of scene requires a technology tool able to capture a substantial chunk of detailed information and evidence very quickly. In this instance, a 3D laser scanner is perfect. What is especially helpful is that the scanner can capture data from the periphery of the scene, and quickly. However, it may be difficult for the laser scanner to see key evidence, such as a tire mark or gouge on a road's surface. Remember, as effective as a laser scanner is at capturing a total scene, it can only document what it can see while scanning. To meet this challenge, it might be best to use a total station because it can usually record critical data points that the scanner might miss. And, the data points picked up by the total station can supplement data caught with the laser scanner.

Drones—Well-Suited for Data Collection at Lengthy Crash Scenes

One trend associated with documenting vehicle collisions is the combined use of drones and laser scanning for certain scenes, especially long, hard-to-access collision scenes. Such scenes are typical in major freeways in large urban areas. In one instance, Mark Johnson, CEO of San Jose, California-based Visual Law, an expert consulting firm offering 3D forensic visualization and animation, was hired to map and record a multi-car collision on a five-lane freeway in Los Angeles, California. A crash sequence involving at least eight cars stretched out for approximately 1,500 ft. The collision was the result of actual impacts or as factors causing avoidance maneuvers among some of the cars involved that led to the impacts. On the day of the collision, Johnson explained, the highway patrol came to the crash scene, without stopping traffic, and collected all kinds of data points using a total station. Patrol officers measured landmarks from the highway's shoulders and determined distances for lanes as well as some other key features. The highway patrol gave Johnson two total station measured points and also wanted Johnson's measurements. However, they did not provide Johnson their total station's measurement determination. "We could have taken a laser scanner to the scene, but that would have required a lot of considerations," Johnson said. "We would not have had the ability to stop traffic. We would be scanning a very busy freeway and could not risk the safety of the scanning operator," he continued. Furthermore, because skid marks and other evidence were on the road surface and the laser scanner reaches only 6 ft high, scanning the highway would have taken all morning and produced a lot of noise. So, Johnson and his team flew a little drone on three separate passes over the crash scene from the safety of a protected berm about 300 ft away from the freeway. The drone flights took about 40 minutes.

"The drone (armed with Pix4D photogrammetry software) flew over the freeway and collected all of the evidence—skid marks, debris, and spray paint markers that the highway patrol had left from their analysis," Johnson said. "We were able to collect that very quickly and safely with a single operator." The Pix4D software identified the same spray-painted markers in multiple photos taken by the drone. By locating the same landmark in multiple photos, the software could determine this landmark's precise location in physical space. The spray-painted marks were made by the highway patrol to designate specific distances along the freeway so that physical evidence could more easily be identified. For post-processing this crash scene, the Pix4D software removed the cars so that by zooming into the photos taken by the drone it is easy to clearly identify the skid marks and the spray-painted markers.

Johnson considers the drone to be the fastest, easiest way to capture data accurately at both crash and crime scenes. What's more, a drone now complements a laser scanner. When a scanner sweeps a debris field or tire mark on a roadway of a crash scene, for instance, it can accurately address all moving objects in front of it during the scanning process and automatically delete them. Images for colorization can be reviewed before the scan is completed. There are no more blocked views of anything in the field of view of the scanner. A drone can take

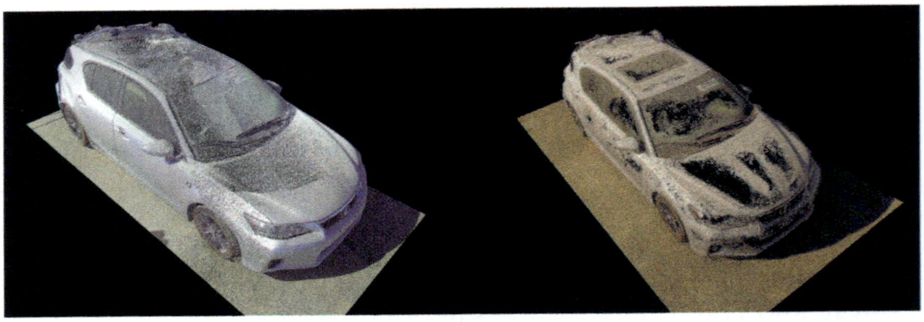

Figure 19.1 A comparison of vehicles documented with both laser scanners and drones to acquire data for accident reconstruction (Photo courtesy of www.visuallaw.com)

hundreds of photographs that overlap, and this also makes it easy to isolate the full debris field along a busy freeway (Figure 19.1).

The drone orthographic image of the crash scene was of very high resolution, enabling Johnson and his team of crash reconstruction experts to determine the character and density of the crash scene's skid marks and examine the various spray-painted measurements made by the highway patrol's total station.

Drones and Laser Scanners Work Well Together; Shadows Controlled

As compelling as drone technology is by itself for lengthy crash scenes, Johnson stresses that the drone *and* laser scanner really work well together and should be considered for these types of scenes. "The scanner gives high resolution to the scene details it captures, and accuracy is straight out of the box," Johnson said. He continued, "With the drone, the data is as good as what the operator gets out of it. The scanner registers and corrects the data. The drone data will document the physical evidence, whereas the laser scanner collects the geometry of the crash scene." When the scanner is running and recording a crash scene, it registers a position on which it focuses very precisely. But skid marks or tire marks from a tire are not physical features. He added further, "The only way the scanner is going to collect those tire marks is as the scanner finishes its pass, its has it own camera that collects the surface of the roadway as a photograph that then is superimposed on a scan." When this happens, the skid marks are visible as a by-product of the scanner collecting this data. But the skid marks are difficult to see "because you're looking at them obliquely, at a very acute angle." "In this sense, the scanner is no better at seeing the skid marks than the human eye." The drone gives a 180-degree overhead view, looking straight down, so it is relying strictly on vision. The scanner is more advantageous in picking up ground surface features. In traffic collisions, skid marks and other surface marks do not have physical geometry and so will not be registered by the scanner in an ideal way and are not as easy to generate a high-resolution view. "But the drone really excels at that," Johnson said. That said, the drone can only see what it's seeing straight down. "It cannot give subtle variations in elevation, but the scanner is ideal for this," he added. "The scanner will let you build a complete cross-section of the roadway and of the surface topography. You put those two together—the drone and laser scanner—and you've got a really powerful solution," Johnson concluded.

A drone is highly effective at mapping and recording 80 percent of what data is needed from a scene, within less than an hour, Johnson argues. It can capture basic physical evidence as well as the configuration of the scene. When a drone is flown over a crash scene, it can give 20 or 30 times the resolution that a Google Earth picture will offer, and the drone's user will get this data on a known time and date that he can control, Johnson continued. This allows the user to control shadows and the amount of coverage. As he has said before, Johnson believes combining laser scanning and drone mapping is optimal because the scanner is limited; anything that it sees blocks the view behind it. If there is a building being scanned, for example, it is impossible to see what's behind it, which is why multiple scans must be taken to overlap and correct for any data being shadowed. "A drone, however, is flying above this building and is generating—not at the same resolution as a scanner—all of the data," Johnson said.

Available Videos at Crash Scenes Aid Reconstruction

The reason this becomes important, Johnson explained, is that many of his firm's cases involve either a dashboard camera or a security camera on a commercial vehicle. There actually will be video footage of an accident scene that was generated by the commercial truck, or by a police car. "When you have that footage, now you can use the drone mapping footage to match up all of the items you see in this video," Johnson said. He recalls a case in the San Francisco Bay Area involving a SuperShuttle whose driver was traveling on Interstate 280 when a car in front suddenly went out of control and collided with the shuttle van. The shuttle had an onboard video camera that was on during the crash and taking a photograph every 30th of a second. Every video frame showed all of the objects in the field of view—street signs, telephone poles, tops of buildings, and guard rails. "All of that visual information is very important because if you're able to locate these objects, you can locate where the vehicle was at any given time," Johnson explained. "A scanner gives you a little of that data, but a drone will give you the whole 3000 or 4000 feet of travel, and every street sign, guard rail, etc., will be located using the drone point cloud." A scanner is limited in what it can see and capture.

Landmarks and Speed of Vehicles Can Be More Easily Determined

Back at the SuperShuttle collision scene, it took a drone, that Johnson had launched, less than an hour to collect data. Meanwhile, a laser scanner was used on the ground at the scene of the crash and collected 400 ft of data, including the space under an overpass. "The drone was able to capture objects 700–1,000 ft away from camera views of the scene and these objects were precisely located,"He added, "We could not have done this project without combining both technologies—the scanner and drone."

A drone is particularly useful whenever landmarks are important, according to Johnson. If only digital photos of a crash or crime scene are available, there is a risk that some key landmarks might not show up in them that could be crucial to faithfully reconstructing the scene. Fortunately, most people have cell phones with cameras (for taking still photos and videos) and some of them might be witnesses to a collision and can record them. Likewise, a dashboard camera in a police cruiser that arrives on the scene also may be able to record parts of a crash scene. Finally, activated surveillance cameras can be present, as well. "If there's an incident, the footage from these sources can be dissected to see who was doing what," Johnson said. All of the information captured by these devices can be evidentiary and helpful when combined with data gathered by reconstruction tools like laser scanners and drones.

In the shuttle bus crash scene, Johnson and his team were able to use the drone data with data collected by the event recorder and dashcam on the shuttle van to precisely reconstruct the van's movements during collision. During the collision, the shuttle van driver's view is obscured and he continues to drive without breaking, unaware of other vehicles swerving toward the van. The shuttle sideswiped another vehicle but continues traveling forward. In doing so, another car that had been struck from behind had crossed its lane and was directly in front of the shuttle van. This move gave the shuttle van driver no chance or time to avoid the collision.

Drones Clarify Details at Officer-Involved Shooting Scenes and Give Valuable Perspectives

Det. Matt Archuleta of the Arvada, Colorado, Police Department, is a fervent believer that multiple technology tools for reconstructing crime scenes give significant advantages. His agency owns three 3D laser scanners that are used on most crime and crash scenes as the primary documentation tool. But increasingly drones are a frequent partner in the effort to thoroughly and accurately document scenes. Det. Archuleta recalls a shooting incident at a convenience store a few years ago in which a laser scanner and a drone were used to comprehensively record the crime's events. The event involved a suspect who was robbing a convenience store. Once the suspect committed the robbery he ran out and confronted a customer pumping gas, unaware that the customer was an off-duty police officer. The panicky suspect immediately began shooting and the officer returned gun fire. The officer was struck in one of his legs by a bullet. After that, the suspect fled the scene, but eventually was caught by the police department's S.W.A.T. team a few hours later.

Det. Archuleta noted that it was a 12' × 12' area where most of the shots from each person's gun had been fired. "We scanned this area and then flew a drone over the location which included the convenience store, a parking lot and an intersection," Det. Archuleta said. "We also had the external surveillance video of this shooting, and there was a surveillance video camera that recorded the robbery as it unfolded inside the store. During the shootout between the suspect and the police officer, some of the officer's bullets struck a rack of propane tanks in front of the store. "With the outside surveillance video we can point out the propane storage rack, and then we can point to where this is in the laser scan of the entire scene," Det. Archuleta explained. After the scanned scene was processed and converted to a 3D model, it was possible to rotate the scene to show the relationship of where the robber parked his car, the location of the officer's pickup truck, and where the officer had moved. After the scene was laser scanned, Det. Archuleta used a drone to fly over the entire scene and record it. "With the drone footage, we have a to-scale overhead view of the scene to show all of these perspectives," the detective said. By combining data sets captured with the laser scanner and drone, Det. Archuleta added, "We can put people (i.e., a jury) virtually in this scene and show what participants in the incident may have seen."

Animating Crime Scenes Can Help Jury Understand Relationships of Events

This kind of technology fusion is what has such a huge impact on a jury, allowing each juror to more clearly understand the course of events at a complicated crime scene in the same way. Additionally, it is why Det. Archuleta will, in certain instances, use animation as part of his presentation of a reconstructed crime scene. For example, he created an animation for a 2014 officer-involved shooting scene that proved to be both dramatic and effective for the jury on the case. The incident itself focused on a suspect speeding in his car and being pursued by police. At one point, the suspect drives off the roadway and stops. As officers approach the suspect's car, he turns it around and begins driving it towards the officers. After officers shouted at the suspect to stop, he refused and shots were fired by the officers, killing him. Det. Archuleta scanned the officer-involved shooting scene and then built an animation for it. "Then we married that animation to the police radio traffic and the time sequence for it," the detective said. "We put this in a 2D diagram that was to scale. The radio traffic lets you hear the cops screaming at the suspect to stop, and then the sound of shots being fired can be heard." This all helped to understand the relationships of what happened," Det. Archuleta concluded.

Roadway, Collision Scene May Not Always Be Ideal for Laser Scanning

In certain instances, it can be extraordinarily difficult to piece together how a crime or vehicle collision occurred, due to numerous factors: Key evidence might be missing, the scene may have been disturbed, eye witness and suspect accounts may have proved conflicting. Yet by combining several methods of scene documentation it may be possible to show how events unfolded and help determine who is at fault. This was exactly the situation confronting Carl Lakowicz, a crash reconstruction expert with Concord, New Hampshire-based Northpoint Collision Consultants, for a complicated crash scene he had been tapped to reconstruct.

Lakowicz and his partners predominantly have used ground-based laser scanning for many of their crash scenes; other technology tools can be used to supplement scanning, if necessary, for capturing all essential scene data. Northpoint Collision Consultants uses two laser scanners that have proven valuable for reconstructing most of its larger crash scenes. When a scanner is brought to a crash scene, it is set up to scan every 50 ft down both sides of a road that often can be a long road, with intersections and driveways. Those portions of the road that involve a driver's perception, reaction, and line of sight, based on the investigation, are scanned. Prior to reconstructing a crash scene, the consulting firm estimates how many feet—based on the speed limit and the area—that a driver would need to account for perception and reaction to a collision with another vehicle. This scenario would ideally have a daytime crash, sunny day, and no view obstructions, and with the driver having a line of sight that could extend a long way down the road. There also may be some skid marks and other evidence in the crash scene. Such an ideal scene allows scanning to pick up nearly all evidence and for an understanding of what the driver probably saw. If necessary, the scanner could even be brought back to the crash scene to capture some additional scans to supplement the original scene scans.

"The dominating thing you must remember with laser scan technology used at an accident scene is that what you see is what you get," Lakowicz cautioned. And laser scanning cannot capture and yield a digital data set without having control points or surfaces common to this data set, also known as the "point cloud." Each point in the point cloud has 3D coordinates that are essential so that the entire point cloud can be seamed together with other point clouds using control points.

Bicylist-Dump Truck Collision Scene Was Disturbed; Point of Impact Was Missing

Therefore, as powerful as 3D laser scanning technology can be for documenting a crash scene under ideal conditions, what happens when these conditions do not exist and scanning cannot capture all of the essential evidence? Lakowicz found the answer to this question when he was hired to reconstruct the scene of a bicyclist who was fatally struck by a dump truck at a highway's intersection. He soon realized that due to complicating factors with reconstructing this scene, it would take more than just laser scanning to solve the problem of who was at fault.

In the incident, which occurred in 2018 in Pelham, New Hampshire, a bicyclist was traveling down a two-lane highway, in a breakdown lane, on a pedal/gas-powered bicycle at about 23 mph. The terrain was flat, and the roadway included a couple of side streets. The speed limit for the highway is 35 mph. The cyclist was approaching a T-intersection that turns off to his right. Lakowicz noted that it was believed the cyclist was going to cross the intersection after leaving his breakdown lane to access a similar lane on the other side of the intersection. Meanwhile, a dump truck traveling in the opposite direction at a determined speed of 24 mph, was making a left-hand turn without slowing and crossed over the same breakdown lane in which the cyclist had just reached. This action effectively cut off the bicyclist's travel path, leaving no time for the bicyclist to take any effective evasive action other than to swerve to the left. At this point, the cyclist ran into the right rear tire of the truck during the collision avoidance swerve maneuver attempt, which killed him (Figure 19.2).

The dump truck's driver pulled over to the side of the road and stopped. About 20 seconds before the accident, a local Pelham police officer in a marked cruiser with an activated dashcam was turning off a side road onto the main highway and was traveling in the same direction as the cyclist. The officer was some 800–900 ft away and closing the gap on the cyclist as he (the officer) was getting up to the

Figure 19.2 Scene of collision between a dump truck and a bicyclist at a T-intersection. Shown is the struck bicycle in the intersection as it was crossing and collided with the dump truck's right rear tire as the truck was turning. The truck's driver claimed he had stopped, then accelerated into the left turn and did not see the bicyclist due to blocking traffic, which resulted in the collision that killed the bicyclist. Images courtesy of Northpoint Collision Consulltants, Concord, New Hampshire.

road's speed limit. As the officer arrived at the intersection, he realized the collision had occurred and removed the bicycle off of the cyclist, throwing it to the side of the road and tried to give first aid to the cyclist.

The police officer witnessed the accident and it was recorded on his cruiser's dashcam, but since the cyclist and bicycle had both been removed from the scene, the collision's point of impact was now gone before any at-scene measurements could be collected. The only major piece of evidence left at the scene that was part of the collision was the dump truck and the cyclist's cut-off clothing left behind by the EMS responders. Another police officer arrived at the scene and was able to retrieve the other responding officer's dashcam video. The original officer failed to mark the collision's point of impact with spray paint.

According to Lakowicz, the requested state police accident reconstruction team arrived and conducted their own investigation and concluded that the fault in the collision was with the cyclist who crossed the path of a turning truck. Attorneys for the estate of the cyclist hired Northpoint Collision Consultants to map and reconstruct the collision scene to see if the state police investigation was correct and if there was any recourse.

Photographs, Total Station, and Dashcam Video Data Were Available; Used with Scanner

The state police had used a robotic electronic total station to map the cyclist-dump truck collision scene, and marked where the bicycle had been thrown to the side of the road, as well as some clothes on the road that had been cut off the cyclist while he was being triaged. The dump truck, curbing, yellow lines in the road, stop signs, and area of the crash scene, all were mapped to help measure distances. Lakowicz and his team had been hired by the cyclist's estate months after the collision. "If the rest of the scene wasn't recorded at the time, it wasn't there for us to use," Lakowicz recalled. He had obtained reports on the collision from the state police and responding officer, plus state police reconstruction analysis, analysis of the dashcam video, and the state police findings in the total station data captured. The reconstruction expert also looked at the video and analyzed it frame by frame, and recorded the timing and was able to locate distances.

"We discovered from the report that the dump truck driver reported he never saw the bicyclist after stopping in the intersection and before making the turn," Lakowicz said. He continued, "The truck driver reported cross traffic was blocking his view. On approach the truck's driver saw a break in the traffic and made his turn. Seeing the truck unexpectedly turning, the cyclist had little opportunity to slow down, but didn't and instead swerved to the left to go around back of the turning dump truck." He further added, "Here's where all of our technology came into play. We used our office's two laser scanners to map 300 feet in both directions of this intersection, which would cover the travel path of the cyclist, the video travel path of the police cruiser, and the truck that was reportedly stopped at the intersection in its approach to the intersection and subsequent left turn." Combined, there was total station and laser scanning data, photos of the scene, and video footage.

Video Footage Was Pivotal; Photogrammetry Was also Used

The video footage showed that the truck was not stopped. It had to cover 68 ft in its turn. The video analysis claimed it took the truck less than three seconds from the time it made its turn to the point of impact. Yet Northpoint Collision Consultants doubted this could happen if, as the state police report said, the dump truck was stopped before turning. Also, this was a heavy, fully loaded landscaping truck. "Our analysis was that the dump truck would have had to be going 52 MPH as it was making its turn to reach the point of impact in under three seconds," Lakowicz said. "We know the dump truck's driver was not starting to turn from a stop. He was traveling at 24 miles per hour into his left turn."

Lakowicz and his team wondered what the average rate of speed would be for a turning dump truck, and after making some calculations they determined that after three seconds of acceleration, the driver would actually be traveling about 12–14 mph at best. "The driver's testimony was false," Lakowicz concluded. "He wasn't stopped but moving. This was proven through the visuals and reconstruction."

Northpoint Collision Consultants knew they had to find the point of impact for the dump truck-cyclist collision scene. The police cruiser's video shows the point of impact, according to Lakowicz. The footage was clear, it was just at a distance. And, the cruiser came within 20 ft of the crash scene. The officer got out of his cruiser to approach the scene and his dashcam was recording the whole time. "At 30 frames per second, we can now find out where the cyclist was in the roadway because the crash scene, including the roadway, was never mapped," Lakowicz said (Figures 19.3, 19.4, 19.5, and 19.6).

Dump-Truck Driver's Testimony Faulty

"Here's where we bring in photogrammetry," Lakowicz continued. Measurements had been taken at the crash scene with the laser scanner and off of the still photos from the video footage. "The photogrammetry software was able to find known reference points so that distances between these points could be determined, triangulation is accomplished and then a diagram can be prepared to show where key identifiers were at the scene," Lakowicz added. "We could then pinpoint where the truck was located at the point of impact."

Figure 19.3 Three-dimensional models of the dump truck-bicyclist collision showing various positions of the truck as it turned and collided with the bicyclist and came to rest, and locations of the struck bicyclist. Reconstruction of this scene required mapping with a 3D ground laser scanner, electronic total station, and photogrammetry, as well as collision scene photos and dashcam video from a local police cruiser showing the collision point of impact. These combined tools enabled an accurate reconstruction showing that the truck's driver inaccurately had claimed he had first stopped at the intersection before accelerating into a turn, which led to the collision that killed the bicyclist. Images courtesy of Northpoint Collision Consulltants, Concord, New Hampshire.

Figure 19.4 Three-dimensional models of the dump truck-bicyclist collision showing various positions of the truck as it turned and collided with the bicyclist and came to rest, and locations of the struck bicyclist. Reconstruction of this scene required mapping with a 3D ground laser scanner, electronic total station, and photogrammetry, as well as collision scene photos and dashcam video from a local police cruiser showing the collision point of impact. These combined tools enabled an accurate reconstruction showing that the truck's driver inaccurately had claimed he had first stopped at the intersection before accelerating into a turn, which led to the collision that killed the bicyclist. Images courtesy of Northpoint Collision Consulltants, Concord, New Hampshire.

Figure 19.5 Three-dimensional models of the dump truck-bicyclist collision showing various positions of the truck as it turned and collided with the bicyclist and came to rest, and locations of the struck bicyclist. Reconstruction of this scene required mapping with a 3D ground laser scanner, electronic total station, and photogrammetry, as well as collision scene photos and dashcam video from a local police cruiser showing the collision point of impact. These combined tools enabled an accurate reconstruction showing that the truck's driver inaccurately had claimed he had first stopped at the intersection before accelerating into a turn, which led to the collision that killed the bicyclist. Images courtesy of Northpoint Collision Consulltants, Concord, New Hampshire.

The laser scanner was effective for delivering the scene in three dimensions. With this information, Lakowicz said he could place a person in the driver's seat of the truck. He could also show the perspective of the scene as observed from the face of the bicyclist.

What did this forensic science mean for the case? "It meant that the driver of the truck inaccurately reported that he had stopped at the intersection before turning," Lakowicz concluded. "It was not possible for him to stop and then accelerate at the speed required in the time that was available as recorded by the dashcam in the police cruiser." Although the dump truck's driver claimed he never saw the bicyclist coming due to cross traffic, he had not even reached the road he was turning onto with a stop and then accelerating. When Lakowicz was challenged on this point in court, he responded by indicating it was inaccurate because the cyclist had to swerve to try avoiding striking the truck. Because the bicycle had been thrown to the side of the road and later removed along with the cyclist, there was little evidence for Northpoint Collision Consultant to use. As a result, "We were able to use technology to account for

Figure 19.6 Three-dimensional models of the dump truck-bicyclist collision showing various positions of the truck as it turned and collided with the bicyclist and came to rest, and locations of the struck bicyclist. Reconstruction of this scene required mapping with a 3D ground laser scanner, electronic total station, and photogrammetry, as well as collision scene photos and dashcam video from a local police cruiser showing the collision point of impact. These combined tools enabled an accurate reconstruction showing that the truck's driver inaccurately had claimed he had first stopped at the intersection before accelerating into a turn, which led to the collision that killed the bicyclist. Images courtesy of Northpoint Collision Consulltants, Concord, New Hampshire.

this," Lakowicz said, adding, "The technology now allowed us to support the lawsuit."

For the crash scene, Lakowicz used FARO laser scanners, and FARO SCENE software to process the crash scene data. FARO Zone 3D was used to build the diagram of the crash, with which Lakowicz also was able to create a 3D model and animations.

The advantages of combining two or more technology tools to reconstruct a crime or crash scene have been the emphasis of this chapter. In addition to today's widely used 3D laser scanner, drones have become a favored, newer technology to capture scene data sets. And these data sets can easily be used with scene data recorded with not only laser scanners but total stations, 3D tablets, and photogrammetry, as well. The use of multiple mapping and documentation tools enables reconstruction experts to tackle scenes whose evidence may be difficult or impossible to extract if only one tool is applied.

Conclusion

As you have observed in reading this book, there is no absolute way to reconstruct a crime or crash scene. Any of the numerous scene mapping and capture technologies explored can be effective. However, accuracy is paramount, and so are sufficient evidence data and crime scene views that can suggest circumstances as to how the incident behind the crime scene may have come about. And what technology is used often depends on what kind of scene is at hand.

The aim of thorough scene reconstruction is, ultimately, to enable a jury to see the crime scene—both in photos and via a 3D diagram—so that jurors can fully understand scene details and a likely course of events. It is equally important that each juror views and understands a crime scene at the same level when it is being presented and explained. In today's courtroom, a compelling 3D model of a crash or crime scene allows a jury to enter it as though they were actually at the original scene; advanced software enables a reconstruction expert to create fly-throughs of the scene and to show a variety of scene orientations. Essentially, the jury is being transported to the crime scene at the time and in the shoes of the suspect, the witness, or the officer. When this happens, the jury can experience multiple scene perspectives, positions, and locations of people, and see various pieces of evidence that can prove critical to a case.

Three-dimensional laser scanning is considered by many law enforcement agencies and reconstruction professionals to be the most powerful and reliable way to capture and preserve a crime scene. And through the use of post-processing and CAD software, a credible, photorealistic representation of the scene, based on point cloud data generated by the laser scanner, has become one of the most significant advances in crime scene reconstruction. The laser scanner's precision enables crime scene investigators to analyze a crime scene with greater accuracy and specificity, but also focus on specific scene aspects.

The upshot of this book has been to demonstrate, through extensive commentary from multiple reconstruction experts, how 3D laser scanning captures and preserves a crime or crash scene, doing so faster than most existing technologies. Why this is so critical is that there might be details from a crime that the reconstruction technician did not know to look for originally. But since a laser scanner captures a scene in its entirety, the scene's detail will be frozen and always available to view and analyze—today, or years after the scene was mapped and documented. Perspectives of a scene and how it came to be are always germane and important; witnesses have different perspectives based on where they were when a crime occurred, but memory may change. Luckily, everything in a crime scene that a laser scanner has recorded is exactly as it was at the time it was scanned.

The wide range of applications for which laser scanning can be applied makes it a compelling and valuable tool in any reconstruction expert's toolbox. As the book has discussed, these include mapping and documenting active incident scenes, bloodstain pattern analysis, officer-involved shootings, vehicle collision damage and crush analysis, suspect height approximation, and risk assessment for public buildings because of the scanner's ability to produce digital floor plans and building layouts that can aid law enforcement and first responders.

Laser scanner training and consistent practice by the operator to become proficient cannot be emphasized enough, and pursuing refresher scanner training is strongly recommended. Remember, whenever a scanner is deployed, it *is practice* that will make the operator more comfortable and experienced as he scans scene after scene. Therefore, every crash or crime scene that can be laser scanned is another opportunity to practice so that when a major, complex scene occurs, you will be ready to scan it.

Although this book has emphasized laser scanning's attributes and its many applications, it is worth reiterating that this technology is *not the only one* for every scene. Many scenes may require the integration of other technology tools; for example, the use of drones coupled with a terrestrial laser scanner or total station for a lengthy and complex crash scene can yield useful scene data and striking views from numerous angles.

Finally, above all, the tools for reconstructing a crash or crime scene are just that—tools. They are only useful to the reconstruction expert who has taken the time to learn these tools and apply them to the crime or crash scene at hand. With these tools, the user can apply his investigative and forensic analytical skills to build a meaningful and accurate representation of a crime scene that will connect with any jury. That representation may just change the outcome of a case.

####

Index

9780367652302